Provence and the
Côte d'Azur

Provence and the Côte d'Azur

A Phaidon Cultural Guide

with over 270 colour illustrations
and 6 pages of maps

Phaidon

Editor: Dr Marianne Mehling

Contributors: Dr Klaus Bennewitz, Corinna Cacoveanu, Gerda Kurz, Dr Marianne Mehling, Siglinde Summerer

Photographs: Ernst Höhne, Franz Mehling, Marion Müllmayer

Maps: Huber & Oberländer, Munich

Ground-plans: Herstellung + Grafik, Lidl

Phaidon Press Limited, Littlegate House, St. Ebbe's Street, Oxford, OX1 1SQ

First published in English 1986
Originally published as *Knaurs Kulturführer in Farbe: Provence und die Côte d'Azur*
© Droemersche Verlagsanstalt Th. Knaur Nachf. Munich 1984
Translation © Phaidon Press Limited 1986

British Library Cataloguing in Publication Data

Provence and the Côte d'Azur.——(A Phaidon
   cultural guide)
   1. Cote d'Azur (France)——Description and travel——
   Guide-books   2. Provence (France)——Description
   and travel——Guide-books
   I. Knaurs Kulturführer in Farbe, Provence und die
   Côte d'Azur. *English*
   914.4'904838   DC608.3

   ISBN 0-7148-2384-8

All rights reserved. No part of this publication may be reproduced, stored in a retrieval system or transmitted, in any form or by any means, electronic, mechanical, photocopying, recording or otherwise, without the prior permission of Phaidon Press.

Translated and edited by Babel Translations, London
Typeset by Hourds Typographica, Stafford
Printed in West Germany by Druckerei Appl, Wemding

Cover illustration: Roquebrune, the old town and Cap-Martin
(photo: Phedon Salou—Joseph Ziolo, Paris)

Preface

The light in Provence is intense and almost harsh. It emphasizes the colours and solidifies the contours, sometimes shimmering in the heat. Many great painters have been influenced by this light, including Monet, Renoir, Signac, Matisse, Dufy, and most notably van Gogh and Cézanne, as well as Picasso, Léger, Chagall, Gauguin, and Kandinsky. It was here, too, that Perret and Le Corbusier brought a new style to architecture and that Vasarély introduced an abstract form of expression to the fine arts. Indeed, there is a greater concentration of modern-art museums in Provence than anywhere else in the world.

There were human beings in the region as early as 400,000 BC and a settled population from 100,000 BC. From around 1000 BC the Illyrians lived here; then around 600 BC Marseille was founded by Greek colonists from Phocaea in Asia Minor. Nice, Antibes, and other trading posts grew up in the fourth century BC. The same period saw the Celtic immigration and the intermarriage of the Celts and the Ligurians. The Romans came in 122 BC. They proceeded to fight the Cimbri and the Teutons and defeat the Celts, until they had made the whole region a Roman province. The culture of the Greeks and Celts can still be seen in the local museums and excavation sites. Whole towns have been excavated, such as Glanum and Vaison-la-Romaine, which reveal the comfort in which the Romans lived. In towns like Arles or Orange, which were the principal Roman settlements, parts of the old Roman buildings have survived, including temples, amphitheatres, and triumphal arches. The Emperor Constantine resided in Arles in 313. Christianity then began to spread all along the coast, and the first monasteries were founded. But Provence remained a region of enduring conflicts and of cruel and fanatical religious wars. These have left their mark on its culture in the shape of small fortified villages in the mountainous interior and of Romanesque monasteries and churches which look like fortresses. But there are also little cloisters and monastery gardens which, with their chiselled capitals and columns set against this landscape, are peculiarly charming, as for example the monastery of Saint-Trophime in Arles or of Saint-Sauveur in Aix. Even if the Gothic architecture in the South of France cannot be compared with the majestic cathedrals of the North, it has nonetheless left us some magnificent monuments in Saint-Maximin-La-Sainte-Baume and above all in Avignon, the old Papal capital. The baroque style, too, was interpreted here in a more moderate form, which can be seen notably in the town houses of the nobility (as in Aix).

One is not overwhelmed by culture in Provence, as one is in Greece, Italy, or in the North of France; one has to seek it out. But this is a very ancient region full of contrasts and cultural treasures which are rewarding to discover.

As with the other guides in this series, the text is arranged in alphabetical order of place names. This gives the book the clarity of a work of reference and avoids the need for lengthy searching. The link between places which are geographically close, but which are separated by the alphabet, is provided by the maps on pages 254–9. This section shows all the places mentioned which are within a short distance from any given destination and which, therefore, it might be possible to include in a tour.

The heading to each entry gives the name of the town, and, below, the name and number of its geographical region (*département*) and a reference to the map section, giving page number and grid reference. Within each entry the particular sites of interest are printed in bold type, while less significant objects of interest appear under the heading **Also worth seeing** and places in the immediate vicinity under **Environs.**

An index of all the towns and places of interest mentioned in the text is included at the end of the book.

The publishers would be grateful for notification of any errors or omissions.

Aix-en-Provence

13 Bouches-du-Rhône   p.256☐D 7

The beautiful, dreamy university city of Aix-en-Provence nestles amidst hills in the heart of the south of France, still exuding venerable culture and history. For all its historical significance, this barely industrialized, quiet, comparatively small cathedral city attracts an equal proportion of foreigners and students with modern and up-to-the-minute art, culture and science. The annual 'International Music Festival' has been held here since 1948. In September there is 'Les Rencontres Internationals de Télévision' and an ever changing array of exhibitions is on display in the museums. A particular attraction for the gourmet is the great variety of restaurants, bistros and cafés with typical Provençal fare and also foreign, but always excellent, cuisine. The climate here is always pleasant even in the sweltering height of summer, as the nights are cool. The magical quality of light in Provence and the richly contrasting colours enabled Paul Cézanne, in particular, to capture its landscapes. He was born here in 1839 and spent most of his life in a house concealed in a garden, called Jas de Bouffan, near Aix-en-Provence. The novelist Emile Zola (1840–1902) spent his youth in Aix and the composer Darius Milhaud (1892–1974) was born here.

History: Excavations have revealed that *Entrement*, the predecessor of Aix-en-Provence, was capital of the Celto-Ligurian Salluvii. It stood on a

Aix-en-Provence, Saint-Sauveur, sibyls on the portal

Saint-Sauveur, portal

hill, which also had a shrine, where human sacrifices were performed (finds in the Granet museum). In 123 BC the Romans totally destroyed this town and, the following year, founded *Aquae Sextiae Saluviorum* in the valley to the S. of the ruins. This, the oldest Roman town in Gaul, became Aix-en-Provence. It was originally planned as a castrum, a stronghold on the land-route to Italy, and was named after the victor, Consul Gaius Sextius Calvinus, the medicinal spring which the Romans developed and the defeated Celtic tribe, the Salluvii—the city is still a spa to this day. From 105 BC onwards, under Gaius Marius, who used it as a base in his campaigns against German and Celtic tribes, the settlement grew into a town, subsequently becoming a Roman colony, *Colonia Julia Augusta Aquis Sextiis,* under Augustus, and at the end of the 3CAD the capital of the Roman province of Gallia Narbonen-

sis Secunda under Diocletian; not being superseded by Arles until the 4C. In the course of the same century it became the seat of an archbishop.

During the Middle Ages the city suffered repeated attacks by the Alamanni, Franks, Visigoths, Lombards and Saracens. In 1189 Aix-en-Provence became the residence of the Counts of Provence and then in the 14C the population was decimated by the plague and the Hundred Years War. Of the once-rich Roman town there remains practically nothing, although the medieval buildings incorporated stones from it. In the later Middle Ages the city was extended on all sides beyond the walls. University founded in 1409.

In the 15C the art-loving King René of Anjou chose Aix-en-Provence as his residence, enhancing its importance and turning it into the cultural centre of Provence. Provence then passed to France in 1481, but Aix did not suffer. In 1501 a 'parlement' was established by Louis XII, and this soon ruled the whole of the south of France. It was unpopular because of the heavy taxes it exacted from the people, but nevertheless it did much to foster the development of the region—the Mistral, the Durance and the parlement were, it was whispered, the three scourges of Provence. In the 16C the city suffered in the Wars of Religion and from another siege. The rule of the nobility and parlement came to an abrupt end with the French Revolution, in which the flawed Count Mirabeau (1749–91), the great orator and writer, played a special role in Aix-en-Provence. From 1705 onwards a bath and other facilities for the cure were built near the original Roman baths.

Religious buildings
Cathedral of Saint-Sauveur (Rue Gaston-de-Saporta, near the Place de l'Université): On the spot where

Saint-Sauveur, portal by
J.Guiramand ▷

Aix-en-Provence, Cathedral of Saint-Sauveur 1 Simple façade of the former Romanesque parish church of Corpus Christi with Romanesque portal **2** Fragment of a wall once thought to have belonged to a Roman building but now recognized to have been part of the wall of a medieval fortress **3** 16C chapel which now contains stone sculptures. Of special note are the 5C sarcophagus of St.Mitre, 2 embossed lions from a stone sarcophagus of 1481, and a 15C group of marble figures including St.Martin. **4** Bay of the former Romanesque parish church of Corpus Domini, which dates from the last third of the 12C (although it is believed by some to have been built at the beginning of the 12C). It had a single aisle occupying four bays (and no transept). The first three bays have a half-barrel vault and the fourth is domed. **5** Baptistery. This is one of the 4 largest baptisteries in Provence, the others being those in Marseille, Riez and Fréjus (diameter 42 ft.) The date of its construction is debated, and must be placed between the 4 and the 11C. It is an octagonal chamber enclosed by square walls; the remains of a floor mosaic still survive. The font, which is made of brick and set deep in the floor, is surrounded by 8 marble columns with Corinthian capitals (Roman booty dating from the 2&3C). Above them is a barrel vault (rebuilt in the 12C) resting on arches. The baptistery is lighted by a circle of windows and by the lantern, which was built during 1577-83, at the same time as the dome **6** The fourth (domed) bay of the Romanesque church of Corpus Domini, built in the form of a crossing, with palmettes, ribs, and the symbols of the Evangelists on the squinches **7** Pointed archway of the rib-vaulted passage into the Gothic Cathedral **8** St.Catherine's chapel (Gothic) **9** The relatively small, flat-roofed cloister was built at the end of the 12C on the site of an earlier cloister. There are

four pillars at each corner, and each side has four round arches supported by figured double pillars. These columns, which vary considerably in style (some are spiralling) and their capitals (mostly Corinthian) are decorated with quasi-classical as well as typically Romanesque figures, some as ungainly as blocks of stone, some quite enchanting, like those of the mythical beasts, which look as if they have been petrified from the living state. During the shimmering months of summer, the columns are quite remarkably vivid and luminescent. Although nothing has been destroyed and some parts have been restored, this cloister is often compared, on account of its beauty, with that of Saint-Trophime in Arles. In the NE corner there is a large figure of Saint Peter. Above the N. row of columns there are e.g. figures and scenes from the life of Christ; on the E. side there are e.g. a remarkable capital, which is said to depict the triumph of the Church over paganism, and some symbolical Biblical figures **10** Former choir (square) of the Church of Corpus Domini **11** Coeur-de-Jésus chapel, containing the Pugets' family vault, which dates from 1464. Opposite it is the chapel of St.Peter, dating from 1463, which was rededicated to the Magdalene in 1808. It contains double columns from the former oratory (4&5C). **12** This area (now the S. transept) was the site of the former chapel of Saint-Sauveur, an early Christian oratory of the 5C which was destroyed as late as 1808 (there are still remains of columns and the floor mosaic). **13** 14C tower (originally a defensive tower). The square base of the tower incorporates square stone blocks from Roman buildings and was completed in 1425. The upper part was restored in the 19C. During the enlargement of the façade, the two stairways were built to connect the tower with the interior of the cathedral **14** The beautiful façade of the Gothic church, built by P. Soquet during 1477-

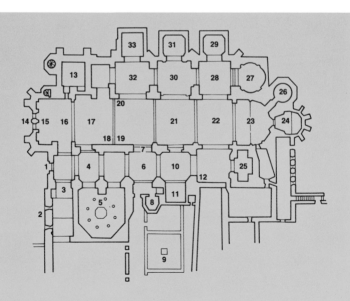

1513 in Flamboyant style. Many of the statues decorating the façade were destroyed during the French Revolution, though some were replaced by copies in the 19C. The most important figures to have been preserved are the Madonna sculpted by Soquet in 1505 in the centre, and, at the top, the beautiful St.Michael **15** The portal (1508-10) by J.Guiramand represents a mixture of the late Gothic and Renaissance styles. It has many figures, including the four major prophets and the 12 pagan sibyls prophesying the life of Christ (carved in walnut). **16** W. entrance, completed in 1513 **17** Second bay of the Gothic cathedral of Notre-Dame, built during 1285-1350. It consisted originally of a single aisle occupying five bays and had a groin vault. The outer walls of the three W. bays were part of the 11C church of the Knights of Malta which had originally stood on this site. They were opened up when the chapels and passages were built on. **18** The main attraction of the cathedral is this triptych, commissioned by the king and painted by N.Froment in 1476, originally for the town's Carmelite church. This is one of the most important paintings executed in Provence in the 15C. The centrepiece shows the burning bush, symbolizing the Madonna and Child, while the wings depict King René and his second wife Jeanne de Lavalle with suppliants **19** Altarpiece dating from the second half of the 15C. The centrepiece depicts the Passion and Resurrection, and the wings show Sts. Maximin and Mitre **20** Picture showing Doubting Thomas, painted in 1613 by L.Finson (Finsonius). **21** Fourth bay of the Gothic cathedral **22** Fifth bay of the Gothic cathedral, containing important Flemish tapestries from the school of Q.Metsys which show scenes from the life of Christ and the life of the Virgin Mary. They were originally commissioned in 1511 for Canterbury Cathedral, but were acquired by Aix in 1656.

There are organ cases, dating from 1724, on both sides (the one on the S. side is a dummy). **23** Choir of the Gothic cathedral. The high altar features a relief depicting Lazarus which was executed in the 17C by Ch. Veyrier. **24** St.Mitre's chapel, dating from 1442. It contains a beautiful late Gothic groin vault, stained-glass windows made by G. Dombet in 1444, and a panel painting by N.Froment which shows the martyrdom of St.Mitre (around 1470) **25** Chapel of Corpus Domini (1739), containing a beautiful grille. Last Supper by J.Daret (17C). **26** St.John's Chapel, built in 1582 as a mausoleum for François Estienne de Saint-Jean-de-la-Sole **27** Chapelle d'Espérance, built in the 17C by Laurent Vallon, and containing a 16C polychrome stone sculpture of the Virgin Mary and, in the altarpiece, a relief by A.Duparc dating from the end of the 17C. The chapel simultaneously constitutes the choir of the church of the brotherhood of Notre-Dame d'Espérance, which consists of the interconnecting side-chapels to the Gothic cathedral. Three further chapels were built on to the N. side of this Church of Notre-Dame-d'Espérance as burial chapels **28** St.Joseph's Chapel, originally St. Gregory's chapel, built as a burial place by Armand de Narzés (d. 1348). **29** St.Maximin's chapel, containing a 16C retablo (Adoration of the Magi). **30** Original funerary chapel of Olivier de Pennart (1467) **31** Tomb (in the wall) of Archbishop Olivier de Pennart (d. 1484). The original recumbent effigy of the deceased has been replaced by one of St.Martin (1457) taken from the tomb of the Puyloubier family **32** Chapel and burial place of the University's theological college, originally built around 1470 as a chapel for Archdeacon Bernard Teyssier **33** Chapel for the University and the poor, containing a stone altar in the wall beneath a crucifix dating from 1470

Saint-Sauveur, portal, detail

Saint-Sauveur, baptistery, dome

Gaius Sextius is supposed to have founded the castrum, the later Bourg Saint-Sauveur, there now stands the cathedral, a mixture of various styles, which, as a result, disappoints at first sight, but on closer analysis reveals rich artistic treasures and historical features spanning a period of some 1500 years.

The existence of a Roman Temple of Apollo, reputed to be the first forerunner of the cathedral, has never been established, although Roman ashlars were constantly being re-used in the Middle Ages. The oldest part of the building, as far as can be established, is the baptistery, the date of which is disputed, some dating it from the 10C, most, however, as early as the 4 or 5C. The columns which surround the deep-set font are certainly of Roman origin. They date from the 2 or 3C AD and originally came from a heathen structure. A small Oratory of Saint-Sauveur, the Holy Chapel, was built around 1070, but pulled down in 1808. An early cathedral presumed to have stood here cannot be proved, but there was certainly a very early church. This was followed by the church of Notre-Dame (the predecessor of the present cathedral), which was built in the 11C for the cathedral chapter.

In the meantime, however, a cathedral of Beata-Maria de Sede in the W. of the city was possibly built as early as the 5C, of which nothing remains today. In either 1103 or at the end of the 12C the parish church of Corpus Domini was built between the church of Notre-Dame, the baptistery and the Holy Chapel to cope with the city's growing population. Its portal still serves as the cathedral's entrance. Also surviving from the basically simple building are parts of the walls (ashlars), the half-barrel vaulting (dome in 4th bay), ornamental moulding, beautiful carved columns with double capitals and images on the springers of the blind arches.

Towards the end of the 12C the cloister was laid out by the cathedral chapter, probably replacing an older one.

In 1285 the building of a new cathedral of Saint-Sauveur was begun under Archbishop Rostan de Noves to replace the old church of Notre-

Saint-Sauveur, triptych by N.Froment, detail

Dame. It was not finished until around 1350 and the façade was not completed until 1513.

Aix-en-Provence did not become a bishopric until 381; in the 6C it was transferred to Arles, but in 826/7 the bishopric was restored. In 1425, the Bishop moved to the new cathedral together with the diocesan administration. 243 ft. long, 39 ft. wide and 62 ft. high, the increasingly important single-aisled building was built from E. with a transept, groin vaulting and plain walls with thin, clustered responds. These walls were subsequently pierced in several places to form passageways to the S. and side chapels to the N.

In the mean time, work was begun in 1322–9 on the tower, the lower part of which was completed in 1425. Then, in the 16C the spireless upper section was adorned with pinnacles. The two slender staircase turrets are later additions; the balustrade and its pinnacles are 19C. In the 14&15C chapels were built on to the N. wall, and in 1697 these were connected to the transept and to each other, and uniformly decorated to produce a sort of side

aisle to the cathedral and, simultaneously, a separate church for the brotherhood of Notre-Dame-d'Espérance. At the end of the 17C three further square chapels were added on to the N.

The present building therefore contains three churches, a baptistery, a cloister and a large number of chapels, as well as monuments from Roman times up to the 19C. The main attraction, however, is not the multi-aisled church itself, but the baptistery, cloister and, above all, N.Froment's *triptych* in the nave, a masterpiece of 15C Provençal painting.

Saint-Jean-de-Malte (corner of Rue Cardinale/Rue d'Italie, next to the Granet Museum): In 1180 the Knights of St.John, who considered it their duty to provide board and protection for travellers, founded a commandery in Aix-en-Provence on the pilgrimage route to Italy (still the Rue d'Italie). In the 13C its chapel was used as a burial place by the Counts of Provence of the House of Barcelona. In 1272–8, in fulfilment of

Saint-Sauveur, triptych

Saint-Sauveur, triptych, King René

a wish of Béatrice de Provence (one of the 5 daughters of Raymond Bérenger V), a Gothic church on a Latin cross ground plan was built in place of the chapel. In 1530 the Knights of St.John became the Knights of Malta, hence the church's name. St.-Jean-de-Malte originally had 4 towers: the 220 ft. high square bell tower on the N. side, which, in spite of its spire and graceful pinnacles, has the appearance of a fortified tower, due to its breadth and massive proportions; completed in 1376. The bells date from 1376, as do 3 smaller watch-towers. The one on the S. side was dismantled down to the height of the chapels in 1693. Of the two staircase towers either side of the W. portal, the one on the right was not built until 1703.

The relatively simple portal with blind tracery and pointed tympanum leads into the single-aisled, four-bayed church with a transept, which is arranged in typical S. French Gothic style: Elongated, room-like with a straight E. wall. The capitals of the slender round responds are foliated. Groin vaulting, extensive, traceried walls and the relatively large

E. window (panes from 1859) create an impression of lightness and height and, at the same time, massive stability. The lower part of the narrow windows in the S. aisle were walled in due to the addition of chapels in 1682–93. On the S. side, in the 2nd chapel after the entrance, is a 13C lavabo. The Resurrection of 1610 was painted by Finsonius. The 13C S. tower was removed in 1693 to bring the 3rd chapel in line with the others. In the 4th chapel is a depiction of Religion by C.Van Loo and a Descent from the Cross after Volterra. In the S. transept: Apotheosis of St.Francis of Paola by Jouvenet. In the N. transept: Reconstruction (1828) of one of the church's old tombs destroyed in 1793. The first chapel after the crossing on the N. side dates from 1331 and contains stellar vaulting and statuettes by Ch.Veyrier (17C). The bust on the tomb in the 3rd N. chapel is also by Veyrier, as are the 4 busts of Apostles in the old baptistery of 1374, which was altered in 1680.

Parish church of Sainte-Madelaine (actually Sainte-Marie-Made-

Saint-Sauveur, sarcophagus

leine, Place des Prêcheurs). In 1274 Raymond Bérenger V gave the Dominicans this church, which stood outside the city walls until the 15C. Church and monastery were rebuilt on several occasions, for the last time with a dome over the crossing in 1691–1703 (Gothic features include 3 rib-vaulted chapels). Church façade by Révoil (1855–60).

Other interesting churches
Saint-Esprit and Saint-Jérôme (Rue Espariat): Built in 1706–16 by L. and G.Valon in place of a former Augustinian monastery. Interesting altar of the Virgin Mary, 1505. In a choir chapel on the right is an altar with the Descent of the Holy Ghost by J.Daret (1653).

Former Augustinian church (opposite Saint-Esprit): Of this there remains only the 16C tower (bell tower of the Augustinians) with a wrought-iron belfry of 1677. An Augustinian monastery founded in the 13C once stood here.

Saint-Jean-Baptiste du Faubourg (Cours Sextius): Built at the end of the 17C by L.Vallon on the site of an older chapel. Interesting marble pulpit by J.-C.Rambot (1704) and high altar (18C).

Chapelle des Pénitents Gris (also: Pénitents Bourras; Rue Lieutaud): 17C, with a moving 16C Descent from the Cross (probably by J.Guiramand).

Chapelle des Pénitents Bleus (Rue du Bon-Pasteur): Dating from 1775, now used as an institute for American universities.

Chapelle des Pénitents Blancs des Carmes: Built in 1654–72. Late Gothic vaulting and baroque façade.

Hospital de Saint-Jacques: Begun in 1519, extended in 1753. Chapel with Renaissance portal of 1542. One chapel contains a 15C altar.

Église de la Visitation: Built together with the Dominican monastery in 1647–52. Late Gothic vaulting, façade by P.Pavillon (1624).

Saint-Sauveur, baptistery

Saint-Sauveur, cloister, capital

Chapelle du Collège de Jesuites (Rue Lacépède): Built around 1680 by L.Vallon in place of an older chapel. Galleries, Corinthian pilasters and stucco inside.

Chapelle des Oblates: Built around 1700 the chapel belongs to the Carmelite monastery.

Secular buildings
Clock-tower (Tour de l'Horloge; Place de l'Hôtel-de-Ville): An emblem of the city, built on Roman limestone ashlars. The clock which strikes the hours was built in 1510, although its associated figures are very recent; the astronomical clock and the wrought-iron belfry date from 1661.

Hôtel-de-Ville: Opposite the clock-tower, it was built in 1655–70 on the site of two older, 14&16C buildings to plans by P.Pavillon. The three-storeyed Italianate building surrounds an inner court and the façade is adorned with sculptures. The Salle des Marriages on the ground floor has a rib vault, as do so many 17C Provençal churches.

Halle aux Grains (S. side of the Place de l'Hôtel-de-Ville): The beautiful grain market with its row of pilasters, built by G.Vallon around 1760, now serves as the post office.

Palais de Justice (Place de Verdun, directly opposite the Madeleine church): Extensive administrative centre, begun in 1787 to plans by N.Ledoux on the site of the old castle of the Counts of Provence, by the Roman Via Aurelia gate. After the French Revolution, from 1822 onwards, it was extended in considerably simplified form by Penchaud, and in 1957 a further storey was unsympathetically added.

Pavillon de Vendôme (Pavillon de la Motte; Rue de la Molle): Built by A.Matisse (known as La Rivière) and P.Pavillon as a luxurious palace in 1664–7 in very elaborate style for Louis de Mercoeur, Duc de Vendôme. The painter J.-B.Van Loo lived here from 1730 until his death in 1745. Temporary exhibitions are now held in the palace, which is furnished with antiques.

Saint-Sauveur, cloister

Saint-Jean-de-Malte

Parc des Thermes: In the NW of the city, where in Roman times the baths had been built and where remains of Roman country villas have been excavated, there is now the Parc des Thermes. Here stands the *Tourreluque,* a 14C observation and defensive tower, the sole survivor of the 39 towers of the medieval city walls.

Hôtels: Aix-en-Provence has so many beautiful 17&18C hôtels that there is not sufficient space here to list them all. However, it is worth looking out for them (there are more than 70) and letting their special magic work on you. Typical features include the yellow stone, rusticated masonry and symmetrical division of the multistoreyed fronts by projecting pilasters. Carved portals, wrought-iron balconies and decorated window frames accentuate the gaiety of these town houses and palaces. The following is a list of the major hôtels. Rue Gaston de Saporta: No.23, *Hôtel de Maynier d'Oppède* from 1730 (now seat of the Institutes d'Études Françaises). No.21, *Hôtel Boyer de Fonscolombe* from the mid 18C. No.19, *Hôtel*

de Châteaurenard (1650) with a well-maintained staircase with wall paintings and sculptures.

Rue Marie et Pierre Curie: No.10, *Hôtel de Galice* from the beginning of the 17C with a beautiful staircase. No.17, *Hôtel d'Oraison* (18C).

Place des Cardeurs: Among others the *Hôtel de Venel* with interesting furnishing and ceiling paintings from the end of the 17C.

Rue Aude: No.13, *Hôtel de Croze-Peyroneti* (1620).

Rue Maréchal-Foch: *Hôtel d'Arbaud* from the end of the 17C.

On the little Place d'Albertas, among others: *Hôtel d'Albertas* (1707, N. corner) and *Hôtel de Boyer d'Eguilles* of 1675 (now Natural History Museum).

Place de Prêcheurs: *Hôtel d'Agut*, 1670. *Hôtel de Gras*, 1766. *Hôtel de Simiane*, 1641.

Rue Mignet: No.6, *Hôtel d'Ailhaud*, 1750. No.22–4, *Hôtel de Valbelle*, 1655.

Rue Emeric-David: No.22, *Hôtel de Carcès* (late-16C). No.16, *Hôtel de Panisse-Passis*, 1739. No.25, *Hôtel de Maliverny*, 17C.

Saint-Jean-de-Malte

Sainte-Madeleine

Rue Emeric-David: No.18, *Hôtel de Lestang-Parade*, 1650, with a small private theatre of the same date. No.26, *Hôtel de Grimaldi*, 1680.

Cours Mirabeau: No.38, *Hôtel de Maurel de Pontevès*, 1650. No.20, *Hôtel- de Forbin*, 1656. No.16, *Hôtel de Mirabeau* (18C). No.14, *Hôtel de 'Raousset-Boullon*, 1660. No.10, *Hôtel d'Isoard de Vauvenargues*, 1710. No.4, *Hôtel de Villars*, also from 1710.

On the N. side of the Cours Mirabeau there are further numerous 17&18C hôtels to admire. No.55, incidentally, is the house in which Cézanne spent his childhood.

Rue du 4-Septembre: No.9, *Hôtel de Villeneuve-Ansonis* (18C). No.11, *Hôtel de Boisgelin* (17C). No.18, *Hôtel de Valori* (or Beausset-Roquefort), mid-18C.

Rue Mazarin: No.10, *Hôtel de Ricard de Saint-Albin*, late-17C. No.12, *Hôtel de Marignane* (17C). No.14, *Hôtel Dedons de Pierrefeu* (18C).

Rue Josephe-Cabassal: No.1, *Hôtel de Caumont* (or de la Tour d'Aigues).

Fountains: Apart from the somewhat weather-beaten, but still elegant, hôtels, the city's appearance is characterized by its numerous fountains, the charm of which is undeniable. The visitor is welcomed by the splendid *Fontaine de la Rotonde*, erected under Napoleon III, in the middle of the spacious Place de Géneral-de-Gaulle, where all the main streets meet: the Avenue des Belges, the Boulevard de la République and the main thoroughfare of the inner city, the Cours Mirabeau. The splendid *Fontaine de Quatre-Dauphins*, one of the city's most beautiful fountains, recalls the fountains of the Romans and was built, after the style of Bernini, by J.C.Rambot in 1667 in the middle of a rectangular square at the intersection of the Rue du 4-Septembre and the Rue Cardinale. By the cathedral, in front of the Archbishop's palace on the Place des Martyrs de la Resistance, is the *Fontaine d'Epéluque* (1618), which was not placed here until 1953. The surround of the basin is 18C.

Music and opera: Aix-en-Provence is a city of music and a music school has been documented since the Middle Ages. The *Opera House*, built in 1756, is on the Rue de l'Opéra, the eastward continuation of the Cours Mirabeau.

Museums

Musée Granet (next to the church of Saint-Jean-de-Malte): In 1838 the museum was installed in the former commandery of 1671, which originally belonged to the church. Along with other collections the museum's principal exhibits are from the estate of the painter Granet (1775–1849). There are finds from Entremont, Celto-Ligurian sculptures, Roman, Greek and early Christian works. In the former cloister there are medieval sculptures, as well as fragments of tombs from Saint-Jean-de-Malte. The paintings in the museum, which also shows temporary exhibitions, are from the 15–20C and vary greatly in quality. Alongside works by unknown masters and a few colossal works from the 19C are paintings by artists ranging from Bouts, Rembrandt and Rubens to Ingres and Cézanne. Among the sculptures are works by Bernini, Giovanni da Bologna, Houdon and others. Local art is well represented.

Musée des Tapisseries: This museum is housed in the former archbishop's palace, which was built next to the cathedral from 1648 onwards. The interior from 1780 has largely survived. Tapestries have been exhibited here since 1905, in particular the famous ones woven in Beauvais, the 6 grotesques tapestries, to designs by J.Bérain (1637–1711), the 9 wall-hangings of scenes from the life of Don Quixote, conceived by Ch.-J.Natoire (1700–77), and a series of 6 original ones designed by J.-B. Le Prince (1734–81). The museum also

Aix-en-Provence, Fondation Vasarely

displays 17&18C sculptures, reliefs and paintings (e.g. by Van Loo, Puget and Finsonius).

Musée du Vieil Aix (Rue de Gaston-de-Saporta): The museum is in the Hôtel d'Estienne de Saint-Jean of 1668 with its beautiful façade and some of the old furnishings, directly opposite the tapestry museum. Interesting collection of dolls, marionettes and santons (Nativity figures). Also exhibits of folklore and arts and crafts, as well as old views of the city.

Musée Paul Arbaud (Rue du 4-Septembre 2): The Arbaud collection, housed in the Hôtel d'Arbaud, also the home of the Académie d'Aix, includes paintings by Van Loo, Fragonard, Granet, Puget and others, and fine old books.

Fondation Vasarely: Follow the Boulevard de la République westwards, out of the city and over a bridge, and on a hill to the left is the unusual structure of the Fondation Vasarely of 1975, which is both a museum (works by Vasarely) and a study centre.

Allauch
13 Bouches-du-Rhône   p.256□D 7

Now a mere dormitory suburb of Marseille, Allauch was once a self-sufficient town with its own walls. Parts of this still survive on the hill top to the E., the original site of the market town, also a square 13C gate tower. The site of the church is now occupied by the Chapelle Notre-Dame, rebuilt in 1859.

The modern satellite town has a 16/17C *church* with an 18C façade (interesting 'Ascension' by Monticelli), 4 17C *windmills* (Esplanade Fréderic-Mistral) and a *local history museum (Oustau Alau)* housed in an 18C town house (Place Pierre Bellot).

Environs: Château-Gombert (5 km. NW): Old village, more or less absorbed by Marseille, in which an international folklore festival is held annually at the start of July. The *church* (18C), which is worth a visit if only for the 'Raising of Lazarus' by L.Finson, also houses other interesting works.

Grottes Loubière (2.5 km. NW): An impressive cave, some 2,300 ft. long, which is divided into a series of caverns.

Ansouis

84 Vaucluse   p.256□D 6

This beautiful little village, site of an important castle since the 10C, is known locally principally as the birthplace of St.Elzéar, who was born here in 1285 as son of the Count of Sabran.

Castle: The *old part* is a massive, only partly preserved fortress from the 12, 13 and 15C, in which the 'Saints' Room' is still shown, where St.Elzéar and his beatified wife Delphine took their vow of chastity. In the *new château*, a very beautiful, early-17C building, the banqueting hall, with its Flemish tapestries depicting the story of Dido and Aeneas, and other rooms decorated with elegant stucco are opened to visitors.

Musée extraordinaire (in the village): This is dedicated to the diver Georges Mazoyer.

Apt

84 Vaucluse   p.256□D 5

Now famous only for its *fruits confits* and as a centre of ochre production, Apt was once capital of Celto-Ligurian Vulgientii and, after its destruction and rebuilding by the Romans in *c.* 40 BC as *Colonia Apta Julia*, a provincial capital on the Via Domitia—the road linking the Rhône valley

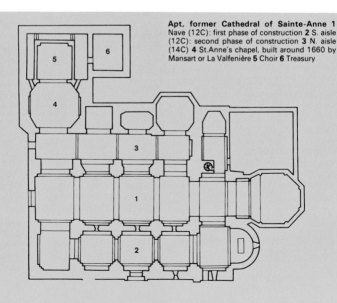

Apt, former Cathedral of Sainte-Anne 1 Nave (12C): first phase of construction **2** S. aisle (12C): second phase of construction **3** N. aisle (14C) **4** St.Anne's chapel, built around 1660 by Mansart or La Valfenière **5** Choir **6** Treasury

and the plain of the Po. Today, however, there are few traces left of its glorious history, apart from the *Pont Julien*, a well-preserved Roman bridge, lying a few km. W. of the town.

Sainte-Anne (a cathedral until the Revolution): Formerly housed in the basilica in the forum, which was totally destroyed in 896, an administrative building with a Gallo-Roman apse, the former cathedral was rebuilt in the 11C on the same site and renovated from the ground up in the 2nd half of the 12C. In the 13&14C the Romanesque building acquired a N. and S. aisle and further additions and extensions followed in the 16–18C.

The *exterior*, a faithful reflection of the various periods of building, does not, therefore, make a unified impression. The beautiful and imaginative baroque *portal*, with St.Anne in the tympanum, is particularly out of keeping with the rest of the building. The only feature to have survived quite unaltered from the Romanesque church is the massive *tower* over the crossing with its stone pavilion roof.

The *clock tower* with its wrought-iron bell tower on the S. side is 16C.

The *interior* also seems stylistically disjointed as a result of the alterations carried out over the centuries. The N. aisle, for example, is considerably lower than the older S. aisle, and the two arms of the transept also differ in width and depth. This is completely compensated for, however, by a visit to the two *crypts*, the upper one of which, in particular, reveals complete expertise and mastery of technique. While the lower crypt, which possibly dates from the time of the old basilica, convinces through its simplicity, the Romanesque crypt above it stands out with its rich and clear spatial division into an apse with ambulatory and five small aisles, as well as its beautiful vaulting.

Museum: The exhibits consist predominantly of prehistoric finds, Gallo-Roman ceramics, Roman bronzes, burial offerings and faience—in the 18C Apt was an important centre for their production.

Also worth seeing, apart from the

Apt, Sainte-Anne

narrow old streets and alleys, is the *Porte de Saignon,* a 14C town gate from the 14C, and the Hôtel-de-Ville, the *former bishop's palace,* built around 1780.

Environs: Caseneuve (8.5 km. NE): Old *château* with beautiful Romanesque façade.

Gignac (14 km. NE): Old *château* and starting point for a walk through the 'Colorado provençal', the impressive ochre quarries of the neighbourhood.

Javon (22 km. NW): 16C *château* restored by the painter P.Vayson.

Lagarde d'Apt (19 km. NE): Highest village at the foot of Mont Saint-Pierre (4,120 ft.), the highest point of the Vaucluse (lavender, honey, goat's cheese).

Lioux (19 km. NW): Small village at the foot of an awesome precipice.

Pérréal: In pre-Roman times the Vulgientii built an oppidum on this 1,551 ft. high hill to the NW. Recently many interesting fossils and even several fossilized skeletons from the Tertiary period have been discovered here.

Roussillon (13 km. NW): Set in incomparably beautiful scenery, this old village is a starting point for excursions to the ochre cliffs and quarries (Val des Fées, Chaussée des Géants).

Rustrel (10 km. NE): 17C *château,* now Hôtel-de-Ville.

Saint-Lambert (25 km. NW): Typical Provençal *château* with massive towers from the 16&17C, now a rest home.

Saint-Saturnin d'Apt (9 km. N.): Of the old château, whose ruins dominate the market town, there remains only a *Romanesque chapel* from the mid 11C.

Viens (22 km. E.): Small, old village with several *Romanesque houses,* a partly Romanesque *church* and a *château* with Romanesque and Gothic elements.

Arles

13 Bouches-du-Rhône   p.256☐B 6

Thanks to the extensive farming in the Camargue, Arles is today an

Apt, Sainte-Anne, chapel

important agricultural market, but its days of glory are long gone. Nevertheless, there are still numerous testaments to its earlier international significance. The rocky plateau in the marshes of the Rhône delta was settled as far back as prehistoric times and in the 6C BC there were already trade links with the Phocaeans. This explains the Greek name *Theline* for the Celto-Ligurian settlement (meaning 'the provider'), although this was later replaced by *Arelate* ('town in the marshes'). Its truly astonishing rise only came about in Roman times. The building of the Via Domitia, the road connecting Spain and Rome, and the subsequent development of the hinterland of Gaul through the Via Aurelia, the Via Regorda and the Via Agrippa, which placed Arles more or less at the intersection of the great trade routes, made it the rival of the Phocaean foundation of Massalia or Massilia, which the Romans named Marseille. It received a further boost from the cutting of the Fosses Mariennes, the canal opened by Marius in 104 BC through the swamps of the Rhône delta, which linked Arles directly to the coast at Fos. Arles profited greatly when it sided with Caesar in his struggle against Pompey, from which Ceasar emerged victorious. So, while Marseille's walls and temples were being pulled down, Arles was declared a Roman colony (46 BC) and veterans of the 6th Legion were settled there (Colonia Julia Arelate Sextanorum). The buildings, castrum, forum, temples, baths, amphitheatre, circus and triumphal arches that its new status called for soon followed and in the course of the 1&2C a Roman town was built along the lines of Rome, provided with water by an aqueduct and surrounded by a wall: *Gallula Roma,* the little Rome of Gaul. And indeed, at the start of the 4C under Constantine, Arles was nearly designated as the new capital of the Roman Empire instead of Constantinople. However the power struggles with Licinius were the decisive factor in favour of Constantinople (330), and Arles had to make do with its rank as a capital and administrative centre of the 4 Roman dioceses (Britain, Spain, N. and S. Gaul). In 879, following the turmoil of the ons-

Apt, fountain in front of the town hall

Arles, town hall

laughts by Goths, Franks, Saracens and Normans, it became capital of the kingdom of Provence. And even in the following centuries, despite the near civil war of the 12C from which the citizens managed to win a temporary consular constitution, the city still had such an aura that both the Emperor Barbarossa (1178) and Charles IV (1365) had themselves crowned King of Provence here. In 1481 the Kingdom of Arelat, which was named after Arles, became part of France together with Provence and declined in importance—although certainly not for such artists and painters as Van Gogh, who brought the city renewed fame. Arles can in fact look back over a long artistic tradition. Its sculpture workshops and studios for carving sarcophagi were, even in Roman times, at the centre of artistic life in Gaul.

Ancient theatre: With a diameter of 335 ft. the building is still an impressive, massive complex, although little remains of the three tiers of arcades of the exterior and the three concentric walls, which once enclosed the semi-circular auditorium. The purpose of this triple ring was to support the three caveae, which comprised 4, 9 and 20 rows of seats, accommodating a total of 12,000 spectators. For this purpose the rings were interconnected by radial transverse walls, the spaces in between serving as staircases for the auditorium—so ensuring the structural strength of the massive building and the smooth circulation of the equally great masses of people.

Les Arènes: Now undoubtedly the most impressive building in Arles and, with dimensions of 446 x 351 ft., the largest surviving amphitheatre in Gaul, it must have seemed even more massive in Roman times. For originally the two tiers of arcades, each with 60 arches, were crowned by an upper, attic storey, the stones of which were removed for other purposes over the centuries—some being used to build the 200 or so houses which until the last century cluttered up the arena itself. There was nothing out of the ordinary about the decoration: projecting Doric pilasters bore a frieze and cornice

Arles, ancient theatre

above the architrave of the lower tier; Corinthian half-columns on the upper tier. One unusual feature was the fact that the outer gallery, instead of being vaulted by round arches, as was normal Roman practice, was covered by enormous slabs, showing Greek influence. The actual *arena*, a 226 x 128 ft. area carved out of the rock, was originally covered with a wooden floor, below which were the machines required for particular productions. The *cavea*, the auditorium, was laid out so that no draught could reach the seats and the building could be smoothly emptied after the performances. The date of the arena is still disputed, but could be late-1C or early-2C. At the time of the Saracen onslaughts, at any rate, the arena was used as a fortress and the ground floor arcades walled up. It was often to fulfil this function over the centuries, and in the 12&13C the fortified watch towers (which stand to this day) were built. It was not until the 19C that the arena was cleared of the houses which had been built to provide shelter during times of danger. Today it is used to stage bull-fights, in which, unlike in Spain, the object is to wrest a cockade from the bull's horns rather than to kill the animal.

Forum (directly S. of the present Place du Forum): Practically nothing has survived of the forum, which was of such prime importance in a Roman city, forming, along with the baths, the centre of public life.

Cryptoportiques (access from the Musée Lapidaire Chrétienne): An enormous, U-shaped, underground complex, 348 ft. long and 236 ft. wide. The two sides of the U consist of two parallel galleries with barrel vaults, which are connected by round-arched openings between huge square pillars. This building, situated below the porticoes enclosing the forum and dating from the 1C BC, probably served as a granary, judging from the air-holes in the vaulting.

City wall: Little remains of the two city walls built in Roman times. Of particular interest are the *Porte de la Redoute*, two semicircular gate towers projecting from the wall, through

Arles, arena

which the Via Aurelia once led into the city (and the aqueduct, about 6 ft. underground), and the now polygonal *Tour des Mourgues*, which was round in Roman times. Much of the adjoining wall is later.

Baths (on the right bank of the Rhône): Of this palatial complex, once some 656 ft. long, all that remains standing is a semicircular apse, the so-called *Palais de la Trouille*, which, due to the alternating layers of cut natural stone and red brick (opus mixtum), is dated as late Roman. At that time the building probably, like all complexes of its kind, housed a cold bath (frigidarium), a luke-warm bath (tepidarium) and a hot bath (caldarium), as well as steam baths, gymnasiums, changing rooms and rest rooms, a library, refreshment rooms and possibly a garden.

Former cathedral of Saint-Trophime: A very early bishopric, Arles seems to have had a cathedral by the city walls as early as the 3C. Around 450 Bishop Hilarius commissioned the first building on the site of the present cathedral, which was initially dedicated to St.Stephan, but in the 10C was placed under the protection of St.Trophimus. Between 1078 and 1152 the nave was rebuilt, tower and façade following in the 2nd half of the 12C. In the 14C the N. chapels were built on, in the 15C the choir was begun and in the 17C the S. side was extended with the addition of side chapels. In 1870–3 a thorough restoration was finally carried out. Today the former cathedral is one of the most interesting examples of the Provençal Romanesque, due firstly to its massive, almost bare interior, and secondly to its uniquely beautiful Romanesque carving.

W. front and portal: Apart from the richly decorated portal, the exterior of the basilica (nave and two aisles) is astonishingly simple. The W. front, taken over from the preceding Carolingian building, was originally entirely plain, in the style of early Christian basilicas. The splendid portal was, as can be seen from the buttresses still projecting above its gable, added later, as were the steps leading

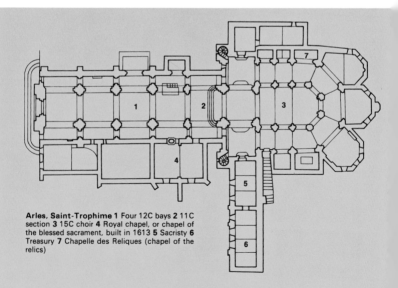

Arles, Saint-Trophime 1 Four 12C bays **2** 11C section **3** 15C choir **4** Royal chapel, or chapel of the blessed sacrament, built in 1613 **5** Sacristy **6** Treasury **7** Chapelle des Reliques (chapel of the relics)

up to and accentuating it—one consequence of these was that the floor level had to be raised by over 3 feet.

Interior: After the incredible sculptural wealth of the portal the interior surprises one with its almost total lack of decoration. The unusually high, narrow room, covered by a longitudinal barrel vault with transverse arches, can thus unfold all the more untroubled in its singularity.

Cloister: The crowning glory of the whole cathedral is the cloister, which, with its unusually rich carving, is probably the most famous in Provence. Provençal Romanesque reveals its most original and most beautiful side here, although only the mid-12C N. and E. walks are Romanesque. The S. and the W. ones were not added until around the middle of the 14C and, in spite of certain concessions to the existing half, were decorated in Gothic style. Particularly famous is the N. side, the oldest part, which still has archaic features, while the E. side heralds the Gothic influence from the N.

Notre-Dame-la-Major (Place la Major): This simple church is mainly 12C Romanesque apart from the portal (1592) and tower (17C). The charm of its interior lies in the tension between Romanesque and Gothic, between the massive, broad nave on the one hand and the narrow aisles and richly furnished choir on the other.

Saint-Blaise and Saint-Jean-le-Moustier: (Rue Vauban): Originally two chapels of the monastery of Saint-Césaire, which was moved into the city from the Alyscamps in 508. Although Saint-Jean-le-Moustier only survives as a Romanesque bay and a most beautiful apse; with Saint-Blaise we can follow the repairs and rebuilding carried out over the centuries. The oldest bay, the third, with its pure round arch vaulting, dates from the start of the 12C, as do the two very narrow aisles and the

domical vault of the crossing. The following bay is from the end of the 12C and the first bay, with its lightly pointed barrel vault and, for acoustic reasons, walled in vases, from the end of the 13C. The elegant window in the W. front is 14C, the porch 17C.

Saint-Genès à Trinquetaille: This simple little single-aisled, two-bayed church from the 12C is dedicated to St.Genesius, a clerk of the court of the city, who was beheaded on this spot in the suburb of Trinquetaille in the 3C for refusing to write an edict for the persecution of Christians.

Les Alyscamps: Of this extensive necropolis, once famous over a wide area, there remains today only an avenue of sarcophagi and a half-ruined church, squeezed between the Canal de Craponne, factories and residential quarters. By far the largest part was sacrificed to the building of the railway and the industrialization of the 19C. Already laid out in Gallo-Roman times along the Via Aurelia outside the city gates, the cemetery, which was probably taken over by the

Arles, Saint-Trophime

Christians around the mid 4C, was already the subject of legends in the 6C. During its reputed consecration by St. Trophimus, for example, Christ is supposed to have appeared in person and various miracles are supposed to have later occurred at the tomb of the saint. This reputation soon led to people from far away having themselves buried in the Alyscamps, the Champs-Elysées, the 'Elysian fields'. Indeed, according to some chroniclers, it was customary in the Rhône valley to let the coffin containing the dead body and a specific sum of money float down the river to Arles, where it would be fished out of the water at the Trinquetaille bridge and be buried. It was taken for granted that the heroes who fell at Roncevaux, while helping Charlemagne throw back the Saracens in the plain of Arles, lay buried in the Alyscamps. It was even believed that the corpses of the Christians were miraculously moved from the vast tangle of bodies on the battlefield into stone sarcophagi.

The church of *Saint-Honorat*, situated at the end of the avenue of sarcophagi and surrounded since the 6C by tiers of tombs, is one of the few cemetery churches and chapels still standing today. The two others, Saint-Pierre-et-Saint-Paul-de-Mouleyrès on the hill to the N. of the Alyscamps and the Chapelle de la Genouillade or Agenouillade on the road to Marseille, are artistically less important, but give one a good idea of the former extent of the old city of the dead. Saint-Honorat, the most famous of all and from early on a much sought-after burial place, dates back to Carolingian times. The intricate masonry from that period can still be seen in the nave, although the regular layers of ashlars from the Romanesque rebuilding at the end of the 12C greatly predominate. The two-storeyed *tower* over the crossing, with its massive base, is considered the most beautiful tower in Provence. Pierced on all sides by large arches, like the Roman arena in Arles, it comes across as monumental and, at the same time, vibrant and elegant. The function of the tower lantern was to display the watch candle on all sides to show the pilgrims the way.

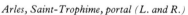

Arles, Saint-Trophime, portal (L. and R.)

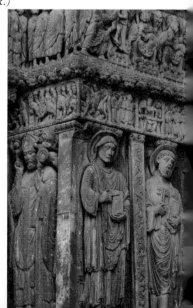

The *interior* of the basilica with its slightly higher nave and two aisles was unfortunately much impaired by the cylindrical cladding of the pillars in the 16C (necessary for support) and the resulting alteration of the proportions. The *crypt* beneath the apse, rebuilt and reduced in size around 1615, once contained the mortal remains of St.Trophimus and St.Honoratus, who was transferred in the 14C to the monastery founded by him on the Iles de Lerins and, like St.Trophimus, later transferred to the cathedral. In the course of the 15, 16 and 17C chapels and wall tombs were added to the church, and to the four bays of the nave which had never been rebuilt.

Hôtel-de-Ville (Place de la République): This building, begun by La Valfenière in 1666 and completed after his death to plans and elevations by J.Peyret and J.Hardouin-Mansart, a master of French baroque, is one of the the the most important works of its time: Not only because of the truly ingenious flat vault in the ground floor hall, which was to be found in every 18C text book on architecture, but also because of the harmonious balance of verticals and horizontals on the façade, the great preoccupation of French baroque. A balanced and, for all its restraint, conspicuous relief is created by the horizontal grooves on the rusticated base and the accentuation of the three storeys by means of cornices, friezes and balustrades on the one hand and by the accentuation of the vertical axes through pairs of columns and double pilasters, continued by vases above the attic storey, on the other. Looming over the whole building is the tower, built back in 1553, the pavilion roof of which was surmounted by a contemporary bronze figure of Mars, the God of War, in the 17C. On the occasion of the building of the Hôtel-de-Ville an obelisk from the Roman circus in Arles was set up in the square in front, the Place de la République, in 1676.

Museums
Musée Arlaten (in the Hôtel Laval-Castellane, Rue de la République): This unusually rich and interesting Provençal history museum, created

Arles, Saint-Trophime, portal

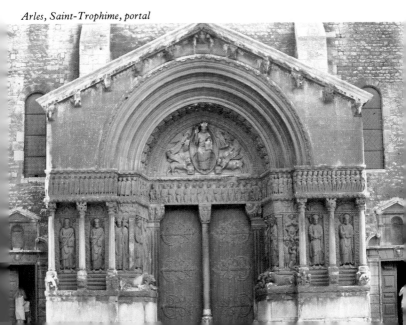

by the poet Fréderic Mistral, is housed in a beautiful early-16C building arranged around an inner court, which will itself repay attention. In the court, furthermore, is the recently excavated Roman complex discussed in the section devoted to the Forum.

Musée Lapidaire d'Art Chrétien (in the former Jesuit church, Rue Calade): Before entering the museum devote some time to the two storey baroque façade with Ionic and Corinthian pilasters and then turn to the lofty two-storeyed hall and the overwhelming, two-tiered altar which fills the whole of the choir. There is also a striking wooden ceiling, carved in the form of a Gothic ribbed vault. Only then should one move on to the exhibits in this relatively small room which, after the Lateran Museum in Rome, contains the most important collection of early Christian sarcophagi; most of which are from Arles' two cemeteries, the Alyscamps and Saint-Genès de Trinquetaille—the majority were even made in local workshops. The oldest pieces, however, such as the Dioscuri sarcophagus (probably early-4C), the sarcophagus (379/95) of Bishop Concordius, the sarcophagus of Hydria Tertulla (c. 340, Rome) and the sarcophagus with columns and showing Christ teaching (c. 400, Rome) had to be imported. Outstanding amongst the *Arlesian sarcophagi* is the Eucharistic sarcophagus from the end of the 4C, a columned sarcophagus with 2 Apostles on each side below an arch, and on top the Israelites crossing the Red Sea. Do not, however, overlook the sarcophagi with just two zones of reliefs or those with friezes, as well as the sarcophagi with very low, stiacciato reliefs, which go back to pagan models. Very beautiful too are the Romanesque capitals and the pillars with carved figures from the cloister of Montmajour abbey. The museum also has a remarkable collection of early Christian coins and ceramics.

Musée Lapidaire d'Art Païen (in the church of Sainte-Anne or Notre-Dame-la-Principale, Place de la Révolution): Behind the simple façade, with its baroque portal framed by double pilasters and entablature, this single-aisled, hall-like church, built 1619–29, houses the most impressive collection of Roman art in Provence. The basis of the collection was laid by Père Dumont in 1793 with sarcophagi and sculptures from the Alyscamps. The collection was, and still is, constantly being added to with new finds uncovered by excavations and construction work. Outstanding amongst the finds from the Gallo-Roman past—statues of gods and other sculptures—are the monumental statue of Augustus, two dancing girls (marble, 1C BC), the great Altar of Apollo and the Venus of Arles (original in the Louvre), all of which are from the ancient theatre; the sarcophagus of Phaedra and Hippolytus (2C) and the Muse sarcophagus, as well as the beautiful mosaic pavements (Orpheus with Lyre, Rape of Europa, Capture of the Golden Fleece, signs of the Zodiac and the seasons), some of which are from Roman villas in Trinquetaille.

Musée Réattu (in the Grand-Prieuré des Hôpitaliers de Saint-Jean-de-Jérusalem, Quai Max Dormoy): This beautiful building, built for the commandery of the Knights of Malta at the start of the 16C and still distinctly fortress-like in character, served as the seat of the Grand Priory of the order in the province after 1615. After the French Revolution it was bought by the painter J.J. Réattu and set up as a museum by the city after his death. Apart from paintings by Réattu, local 17&18C works are exhibited, as well as works by artists who painted in Arles: Vlaminck, Léger and Picasso. Alongside these much space is devoted to photography, the ultimate intention being to create an international centre for this art form.

Also worth seeing: *Porte de la Cavalerie*, 17C, on the Place Lamartine. *Hôtel de Lalauzière* (Rue de la République), baroque portal. *Renaissance portal* of the chapel of the Hôpital du Saint-Esprit (Rue Dulai). *Lock bridge* at the S. end of the industrial zone, which is exactly like the one Van Gogh painted in 1888 half a mile away. Finally, the *Boulevard des Lices*, with its plane trees and inviting street-front cafés.

Events: *Bull-fights* during the tourist season, *festivals of traditional costume* (early July), the *Festival d'Arles* (in the 2nd half of July), which is entirely devoted to dance and is visited by young, choreographers from all over the world, and the equally international photography festival in July and August.

Environs: Camargue (S. of Arles): Strictly speaking the island between the Petit and the Grand Rhône, but more broadly the boundless plain, swept by the cold Mistral, between the Étang de Mauguio or de l'or in the W. and the Étang de Berre: in short, the Rhône delta with its infertile grasslands, reed-choked marshes and flat lagoons, known throughout the world as the home of flamingoes and fighting bulls. The real lords here are the Gardians, a kind of French cowboy, who banded together as long ago as 1572, as the Antique Confrèrie des Gardians, and each April stage a great festival with traditional games in the amphitheatre in Arles. They live in 'cabanes', tiny dwellings with a semicircular extension at the back of the house with a kitchen equipped with an enormous hearth, which is simultaneously used as a living room. Although it did not become France's rice-growing area until after the 2nd World War and the loss of the Indo-Chinese colonies (before then rice, introduced in the 16C, was grown only to desalinate the muddy soil and was fed to animals), the Camargue had from early times attracted people with its strange, melancholy charm. The Greeks of Marseille are supposed to have built a temple to Artemis of Ephesus here, and although its site

Arles, Saint-Trophime, cloister, Entry into Jerusalem (L.), and the Annunciation (R.)

has not yet been discovered, its existence is supported by the excavation of numerous Attic pottery fragments from the 5&4C BC and Gallo-Roman finds. We know for sure, however, that the citizens of Arles, as far back as Roman times, used the grasslands of the delta for breeding livestock and growing corn and exploited the woods, which were still extensive at that time, for their shipyards. In the Middle Ages whole series of watchtowers were built and several large abbeys founded in the clearings (Psalmody, Ulmet, Sylveréal), all indicative of the growing economic importance of the area. Systematic development was not, however, begun until the 16C with the building of dykes.

The *Musée Camarguais* (in Mas du Pont de Rousty, 11.5 km. S. of Arles) offers a wealth of information on the area.

Château de l'Armellière (15 km. S.): Beautiful square castle with machicolations and flanked by towers, built in 1607 by a former royal officer.

La Crau: This area was once so inhospitable to man, consisting only of rocks and swamps covering an area of some 77 square miles, that it was said that Zeus had let it rain pebbles and stones to assist Heracles in his fight with the giants Albion and Bergion, who barred his way to the Hesperides. In fact the river Durance was really to blame, the delta of which once opened directly into the sea at Lamanon.

Mas de Méjanes (22 km. SW): Old Provençal estate going back to the 11C.

Aups
83 Var   p.258□F 6

A delightful landscape extends from the foot of the Espiguières Hills, nestled in which is this old village. The walls (12&16C) with gates and a clock tower are the main feature of the Old Town.

Church (late-15C): S. French Gothic in style, it contains (2nd chapel on the right) a 16C triptych, a Martyrdom of St.Bartholomew (1646) and a Presentation in the Temple (18C, by Dandré-Bardon). The beautiful wooden panelling is 17C.

Museum (Rue Albert Ier): 300 paintings of the Parisian School are exhibited in this former Ursuline chapel.

Also worth seeing: E. of the village, on a rocky height, stands the *chapel of Saint-Marc*. A 90 minute walk to the NE takes one to the *chapel of Notre-Dame-de-Liesse*; beautiful setting.

Environs: Ampus (18 km. E.): The former Roman Antea has a Romanesque *church* and the *chapel of Notre-Dame-de-Spéluque* (both 12C).

Baudinard-sur-Verdon (16 km. NW): 12C Romanesque *priory of Valmogne*.

Cotignac (15 km. SW): 2 square *towers* dominate the town, some of

Arles, Saint-Trophime, Roman sarcophagus

whose *houses* still date from the 16–18C (Renaissance *hospital*). The *church* was built in 1514. Standing on a rock is the *chapel of Notre-Dame de Bon Secours* and 1 km. NW of Costignac is the famous *pilgrimage chapel of Notre-Dame des Grâces* (1519).

Entrecasteaux (18 km. S.): Le Nôtre laid out the gardens of the 17C *château*. The Gothic *church* was built in the 14C.

Tourtour (15 km. SE): Medieval village with *ruined fortress*; former *château*.

Villecroze (8 km. SE): This place derives its name from its *cave dwellings*. 11&13C Romanesque *church*.

Avignon

84 Vaucluse   p.256□B 5

Avignon's turbulent history reaches, as recent excavations have shown, back through the Bronze and Iron Ages into the Neolithic. The site on the Rhône, protected by a 197 ft. high limestone cliff, seems to have attracted new settlers continually. In Celtic times, for example, the Cavarii, who were driven out by the Romans around the 1C BC, and in post-Roman times the Burgundians, Visigoths and Ostrogoths, Franks, Saracens and Normans. Under Hadrian *Avenio*, as the future papal city was called by the Romans, acquired the status of a Roman colony, on account of its strategic importance, and the soldiers and officials, who were not prepared to do without their comfort, built villas, baths, theatres and even temples. In the 12C the city, which had grown prosperous through trade and commerce and had even belonged temporarily to the Holy Roman Empire, was elevated to a city republic with a consular constitution (consul = elected representative of the citizens). However, as a result of opposing the French King in the Albigensian Wars, its walls and 300 fortified houses were dismantled in 1226. Some 50 years later (1274) the city, again as a result of the Albigensian Wars, fell to the Holy See and, at the beginning of the 14C, became the residence of the popes, who no longer felt secure in Rome. This brought Avignon to the pinnacle of its fortunes and much new building was undertaken, while the Holy City, on the other hand, suffered a sad decline. The Palace of the Popes was built; *Livrées* and *Cardinalizes*, town houses for temporal and spiritual dignitaries, shot out of the ground; a university was founded and the city enclosed by a strong wall. Out of the Romanesque there grew a typical Gothic city with over 60,000 inhabitants, a successful, rich community. Even the Pope's return to Rome could not shake the city's sound economic base, even though it was accompanied by a noticeable fall in population, and in spite of increasing neglect from the Papal legates (later even replaed by deputy legates) the city continued to maintain its economic and cultural importance. In 1791 it finally passed to France and in 1797 even the Pope consented to its annexation. Today Avignon forms a conurbation with over 150,000 inhabitants, covering an area nearly four times as large as the old medieval city.

Palais des Papes: The Palace of the Popes, built mainly by Popes Benedict XII (1334–42) and Clement VI (1342–52), is more like a fortress than a palace. Enormous and solid, it towers over the city, appearing at first sight as if poured from one mould. Closer inspection reveals, however, that the N. part, the *Palais Vieux* (Old Palace) of the former Cistercian monk, Benedict XII, is simpler and more severe than the more luxurious S. section, the *Palais Neuf* (New Palace) of the Prince of the Church, Clement VI, who lived in great style. After the Pope's return to Rome the palace still served for a time as residence of the Papal legates and deputy legates, but deteriorated rapidly.

During the Revolution it was to be razed as the 'Bastille of the South', but this was prevented by the indestructibility of its masonry. So it shared the fate of many important buildings—it was used as a prison and converted into barracks in 1818. In 1900 it became the property of the city and the structure—badly damaged in the course of the centuries—was restored. The *Old Palace*, built around a cloister by P.Poisson on the site of the earlier bishop's palace, consists of 4 sides and a series of towers, several of which (Tour de Trouillas, Tour de la Glaciere and the kitchen, which was added later by Clement VI) were combined into a tower block. Characteristic of this part are the enormous buttresses and tall pointed blind arcades running around the outside, with comparatively tiny windows and battlements, and, for the 14C, very old-fashioned machicolations for hot pitch, oil and water. At one time the Tour de Trouillas also had battlements. These towers served various purposes, as their names suggest. The two corner towers (the *Tour de la Campane* and the *Tour de Trouillas*) were used primarily for defence, the *Tour Saint-Jean* in front of the Aile du Consistoire on the E. side was a chapel and the *Tour des Anges* or *du Pape* with the addition of the *Tour de l'Étude* served as a residence and study for the Pope. The *New Palace* to the S. (the S. and W. wings forming a right angle, the Tour de la Garde-Robe and the Tour Saint-Laurent), built by Jean de Louvre, most obviously distinguishes itself from the old one by the larger windows on the S. side and blind arcades reduced to half-height on the W. front with a parapet walk above. It is architecturally interesting that the S. wing, although consisting of one vast room on the upper floor, is supported (apart from by the blind arcades) by just a single enormous flying buttress in the centre of the outer side and by the narrow three-storeyed staircase on the court side.

Interior: Old Palace: The main entrance on the W. front, which is crowned by two slender turrets, leads into the Cour d'Honneur, the main courtyard of the New Palace, and this in turn opens through a gate in its NE corner into the *Cour du Cloître* of the Old Palace. This irregular cloister court, once surrounded on all four sides by two-storeyed galleries, is now bordered by four wings meeting each other at irregular angles: The *Aile du Conclave* to the S., the *Aile des Familiers* to the W., the *Chapelle de Benoît XII* to the N. (the two latter wings are now used to house and look after the archives) and the *Aile du Consistoire* to the E. Here the Pope would receive kings and their envoys in the *Salle du Consistoire* on the ground floor, while the *Grand Tinel* above it was used as a banqueting hall. Displayed on the ground floor today are 18C tapestries and on the upper floor the frescos taken from the tympanum of the cathedral. The *Tour Saint-Jean*, reached from the Aile du Consistoire, also has some beautiful frescos by M.Giovanetti. Its two chapels, the *Chapelle Saint-Jean* on the ground floor, dedi-

Avignon, town wall

cated to St.John the Evangelist and John the Baptist, and the *Chapelle Saint-Martial* on the first floor, were both decorated by M.Giovanetti with scenes from the lives of the saints. In the 19C the frescos and plaster were detached from the wall and sold by the soldiers billeted in the palace, so that now the lower half of the walls of the Chapelle Saint-Jean, which was once completely frescoed, are bare. An idea of the former, almost miniature-like, beauty of this chapel is provided by the Chapelle Saint-Martial, the walls, vaults and ribs of which are still to a large extent covered with frescos. The Aile du Consistoire also leads to the *Aile du Conclave*, the upper floor of which was used for conclaves or to accommodate important guests (the ground floor was reserved for servants of the Pope). The wing now houses a local history museum.

Via what was the treasury of the old bishop's palace one proceeds from the Aile du Consistoire to the *Tour des Anges*, standing outside the original square of the old palace, which was added as a residence for the Pope and consists of a treasure chamber, chamberlain's room, Papal chamber, upper treasure chamber and large library.

New Palace: Clement VI, for whom the old Papal apartments appear to have been insufficient, had a new tower, the *Tour de la Garde-Robe*, built next to the old one and the 'new bedroom' of the Pope, the *Chambre du Cerf*, named after its beautiful wall paintings, installed on the 3rd floor. The frescos covering all the walls were painted in 1343, probably under the direction of M.Giovanetti, and depict hunting and fishing scenes ('cerf' means deer) and bathing and fruit-picking youths of almost indescribable fineness and harmony of colour. Likewise the other parts of the Old Palace failed to satisfy the requirements of the urbane and extravagant Pope and so, as well as the *Aile des Grands Dignitaires*, the wing for great dignitaries, he also had yet another large reception room and a large chapel built. The *Salle de la Grande Audience*, a two-aisled hall on the ground floor, has an elegant vault, originally painted by M.Giovanetti, with imaginatively carved consoles.

Unfortunately only two of the vault paintings survive: the 'Prophets' and the 'Erythraean Sibyl'. The *Papal Chapel* on the upper floor has beautiful, slender groin vaults and the nave, 171 ft. long, 49 ft. wide and only 66 ft. high, seems really broad, due to the absence of a central row of columns. In N. France such an arrangement of space would have been quite unimaginable for a Gothic chapel, but Avignon is in the South and this is one of the region's most beautiful Gothic religious buildings. Its beauty is in no way lessened by another characteristic feature of S. Gothic—the blank walls unrelieved by windows.

As in the other rooms, practically nothing remains of the original furnishing. The *staircase* connecting the chapel and audience hall was built on in the courtyard and provides support against the outward thrust of the main wing. From the large window in the

Avignon, Palais des Papes

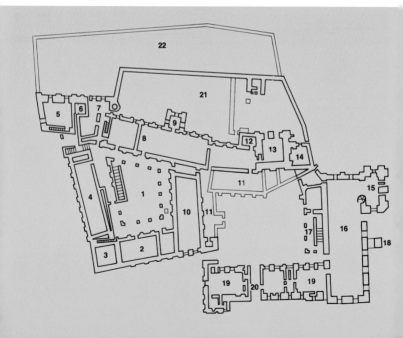

Avignon, Palais des Papes (ground floor) 1
Cour du Cloître **2** Aile des Familiers **3** Tour de la
Campane **4** Chapelle de Benoît XII **5** Tour de
Trouillas **6** Oubliette tower(?) **7** Kitchen tower **8**
Aile du Consistoire **9** Tour Saint-Jean **10** Aile du
Conclave **11** These parts of the palace are no
longer standing **12** Tour de l'Étude **13** Tour des
Anges **14** Tour de la Garde-Robe **15** Tour Saint-
Laurent **16** Large audience chamber **17** Staircase
18 Flying buttress **19** Aile des Grands Dignitaires
20 Entrance **21** Garden of Benedict XII **22** Garden
of Clement VI and Urban V (partially destroyed)

Avignon, Palais des Papes (upper storey) 1
Old dressing-room **2** Grand Tinel **3** Chapelle
Saint-Martial **4** Private apartments of the Pope **5**
Pope's bedroom **6** Chambre du Cerf **7** Grande
Chapelle de Clement VI **8** Chamberlain's room **9**
Notary's room **10** Fenêtre de l'Indulgence **11**
Cour d'Honneur **12** These parts of the palace are
no longer standing

chapel ante-room, the *Fenêtre de l'Indulgence*, the Pope would give his blessing to the faithful gathered in the Cour d'Honneur below.

Cathedral of Notre-Dame des Doms:

This Romanesque building dating from the mid 12C, a single-aisled nave with later side chapels (14–16C), is distinguished by a porch almost Roman in style, also added later, and a W. tower, a relatively rare feature in Provence. Pure Romanesque up to the 2nd storey, this was continued with great sensitivity in the 15C and in 1859, less successfully, it was crowned by a gilt lead figure of the Virgin Mary.

Interior: The original character of the interior, marked, as in so many Romanesque churches in Provence, by vertical emphasis, was completely destroyed by the installation of baroque galleries (1670–2), much to the detriment of the overall effect. Thus the articulation of the wall, extremely effective in all its simplicity, which accentuated the massiveness of the windowless side walls and the pointed barrel vault, was more or less lost.

This arrangement impressed through a clear, broad division of the surfaces by rectangular pilasters, continuing into the ribs above the carved warriors, and the double, bay-wide blind arches set in recesses. As in many Romanesque churches in Provence—the old cathedrals of Apt and Marseille for example—the *dome* over the crossing is an architectural tour de force. The rectangular crossing is turned into a square by means of four arches on the narrow sides, one above the other and each projecting by one stone's width. Above this squinches form an octagon supporting fluted columns at each corner, alternating with semicircular arches. These in turn bear a cornice and the dome, which is traversed by bands of stone and was painted in the 17C.

Outstanding contents: The tomb of John XXII (4th S. side chapel), attributed to the English sculptor H.Wilfred (1345); a 12C white marble bishop's throne (choir); a beautiful 14C figure of the Virgin Mary (3rd N. chapel) and a Romanesque altar, a table altar supported by 5 columns (1st N. side chapel).

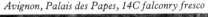

Avignon, Palais des Papes, 14C falconry fresco

Augustinian church (Rue Latte-lerie): Of the former monastery church built in 1372–7 by J.Laugier, who collaborated on Saint-Didier, there remains only a fortified tower, which, despite its tall bell-arches and typical Provençal iron belfry, looks more like a keep than a church tower.

Chapelle de l'Oratoire (Rue Saint-Agricol): Built by F.Delamonce, J.A.Brun and J.B.II Péru in 1730–50, this chapel displays the influence of the Italian baroque, with multiple overlapping ellipses, circles and rectangles. Thus, the outer walls form a rectangle, while the nave and dome are oval and the choir and ring of chapels arranged around the nave are circular.

Chapelle des Pénitents-Blancs (near Les Halles): 14C Gothic, with a nave and two aisles and a later façade.

Chapelle des Pénitents-Noirs (N. of the cathedral): The Brotherhood of the Black Penitents, founded in 1586, who laid the main stress of their work on active charity, was particularly widespread in S. France. It is not immediately apparent that this baroque building, built in the first half of the 18C by Th.Lainée and J.B. Franque, is a church and the only feature of its two-storeyed façade which reveals it as such is the relief below the arch segment which interrupts the entablature. The interior, in which white and gold predominate, similarly seems at first sight more like a salon.

Chapelle Saint-Charles (Rue Saint-Charles): This mid-18C chapel has an unfinished cloister and inside it displays rococo and neoclassical features. The extremely shallow groin vault is of particular interest.

Chapelle du Saint-Sacrement (formerly Chapelle de la Visitation; Rue Paul Sam): This single-aisled building, built in 1631–8 by La Valfenière, was richly painted and stuccoed inside by A.Borde. The two-storeyed façade is a fine example of Roman baroque stamped by French classicism.

Franciscan monastery (Rue Bon-

Avignon, Palais des Papes, 14C fresco of a deer-hunt

neterie): Only the Gothic tower of this monastery still stands, the rest being destroyed during the Revolution. The tomb of Petrarch's Laura (d.1348) is supposed to have been discovered in its chapel in the 16C.

Saint-Agricol (Rue Saint-Agricol): Astonishingly it appears that St.Agricol, who is supposed to have founded the church in the 7C, never actually existed, but was merely an amalgam of various figures. The church itself was first mentioned in the 11C but in its present form it dates back to the 14C. In the 15C the basilica (nave and two aisles, no transept) was extended by one bay and the façade rebuilt. The tower was begun in the 16C and completed in the 18C. Apart from the pointed windows and the W. façade, typical of the style favoured in Avignon in the 15C, the church does not actually look like a Gothic building from the outside due to the horizontal parapet of the nave. *Inside* too the soaring Gothic of the N. is checked by the broad pointed arches supporting the rib vaults. Note the beautiful white marble holy-water stoup (early-

16C) and the Renaissance altarpiece (by the sacristy) by I.Boachon (1525). The high altar (choir) of 1773 is by Péru.

Saint-Didier (Place Saint-Didier): This single-aisled building consecrated in 1359, the largest church to be built in Avignon during the residence of the Popes, is distinguished, like the palace of Benedict XII from the same period, by an astonishing lack of decoration. The walls are unbroken, the windows extraordinarily small for a Gothic building, practically concealed between sharply projecting flying buttresses. Far more striking is the square *tower* with its surprisingly large, pointed bell arches above an almost totally featureless substructure. The *interior*, just as plain as the outside (decoration was avoided even on engaged columns and capitals), is distinguished, like many Gothic churches in and around Avignon, by an un-Gothic broadness.
Items to note: The Bearing of the Cross by F.Laurana (1st S. chapel) 1478, one of the earliest Renaissance works in France; the hexagonal 15C

Avignon, Cathedral of Notre-Dame des Doms

late Gothic pulpit with lavish Flamboyant decoration; the statue of St.Bénézet by J.Péru (*c.* 1700), as well as the modern glass panel depicting the building of the Saint-Bénézet bridge and the late-14C frescos, which were only discovered in 1953.

Saint-Martial (Rue Henri Fabre): The 14C former Benedictine church, now Protestant, conforms to the usual pattern in Avignon in the 14C, apart from its more lavish ornament, particularly in the choir and the Flamboyant tracery, which almost outdoes itself, on the outside of the apse. The tower, although less squat, is similar to Saint-Didier's.

Saint-Pierre (Place Saint-Pierre): This single-aisled Gothic collegiate church (1358), begun around the same time as Saint-Didier and completed at the end of the 15C with the addition of two bays and several side chapels, is far less cold and austere than Saint-Didier. The windows, for example, are traceried throughout and the tower, the most beautiful in the whole of Avignon, rises more gracefully from the body of the church. Particularly richly decorated, however, is the beautiful façade (1512), which was inspired by the side portal of the old cathedral of Carpentras and literally overflows with the most varied Flamboyant ornament. There is a famous portal with a large figure of the Madonna on the central pier (18C), attributed to Péru or sometimes to Bernus, and A.Volard's splendidly carved doors (1551).

Items *inside* include the splendid choir, furnished entirely in baroque style; the Gothic white-stone pulpit (15C); the stone altarpiece (chapel on left of choir) by I.Boachon (1526); the mid-15C Entombment of Christ in the chapel to the right of the choir; the 'Adoration of the Shepherds' by Simon de Châlons and the 'Immaculate Conception' by N.Mignard on the wall between the old side chapels.

Saint-Ruf (Place Saint-Ruf): While its adjoining monastery, founded in Carolingian times and rebuilt in 1039, was totally demolished after the ravages of the Albigensian Wars and the Wars of Religion, a few ruins

Avignon, Saint-Didier

Avignon, Saint-Didier, portal

Avignon, Saint-Didier, glass panel

remain of the monastery church, which reveal antique and oriental influences (the order of regular Augustinian canons was entrusted with the building of Christian churches in Syria and Palestine).

Templar chapel (in the Hôtel du Louvre, Rue Saint-Agricol): The first Gothic building in Avignon, a double chapel built around 1275 with traceried windows, a restrained pointed-arch vault and almond-shaped ribs. Only the upper part remains today and is now a banqueting hall.

Celestine monastery (Place des Corps-Saints): Only a few parts still survive from this monastery, which was long used as barracks. The church itself was built in 1394–1402 on the site of Avignon's old cemetery for the poor, where Cardinal Pierre de Luxembourg, who died in the call of

Holiness, aged 19, had himself buried. His tomb, at which miracles are supposed to have occurred, attracted flocks of pilgrims.

The exterior of the building, which was extended in 1422–4 and left unfinished, remains, with the exception of the monumental portal rebuilt in the 17C, within the bounds of S. French Gothic in its simplicity. The two-aisled interior, however, does not. Its overwhelmingly lavish decoration is reminiscent of the Gothic of the N., as is the transept, so rare in the S. The architect P.Morel of Lyon has produced a masterpiece of Gothic ornamentation, the crowning glory being the lavish vault of the apse, the keystone of which bears an enthroned Christ in an oval wreath of cherubs.

Hôtels: It was not just church building which enjoyed an unprecedented surge during the residence of the Popes. The demand for splendid, palatial dwellings for the various dignitaries also grew. By 1376 31 cardinal's palaces, or *Livrées cardinalices*, had already been built. These were so named because the town dwellings were allocated by a commission made up of one Papal chaplain, a knight and a citizen (livrer means deliver).

Having grown rich through trade and commerce, Avignon enjoyed a second upsurge of palace building with the baroque—or French classicism, as the French version of this style is described; which is characterized by a (Gothic) flatness and a far more restrained use of decorative elements. Thus most of the city's numerous and beautiful palaces are either Gothic or classical.

Hôtel des Monnaies (Place du Palais): The former mint, now the School of Music, a beautiful 17C baroque building (1619), shows obvious Italian influence. The massive ornamentation of the two windowless upper storeys is the dominant feature

Avignon, Saint-Dider, glass panel ▷

LA VOCATION
DV SAINT

of the three-storeyed façade, which is surmounted by a balustrade with winged dragons and eagles, and has a solid rusticated lower storey with a rounded portal and rectangular windows.

Other Italianate baroque palaces are to be found in the Rue du Roi-René: The *Hôtel de Fortia de Montréal* built in 1637 by La Valfenière, the 18C *Hôtel Honorati de Jonquerettes* and the *Hôtel des Ducs de Crillon*, an Italian palazzo arranged around a courtyard and built for the Dukes of Crillon in 1648.

Hôtel de Villeneuve-Martignan (Rue Joseph-Vernet): Almost classical in contrast is this relatively austere single-storeyed building arranged around an entrance court. Built in 1742–54 by Franque and son, its effect relies chiefly on the harmony of its proportions. The Musée Calvet has been housed here since 1833.

Apart from the Rue Joseph-Vernet (*Hôtel de Lescarène*, mid-17C, Nos.34,35,64,83,87), there are a number of other streets with French baroque palaces, where the emphasis

is more on architectural devices than on ornament: Rue du Four, *Hôtel de Galéans des Issarts*, 1681; Place de la Miranda, *Hôtel de Vervins*, 1687 and the Rue Banasterie *Hôtel de Madon de Châteaublanc*.

Maison du Roi René (Rue du Roi-René): The titular King of Naples and Jerusalem, Duke of Lorraine, Count of Provence and Anjou, had this splendid residence built for himself in 1476, incorporating a series of buildings (including an old Livrée cardinaliste), in order to dedicate himself to the renaissance of Provençal minstrelsy. Several painters, including N.Froment, were involved in the interior decoration up until René's death in 1480.

Just a few feet away there once stood the *Convent of Sainte-Claire*, in the chapel of which Petrarch saw Laura for the first time (6 April 1327), an event still commemorated by a plaque on house No.22.

Palais du Roure (Rue Racine): This Gothic palace, heavily reworked at the start of the 17C, was converted at

Avignon, Saint-Pierre

Avignon, Saint-Pierre, portal

the end of the 15C by La Coque out of a tavern and 2 small neighbouring houses. In 1891–9 it was used as the editorial office of Mistral's new Provençal magazine 'L'Aïoli', and in 1918 Mme. Jeanne de Flandreysy, who started an important collection of prints and manuscripts, set up a salon here, which included painters and writers. Her collections and the Gallo-Roman library of her husband, the historian and archaeologist E.Espérandieu, form the basis of the small museum now housed in the building.

Pont Saint-Bénézet: This bridge, made famous in the song 'Sur le pont d'Avignon' and one of the four Rhône bridges between Lyon and the Mediterranean, used to span the river and the Ile de la Barthelasse with 22 arches. Legend has it that it was built in 1177–85 by St.Bénézet, a shepherd, at the behest of an angel. Destroyed during the Albigensian Wars, in 1226 it was rebuilt in 1234–7 on the same spot, but higher. At the same time the Romanesque *Chapelle Saint-Nicolas* on the second pier was adjusted to the

new height by adding an intermediate vault, thus dividing it into an upper and a lower chapel. This is why the lower chapel has a Romanesque apse, but a later, Gothic-arched vault, while the upper chapel has the old barrel vault and a Gothic apse, added on in 1513.

Town walls: The surviving ramparts, originally surrounded by a fosse, were built in the second half of the 14C by Innocent VI and Urban V in order to protect the city from the 'Grandes Companies', roving gangs in the 14C. Little remains of the earlier walls (the 1st Roman wall from the 1C, the 2nd, smaller wall from late antiquity and the 3rd, medieval wall from the 12C, which had to be demolished in 1226 after the siege by Louis VIII). The battlemented, machicolated wall was defended by 35 large and 56 smaller square towers with a magazine on the ground floor and a look-out post on the top floor. The latter could be entered from the battlements or via a staircase in the wall and had holes in the floor for defence

Avignon, Saint-Pierre, portal, Annunciation (L.); Saint-Pierre, Adoration of the Shepherds (R.)

against attack from below. The 7 city gates, also guarded by large square towers, were further secured by portcullises and draw-bridges.

Tour de l'Horloge (Place de l'Horloge): The tower built in 1354, the only surviving part of the medieval Hôtel de Ville was heightened around 1470 with the addition of two storeys for clock and bell. The square in front of it, which had served the Romans as a forum, is now the meeting place for the artistically inclined.

Museums: *Musée Calvet* (Rue Joseph Vernet): This museum, now housed in the baroque Hôtel de Villeneuve Martignan, was founded by Esprit Calvet (1728–1810), a professor of medicine, who bequeathed his extensive library, as well as his various natural history and coin collections etc. to his native city, in order to make them available to all. The foundation, which has since been rounded off by further donations and judicious purchases to complete collections, includes a very fine collection of ironware (including numerous

Montfavet (Avignon), fortified church

Gothic locks), Greek antiquities (replica of Praxiteles's Apollo, a *woman combing her hair* from the early 4C BC, a *woman with doll, c.* 360 BC); prehistoric finds from the vicinity (burial objects from the Neolithic and the 1C BC), as well as an important picture gallery with works by Peter Breugel the Elder, Ribera, Canaletto, Le Nain, David, Géricault, Delacroix, Corot, Manet. New exhibitions are constantly being organized.

The *Musée Lapidaire*, affiliated to the Musée Calvet, is housed in the former chapel of the Jesuit College, which was built to plans by La Valfenière in 1620–45. Its baroque façade, with sculptures by Bérangier (1661), is one of the most beautiful in the whole of France. The museum includes examples of Greek and Egyptian art, pre-Roman Gallic sculptures from the Rhône valley and also medieval works, including a 12C figure of an angel from Apt and small Romanesque columns and capitals from Carpentras cathedral.

Petit Palais (Place du Palais): This beautiful palace near the cathedral and the Palace of the Popes, which in times of emergency was combined with them to form a single defensive system, has been a museum since 1976. Begun in 1317, the fortified Gothic building, with battlements and corner towers, was originally an archbishop's palace. However, after the Revolution it was used to stable horses, becoming a seminary after being won back by the archbishop (1826) and in the 20C, after the secularization of the church estates, a technical school. The collections of medieval art housed here today are thoroughly worthy of the beautiful 14&15C building with its typical Gothic mouldings and windows divided by transoms and mullions formed by slender little columns. Exhibited here are the *Collection Calvet,* culled from the Calvet and Lapidaire museums, which includes pictures and sculptures from Avignon, and the *Collection Campana* with important Italian paintings from the mid 13C to the start of the 16C, particularly of the Italian Quattrocento. Its collector, the classically educated Marquis Campana di Cavelli (1807–80), head of the Monte di Pietà in Rome, a sort of predecessor of pawnshops, who, while acquiring the collection, did not always differentiate between the moneys administrated by him and his own private wealth, was sentenced to 20 years in the galleys in 1857. This was later reduced to exile and the confiscation of his fortune at the intercession of Napoleon III.

There are beautiful works to be seen, such as: The 15C *tomb of Cardinal de Lagrange*; a *Madonna and Child* by Botticelli, a Carpaccio, a *Madonna and Child with 2 Saints and 2 Donors* by E.Quarton, the founder of the School of Avignon; *2 angels*, remains of a stone altarpiece by A.Le Moiturier of Avignon; a *Madonna and Child* by T.Gaddi.

Events: The *Semaine d'Art en Avignon*, inaugurated by Jean Vilar in 1946 as part of the New Provençal movement, has enjoyed a continent-wide reputation for many years. It has subsequently developed into a straightforward theatre festival.

Environs: Château de l'Armellière (15 km. S.): Beautiful château, built in 1607 by an officer of the King, arranged in a square with flanking towers and machicolations.
Entraigues-sur-Sorgue (11 km. NE): Remains of the medieval *town wall*; a *tower* built by the Templars in the 2nd half of the 12C.
Mas de Méjanes (22 km. SW): Ancient Provençal estate going back to the 11C with an old watch-tower.
Montfavet (4.5 km. E.): Beautiful 14C *fortified church* with carved door lintel and tympanum, as well as a few 14C altars.
Vedène (9 km. NE): 2 *towers* of a 12C medieval castle, 17C *belfry*.

Barbegal

13 Bouches-du-Rhône   p.256□B 6

3 km. S. of Fontvieille are the arches of an *aqueduct* from Augustan times, which assured the supply of water to Arles under the Romans. The water collected on the S. slope of the Alpilles simultaneously drove a full-scale *flour mill*. This structure, probably dating from the 1C BC and still most impressive even in ruins, consisted of 16 mills altogether. The

Barbegal, aqueduct

wheels were arranged in pairs and driven by water falling over 66 ft. The mills themselves were built alongside the wheels.

Barbentane

13 Bouches-du-Rhône   p.256☐B 5

Although this area was inhabited during Roman times, Barbetane's real history begins in the 9C, when King Boso gave the district to the archbishop of Arles. Soon a settlement grew up around the castle to the S. of the Ile Barban, at that time an island in the Durance, whose name has endured to the present day. By the 12C the town, which in the mean time had become the property of the bishop of Avignon, had developed to the extent that it became self-governing. The 15&16C former Hôtel de Ville, which is still standing, is a magnificent testament to the civic pride of this period.

Notre-Dame-de-Grace: This was originally built as a single-aisled Romanesque church in the 13C, but a N. aisle was added at the end of the Middle Ages and a S. aisle and a sacristy in the 19C. The W. porch and tower, the top section of which was lost in the Revolution, date from the 15C. Despite this, the exterior appears uniform, and the late Gothic bell-chamber, with its narrow bell arches and alternating narrow buttresses and eccentric water-spouts, has its own harmony of construction. The *interior* also gives an impression of unity, despite the fact that the two W. bays with Romanesque half-barrel vaulting are followed by a pair with Gothic rib vaulting, since the use of rectangular ribs throughout obscures the change.

Château: This fine classical building was begun in 1674, and its most attractive characteristic is its very fine proportions. The harmony of the whole is established by the two clearly divided storeys, the size of the windows and the elegant terrace enclosed by balustrades and leading to a long, rectangular pool flanked by parterres. The clarity of the lines and

Barbegal, aqueduct

the simplicity of the design—a slightly projecting central section crowned by a curved pediment, and a portal flanked by pilasters, a pronounced cornice with the 'pots à feu' framing the dormer windows above it — are classic examples of the French baroque borrowing from antiquity. The *interior furnishings* are quite different—Italian in style and dating from the 18C, and some of the pieces are already beginning to display a tendency towards rococo.

Maison des Chevaliers (near the church): Although originating from the 15&16C, this former Hôtel de Ville has, like almost all Provençal town halls, an open ground floor vestibule, which opens on to the street through two broad, flattened arches. This vestibule was where the council meetings took place. Above it is a loggia-like gallery which runs across the whole length of the façade and has a colonnade supporting the roof. Often there was also a beffroi (belfry), a tower which might be situated near the town hall (as at Aix) or built over a town gate (as in Noves or Salon).

The only remains of the **bishop's castle** are the cellar and the 14C keep, which were built by Cardinal Anglic Grimoard, and the *Tour Anglica*, a huge 130 ft. high square tower flanked by a turret with a spiral staircase and latrines.

Also worth seeing: The two 14C *fortified gates* at either end of the old town's main street; the 17C *Maison Chabert* which is the modern town hall, and a number of other old houses scattered throughout the town.

Barcelonnette

04 Alpes-de-Haute-Provence   p.254☐G/H 3

This is the northernmost town in Provence, and is situated in the mountainous countryside on the right bank of the Ubraye. Raymond Bérenger IV ordered a fortified village to be built here in 1231 and the original name of *Barcelone* refers to the fealty of Counts of Provence to the Lords of Barcelona—it was not known by its present name until some five centuries

Barbentane, Maison des Chevaliers

Barbentane, château

later. In 1381 Count Rouge de Savoie became lord of the town and bestowed privileges on it. During the border conflicts at the end of Louis XIV's reign, Marshal Berwick, son of James II of England, defended the town, and the Treaty of Utrecht (1713) turned the entire Ubraye valley over to France.

Church (1923–8): This modern structure houses a 17C pulpit which bears the Dominican emblem, a dog with a torch.

Tour Cardinalis (Place Manuel): This tower, which has a stone spire, is the remnant of a 15C Dominican monastery.

Museum: This is now housed in the Hôtel de Ville and contains prehistoric and antique Gallo-Roman items, and also some examples of Mexican folk art.

Also worth seeing: There is a *fountain* in the centre of the town, the Place Manuel, with a medallion of Manuel, the French politician and native of the town, by David d'Angers.

Environs: Allos (36 km. S.): On the edge of this attractive village is the 13C Provençal Romanesque church of *Notre-Dame de Valvert*.
Colmars (44 km. S.): This is a small mountain town protected from above by the well-preserved *Fort de Savoie* and from below by the *Fort de France*; the latter being connected to the town by a fortified path. The town itself is protected by embrasured 17C *walls*, and is entered through the *Porte de Savoie*, to the N., and the *Porte de*

Barcelonette, fountain, Place Manuel

France to the S., which has a sundial. The right wall of the 16&17C *church* is battlemented and forms a section of the town wall; the sacristy is also battlemented.

Faucon-du-Caire (2 km. E.): This was the birthplace of St.Jean de Matha and has an old *church* and a *former monastery*.

Faucon-sur-Ubaye (2 km. NE): *Church* with an unusual bell tower.

Le Lauzet-Ubaye (23 km. W.): *Church* with a unique, rustic style pulpit. There is a *Roman bridge* over the river.

Saint-Pons (3 km. W.): The narrow 15C *church* has a tower on the N. side with bell arches. The frieze of round arches which runs round the apse and the N. side is older. The two portals, which have rather clumsy and awkward figures on them, are contemporary with the church's building.

Thorame-Basse (63.5 km. S.): On the hill are the *Tour de Piégut* and the *Chapel of Notre-Dame*; 8.5 km. further on is the *Church of Saint-Thomas*, which is frescoed inside.

Thorame-Haute (56.5 km. S.): The buildings of the *Château Saint-George* rise out of a fertile plateau. The *church* has 18C paintings and a Gothic choir.

Barjols
83 Var   p.256☐F 7

The area at the confluence of the Eau-Salée and the Écrevisses is known as the 'Tivoli of Provence', a title which refers to the countryside around the town. The old part of the town, which has a market place with plane trees at its centre, contains many fine fountains and the *Hôtel de Pontevès*, which has a Renaissance doorway.

Former Collegiate Church (11C): This building was part of a foundation by Archbishop Raimbaud of Arles. It was subordinated to the Pope in 1160, and the Romanesque structure was extended in the Gothic style, beginning in 1537. The right aisle dates from this period, and the 17&18C row of chapels was built on the site of the old Romanesque cloister, of which only the walled-up arcades (on the S. side) and the base of the barrel vaulting are still standing.

There is a square bell tower with a glazed tile roof overlooking the rib-vaulted nave and two aisles. The choir, to the E., has a straight end wall. The almond-shaped, pointed compartments in the rib vaulting stem from around 1300, as do a few of the capitals. The interior includes the Romanesque *relief*, which was moved in 1546 from the tympanum to be the antependium to the altar of St.Marcellus (in the left aisle). The Majestas Domini, the enthroned Christ in a mandorla, is depicted in two panels; the mandorla extending into the upper panel in a zigzag line, signifying rays of glory. The Hand of God is an unusual motif in this context: appearing out of a cloud in blessing. In contrast with this rather clumsy work is the head of Christ, which cannot be dated precisely, although a comparison with the St.Serenus altar in the Old Cathedral of Marseille suggests that it might be from the end of the 12C. There is a fine 16C font and the organ case is 17C.

Environs: Correns (14 km. SE): *Fort-Gibron* stands outside the old town, which is laid out on a grid pattern.

Fox-Amphoux (10.5 km. NE): This was once the Roman Fors Castrum, and was actually settled in the Bronze Age. The village is dominated by the *church* and the *Château des Barras* (1755–1829).

La Verdière (17 km. NW): The *church* and an impressive *château* are both of historical and cultural interest.

Barjols, Hôtel de Pontevès, Renaissance doorway

Pontevès (Barjols), ruined castle

Montmeyan (15.5 km. NE): This small, old village has remains of old *walls* and a medieval *castle*.

Pontevès (3 km. E.): The site of the ruins of a stately *château*.

Saint-Julien (25 km. NW): Situated on a cliff-top, the town commands a picturesque view. There is a group of old houses around the Romanesque *church*, and sections of the 13C *town walls*.

Saint-Martin (19 km. NW): A 19C wing has been added to the rebuilt 17C *château*. The battlements on the towers have survived.

Tavernes (5.5 km. N.): This small village is dwarfed by a mountain peak, on which the *Chapelle Notre-Dame de Bellevue* is situated.

Varages (11 km. NW): The faience industry reached this area around the end of the 17C, and there is a small museum containing a variety of pieces. The 19C *church* has an altar to St.Claudius, the patron saint of faience craftsmen.

Vinon-sur-Verdon (38 km. NW): This small village is situated in the extreme NW corner of the Var department; its small *church* dates from the 16 or 17C.

Beuil

06 Alpes-Maritimes   p.258☐H 5

The Romans settled in the Cians valley in antiquity, but nothing of interest has survived either from this period or from the Middle Ages. However, from the point in the 16C when Grimaldi of Monaco took control of Beuil, the history of the area seems to be an unbroken chain of uprisings and violent battles. Duke Hannibal of Beuil, whose policy it was to resist outside interference, is recorded as a valiant leader, and his murder in 1621 was a great loss for the local people. Beuil is now well-known as a winter sport resort.

Chapelle des Pénitents: This cha-

pel was built in the 17C, with a bell tower the only remnant of the 15C structure which previously occupied the site. The interior contains an altar of the rosary.

Also worth seeing: The 16C *church*. Beuil provides a good base for excursions into the beautiful mountainous countryside.

Environs: Châteauneuf d'Entraunes (18 km. NW): F.Bréa painted an altarpiece for the local *church* in 1524.

Entraunes (38 km. NW): This small village is situated at the confluence of the Bourdoux and the Var; its *church* has an oddly-shaped bell tower. The frescos in the *Saint-Sébastien Chapel* were painted by A. de la Cella in 1516.

Guillaumes (21 km. NW): This small market town is named after its founder, Guillaume II of Provence (*c.* 1100). The *church* dates from 1699, and has a fine bell tower and a modern fresco on the ceiling from 1932. The *Château de la Reine Jeanne* affords a fine view over the village. The *Priory*

Pontevès (Barjols), portal of the ruined castle

Chapel of Notre-Dame de Buye stands by the road out of the village.

Marie (32 km. SE): There is a medieval ruined *castle* here, and the *church* contains a fine old figure of the Madonna.

Péone (15 km. NW): The *church* is 19C, and stands at the foot of a high chalk cliff.

Roubion (12 km. E.): 12C *town walls*, pierced by gates, surround Roubion; its houses (18C) are grouped round a square which has the 18C *Fontaine de Mouton*. The *Chapel of Saint-Sébastian* was painted in the 16C with scenes from the life of the saint.

Roure (20 km. E): The altar of the Ascension (1560) in the *church* is attributed to F.Bréa; another 16C altarpiece depicts St.Lawrence and St.Gratus. There is a *Chapel of St.Sébastien* above the town which has frescos by A. de la Cella dating from 1510.

Saint-Martin d'Entraunes (32 km. NW): This is a Romanesque church built in typical Provençal style with a later Gothic side portal (15C) which bears the coat-of-arms of the Templars.

Saint-Sauveur-sur-Tinée (24 km. E): The *church* is 15C, but its bell tower is from 1333. A marble statue of St.Paul, dating from 1404, is housed in a niche in the exterior wall.

Valberg (6.5 km. W): The *Church of Notre-Dame des Neiges* was built in this well-known winter sports resort in 1939–45 by P.Labbé. The frescos on the façade are by Cassarini, those in the interior by G.Mangin.

Villeneuve d'Entraunes (27.5 km. NW): The *church* has a fine holy water vessel and some old figures of the saints, some in their original polychrome form.

Boulbon
13 Bouches-du-Rhône   p.256☐B 5

This small farming village achieved great strategic importance in the Middle Ages on account of its position on the Avignon-Tarascon road, in the shelter of an outcrop of rock, which rises steeply out of the plain. A mighty testament to its former significance is the massive *fortress* built here

Boulbon, Saint-Marcellin

Boulbon, Saint-Marcellin, portal

around 1400 by the Counts of Provence to guard their borders. It comprises several sections of walls, defended by towers, which encompassed the whole rock, and indeed in places seemed to actually grow out of it. Equally impressive is the square tower, possibly one of the many watch and signal towers in Provence, which probably dates from an earlier period.

Chapelle Saint-Marcellin: Outside the village's still partly intact walls there is a very beautiful, single-aisled, three-bayed church with a spireless bell tower and a low, semicircular apse, as well as even lower flanking side chapels, which seem like a false transept. This little cemetery chapel, dating from the 2nd half of the 12C, is distinguished, like many Romanesque buildings in Provence, by plain, extensive surfaces and walls and vaults whose structure is reminiscent of Roman arches.

Chapelle Saint-Julien: About 2 km. N. of the village there stands a small, isolated single-aisled chapel with two bays, a polygonal apse and a buttressed nave. Again, it is plain in the extreme and it may once have been a pilgrimage chapel. At any rate, the two blind arches in the S. wall were originally open, and may very well have been used as entrances and exits during processions.

Briançon
05 Hautes-Alpes   p.254☐G 1

Right at the confluence of the Durance and the Guisane the Romans founded *Brigantum,* from which present-day Briançon developed. The picturesque town is the highest in Europe, standing at an altitude of 4,347 ft. In the Middle Ages it was subject to the Counts of Albon and in 1590 it became part of France. The important upper town (Ville Haute) was enclosed by ramparts after Briançon had been put to the torch. The fortifications were built in 1693–1722 to plans by Vauban, the military architect, and incorporated the church. The lower town (Ville Basse or Sainte-Cathérine) lies outside the fortifications.

Boulbon, Chapelle Saint-Julien

Fort du Château (to the E.): The centre of the well-preserved fortifications is the *citadel* , at the foot of which stands a large statue (allegory of France) by A.Bourdelle (1861–1929).

Porte de Pignerol (to the N., by the Campus Martius): This *entrance gate* to the old town is well suited to the rocky terrain. Above the round arch with simple Doric pilasters are sharply projecting bastions.

Notre-Dame (to the NW): A vaulted passage leads to one of the Vauban's few religious buildings (1705–18), although the exterior is very much fortress-like in form. The two-storeyed façade, flanked by two towers, is embellished only with flat pilasters and niches on the ground floor, and the main portal is flanked by two stone lions. Even the towers seem stocky and, without any interlinking vertical articulation, the individual storeys seem simply piled on top of each other. The interior of the basilica, with a nave and two aisles, adds to the heavy, massive impression.

Thick pillars and blind arches support a high groin vault. The crossing is vaulted by a small lantern dome. The choir (semicircular apse) is the same width as the nave. Here there are two gilt figures of St.Peter and St.Paul. In the small sacristy there is a 16C 'Adoration of the Magi' by a German painter.

Also worth seeing: In 1734 Marshal Asfeld commissioned the *Pont d'Asfeld* (SE), with a 131 ft. span across the Durance valley at a height of 184 ft. The associated gate is the *Porte d'Asfeld* (NE); the *Porte d'Embrun* is the S. exit from the upper to the lower town. The steep, narrow main street of the old town is the *Grand'Rue*, down the centre of which runs the *Grande-Gargouille*, a medieval water channel. There are a few Renaissance *houses* (e.g. Maison des Templiers) and *portals* (17&18C).

Environs: Col du Lautaret (28 km. NW): The Romans built a small temple *(Altaretum)* here, and it is from this that the pass takes its name. A *chapel* was built here in memory of

Briançon, Notre-Dame and the upper town

Resistance members killed in the war.
L'Argentière-la-Bessée (16 km. SW): This village takes its name from the old silver mines. In the 12C the Hospitallers built a small *chapel of St.John* here in typical Provençal Romanesque style. A square, two-storeyed E. tower rises above the single-aisled, three-bayed nave, which ends in a half-domed apse. This is lower and narrower than the barrel-vaulted nave, the walls of which are articulated only by half-columns. The *parish church* of the village is early-15C, but was largely rebuilt in the 16C. Note the S. wall of the choir with frescos (1516) depicting the Virtues and Vices, as well as the unusual theme of the difference between Heaven and Hell (probably Lombard or Piedmontese influence). *Ruined castle* (13C).

Le Monêtier-les-Bains (14.5 km. NW): Famous for its *hot springs*, it has a 15C *church*.

Les Vigneaux (17.5 km. SW): The 15C *church* has a Romanesque bell tower, as is common in this region. There are wall paintings inside dating from 1552.

Névache (20 km. N.): The late-15C *church* still retains its original portal, the beautiful doors of which date from 1498. The interior panelling is 16C, as are the canvas wall paintings. The former archive room contains a curious iron door.

Plampinet (14.5 km. N.): The inhabitants of this narrow valley built a *church* in the 16C, which has undergone a few alterations in the course of time. Frescos still survive from the original structure.

Saint-Chaffrey (5 km. NW): The 14C *village church* was extensively restored in the 16C. The later S. chapel contains interesting *wall pantings*, thought to be the work of J.Baleision of Piedmont, which depict the legend of St.Sebastian and are similar to the cycle in Venanson and the paintings in Lucéram and La Brigue. The 15C technique of miniatures shows in the warm coloration and sure choice of colour. There are even Gothic elements in the lively narrative style and the conception of the scenes. The frescos have survived best on the S. and W. walls. Where the plaster has come off one can see the cartoons beneath.

Val-des-Prés (8 km. NE): The *church* still has its old Romanesque tower.

Vallouise (22.5 km. SW): This picturesque mountain village has a 15C *church* with a projecting portal.

Brignoles
83 Var   p.256□F 7

During the French Revolution this town on the Roman Via Aurelia was the préfecture of the département of Var, a position which it has held again since 1975. Reputedly the birthplace of St.Louis of Anjou (1274–97), it was converted to Christianity at an early date. The first documentary references date from 558, but there are no more until 1011, at the time of the Saracen invasions. The Dukes of Provence made Brignoles their summer

Brignoles, castle chapel, portal

residence on account of its pleasant climate. François I stayed here during his Italian campaign. In 1525 and 1536 the town was plundered by the troops of Charles V. Huguenots settled in the region at the time of the Wars of Religion (1563). Anne of Austria, Mazarin and Pope Pius VII are amongst other famous figures to have stayed in the town, the older part of which is spread out on the hill.

Saint-Sauveur: Only the portal remains of the Romanesque building which preceded this church (also known as Saint-Jean). The 15C single-aisled nave was built in southern French Gothic style, the transept and choir being added in the 16C. On either side of the high altar (1585) there is a 15C gilded wooden relief: one depicts Abraham's sacrifice of Isaac and the other Manna raining from Heaven. A beautiful 15C carved door leads to the sacristy, which contains a Descent from the Cross by the local artist B.Parrocel. A side chapel to the left has an interesting wooden Pietà.

Musée du Pays Brignolais: Housed in the former castle (13C) of the Dukes of Provence; alongside exhibits connected with local history (Salle des Gardes), is one of the oldest pieces of work from Roman Gaul: the famous *sarcophagus of La Gayole* (late-2C). Imported into Gaul, it was re-used in the 6C, as an inscription on the upper edge indicates, for the tomb of Syagria, the founder of the chapel of La Gayole; finally being brought to Brignoles in 1890. The slightly damaged sarcophagus is 7 ft. 4 in. long and 2 ft. 7 in. high and is decorated with a single frieze of Biblical scenes, mixed with heathen images, although the question arises as to whether Christian motifs are possible, considering its early date.

Environs: Cabasse (14 km. NE): Numerous prehistoric *dolmens* have been discovered here. The 16C *church* has a beautiful wooden altarpiece (1543) by Imbert d'Aups.
Forcalqueiret (11 km. S.): Near the village is the *ruined castle* of Castellas.
La Celle (2.5 km. S.): The *convent*,

Brignoles, Saint-Sauveur, detail of portal

Brignoles, Saint-Sauveur, sacristy door

which was once inhabited by Benedictine nuns, was dissolved in 1660, after which the buildings either decayed or were used for other purposes. The convent church (*c.* 1200) is a typical example of Provençal Romanesque. The chapterhouse (13C) is the only building of the convent still standing.

La Gayole (7 km. W.): The little *chapel* is probably Merovingian.

Le Val (5 km. N.): The beautiful wrought-iron *bell tower* is 18C.

Montfort-sur-Argens (12 km. NE): The *chapel of Notre-Dame de Spéluque* is underground. The *château* was built in the 13&16C.

Méounes-les-Montrieux (22 km. S.): The 16C *church* contains two marble statues (17/18C).

Montrieux-le-Jeune (25 km. SW): The *Charterhouse* (closed to visitors) dates back to the 12C.

Signes (32 km. SW): The village *church* has an 11C portal.

Cannes

06 Alpes-Maritimes   p.258☐H/I 7

The hill now known as Le Suquet was used in the 2C BC as an observation point by the Ligurian tribe of the Oxybii. Feeling threatened by these neighbours, the Greek colonists in Antibes asked for help from the Romans, with the result that the Oxybii were conquered in 154 BC by Roman troops commanded by Quintus Opimius. After that, Greek settlers from Marseille founded a

Cannes, harbour and hill of Le Suquet

defensive settlement on the site known as *Castrum Marcellinum*. During the 4C, a monastery appeared on the island of St.Honorat. In 1070, the monks there had the hill of Le Suquet fortified, following orders from the Dukes of Provence. The small settlement of *Portus Cannis* then grew up in the 11C around the new observation tower. Its population was granted exemption from taxation in 1131 by Raymond Bérenger, who gave the place the name of *Castrum Francum*; this had changed, in documents from the early 13C, to *Castrum Canoïs*. The following centuries brought various periods of war and destruction and the population was decimated by the plagues of 1347 and 1580. The plundering progress through these parts of the troops of Charles V in 1536, and of Charles-Emmanuel of Savoy in 1590, resulted in devastation. The town was able to hold off the Spaniards, but not the troops of the Austrian Empress Maria-Theresa, who retreated here during the War of the Austrian Succession. In 1788, thanks to the secularization of the period, Cannes became independent of the monastery of Lérins, whereupon it spread along the coast, and in 1838 this plain little fishing village underwent a considerable expansion. Its growth during the 19C can be attributed to the English politician Lord Brougham, who discovered and publicised Cannes' pleasant climate and lovely situation. The modern town, which has grown out of the old one on the hill of Le Suquet, is a world-famous resort and hosts an international film festival.

Tour du Suquet (on the S. side of the church): Work was begun on this *observation tower*, which is square and 72 ft. high, in 1070, under Adalbert II, the Abbot of the monastery on the Iles de Lérins, but was not completed until 1385. The door which forms its entrance is at first-floor level, as in a keep, so that, in the event of danger, the ladder could be pulled up and entry prevented.

Notre-Dame de l'Espérance (on the hill of Le Suquet): According to

Antibes (Cannes), former cathedral

Vallauris (Cannes), chapel, fresco by Picasso

an inscription, the construction of this church, which is typical of the Gothic of the South of France, was begun in 1521 and finished in 1648. The simple interior is of no great architectural interest, but does contain some altars and figures which deserve mention. The high altar is crowned by the eponymous gilded wooden statue of the Madonna, which dates from the 17C, and there are several bust reliquaries and paintings which date from the same period. The sacristy contains a wooden statue of St.Anne, which was carved around 1500, and a 16C figure of the Madonna. To the left of the choir is the small *St.Anne's Chapel*, built in the typical Provençal Romanesque style of the 12C.

Musée de la Castre (by the tower): This building, which used to be a castle, now houses an exhibition of objects from antiquity discovered in the Mediterranean region. They were collected by the Dutch Baron Lycklama.

Also worth seeing: On the N. side of

the Place de la Castre are some remains of the *old town wall*, which was built in the 14C. Near the casino is the church of *Notre-Dame du Bon Voyage*, which contains an iron reliquary holding the remains of St.Honoratus.

Environs: Antibes (11 km. NE): This area was still inhabited by Ligurians and Etruscans when, in 350 BC, Greeks from the city of Phocaea arrived here and founded the colony of Antipolis. Having repelled the Ligurian threat with Roman help (in 154 BC), they achieved independence from Marseille in 42 BC. Antibes grew continuously in importance, and even became the seat of a bishop in the 5C. In 1386 it passed into the hands of Marc Grimaldi of Monaco, but was sold to the French Crown by Alexander Grimaldi in 1608. Throughout the Middle Ages, it suffered from raids by pirates, with the result that nothing has survived from the ancient, and immediately subsequent, period. Following the devastation caused by the soldiers of Charles V,

Vallauris (Cannes), chapel, fresco by Picasso

Vallauris (Cannes), man and sheep

Henry IV had fortifications built here, whose walls were subsequently strengthened by Vauban and proved strong enough to withstand the Austrian attacks of 1707 and 1815. For inexplicable reasons, these walls, which were still then in a good condition, were demolished in 1895. The Grimaldis built their *château* on top of the foundation walls of a Roman castrum, and its massive fortified tower survives from the earliest phase of construction (during the 14C). The buildings were extensively restored in 1830. The *Chapel of Saint-Jean* (in the NW part of the town) is a square, domed building with an arcaded porch. The *old cathedral* was built on the site of an earlier, 12C, Romanesque church, of which it retains the choir (which was altered in the 15C) and the transept. A square tower, dating from the 12C, stands beside the church, whose two-storeyed façade is now baroque. The nave, which was rebuilt in the 17C, contains altarpieces from the same period. The left side apse contains a stone mensa on which stands a wooden figure of Christ dating from around 1447. The rosary altar in the right transept chapel was painted in 1515 and is by the school of Bréa. The old château now houses a *museum*, the Musée Picasso, which displays, as well as collections devoted to local history, numerous paintings, gouaches, and drawings by Picasso, in addition to some 200 ceramics which he made in 1946. The Bastion Saint-André survives from Vauban's original fortifications and today houses the *Musée Archéologique*. Its Greek and Roman finds offer a survey of local history stretching back 3,000 years. The item of the greatest interest is the wreck of an Etruscan ship which was discovered off Cap d'Antibes in 1955. On the hill of La Garoupe is the chapel of *Notre-Dame du Bon Port* and, to its left, the prayer chapel of *Sainte-Hélène*, which was built on the foundations of a sanctuary dating from the 5C. The former consists of two 13&14C aisles, each of which contains a beautiful wrought-iron grille, which date respectively from 1587 and 1672. The walls of the interior are decorated with a fresco, painted by J.-H. Clergues in 1952–3,

Antibes (Cannes), panorama

which depicts scenes from local history.

Biot (19 km. NE): It was on a cliff overlooking what may well have been the valley of Brague that the Oxybii were defeated by the Romans in 154 BC. Members of the Order of the Knights Templar came here in 1209, and in 1470 King René settled a small community of 48 families here, and placed it under the joint authority of the Hospitallers and the bishop of Grasse. The 13&14C *church* stands on an arcaded square.

Golfe-Juan (6 km. NE): It was here that Napoleon landed on his return from the island of Elba. The event is commemorated by a mosaic on the quay.

Le Cannet: The old town, which rises in terraces up the side of a hill, is now a N. suburb of Cannes. It retains two medieval towers, the *Tour de Calvis*, dating from the 12C, and the *Tour des Danys* (meaning 'the brigands' tower'), which has 15C trap-doors.

Mandelieu (8 km. W.): The *church* was built in the 18C. The *ruins* of the 12C *Chapelle du San-Peyre* stand on a cliff outside Mandelieu.

Mougins (7.5 km. N.): At the beginning of the 13C, this town was bigger than Cannes and more important than Vallauris. In the old town, which stands on the hill, one can still see the remains of the *walls* and also a fortified gate dating from the 14C. The church of *Saint-Jacques le Majeur* was completed in 1644; above it soars its bell tower. 2 km. SE of Mougins is the hermit chapel of *Notre-Dame de Vie*, which was built by the monks from Lérins in the 12C (it was rebuilt in 1646). The interior contains a miracle-working stone cross dating from the 15C and 17C wooden furnishings.

La Napoule-Plage (8 km. SW): When the château was built, 3 square towers which had formed part of a 14C fort were incorporated in it. The château was extensively restored in 1919 by the sculptor H.Clews, several of whose works are exhibited here.

Saint-Pierre (17 km. NE): The *Musée Fernand Léger* was built in 1959 by the architect A.Svetchine on his own land. The outside of the building is dominated by two vast works based on the works of Léger, a mosaic measuring 4,300 sq. ft., which occupies the S. front, and a window (29 ft. 6 in. × 16 ft. 6 in.) which decorates the entrance hall. Inside the museum, innumerable works by this many-sided artist are exhibited, providing a survey of his entire oeuvre.

Tanneron (20 km. NW): Large parts of this village, and above all of the mimosa plantations which provide the main income for its perfume industry, were destroyed in a disastrous fire in 1970. 1,000 ft. above the village stands the chapel of *Notre-Dame de Peygros*, from which there is a wonderful view over the neighbourhood.

Théoule-sur-Mer (10.5 km. SW): The large building on the sea-shore has stood here since the 18C.

Vallauris (8 km. NE): The name derives from the Latin *Vallis Aurea*. In 1227 the monks of Lérins incorporated Vallauris within their priory, building a convent here in 1227 which did not long survive and a castle which was destroyed by Raymond de Turenne in 1568. Today the town is one of the principal centres of French pottery, the craft having been practised here since antiquity; bricks were being fired here as early as the reign of the Emperor Tiberius. In 1501, D.Lascaris settled a number of Genoese families here who were very active and Picasso brought new life to this art in 1950. The old *château* was restored again recently and has been converted into a *museum* of ceramics. The buildings of the medieval priory were rebuilt in the 16C.

Caromb

84 Vaucluse   p.256☐C 4

Church: This is an attractively

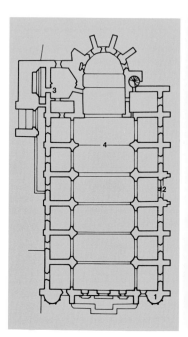

Le Barroux (Caromb), castle

situated old wine-growing village, which still retains parts of its old walls and gates, a beautiful iron belfry in the bell tower (1523), and an old fountain in front of the Hôtel de Ville (16C). It possesses, in addition, a church which is richly furnished and deserves a visit. The exterior of the 13C nave comprises six bays reinforced by buttresses together with a simple Gothic portal and is as devoid of decoration as many other Romanesque churches in the Provence. So the *interior*,is all the more surprising, with its rectangular pillars and horizontal cornice, to discover the remains of frescos as well as wooden figures whose gilt still gleams, on the pulpit, the organ, and the 16C high altar, which is dominated by a 15C figure of Christ in the Spanish style.

Environs: Le Barroux (6 km. N.): A lovely little village with a Romanes-

Carpentras, Cathedral of Saint-Siffrein: 1 Polygonal towers (which, like the nave and choir, date from the 15C) **2** Porte Juive in the S. portal, which was built in 1470/80; above it is the chapterhouse **3** Cloister of the 12C Romanesque church which originally occupied this site. The cloister was demolished in 1829 to make way for a prison **4** Bay beneath Romanesque dome

que church and a *château*. The latter was built in 1539–48 on the site of an old fortress belonging to the feudal owners of Les Baux and is typical of the transition from castle to country seat.

Carpentras
84 Vaucluse   p.256☐C 5

Carpentras, which is a centre of local traffic, has long been important. Today, its market for truffles, vegetables and fruit make it one of the most important centres for agricul-

Carpentras, cathedral, S. portal

Carpentras, triumphal arch, detail

tural produce in France. Under the Gauls, it was known as *Carpentoracte* and was the capital of a tribe called the Memini; then it was conquered by the Romans, either under Julius Caesar or during the reign of Augustus. In the 3 or 4C it was the seat of a bishop and from 1274 until 1797 it was the capital of the Comtat Venaissin and thus the property of the Holy See. It became a favourite resort of the Popes, especially Clement V, and prospered so much that it soon grew beyond its boundaries, acquiring a second town wall in the second half of the 14C. However, when the Papacy returned from Avignon to Rome, the town began to decline, and its fortunes did not change again until the construction of the railway and canal in the 19C.

One cannot discuss the history of Carpentras without mentioning Malachie d'Inguimbert (1683–1757),

who was himself born in this town and was its bishop from 1735 until his death. In this office, he endowed Carpentras with the most beautiful rococo buildings in the Provence.

Monumental gate (in the courtyard of the Palais de Justice): This monument, whose carving is rather coarsely executed, dates from the 1st half of the 1C and celebrates Augustus's victory over the Gauls. It doubtless served originally as the gate of the Roman town; later it was used as the porch in a side portal of the Romanesque cathedral, which was later destroyed, except for a few remains.

Cathedral of Saint-Siffrein: The Gothic building which we see today dates from the 15C—the foundation stone was laid in 1405. It stands on the site of an earlier, Romanesque structure, which comprised a single aisle of five bays. Part of this original building collapsed in 1400 and little of it survives except a dome with some impressive relief figures on the squinches. The present structure resembles the majority of Gothic churches in the S. of France in possessing a single aisle of six bays, with side chapels but no transept. A feature of particular interest is its sumptuously Flamboyant S. portal (1470–80), known as the *Porte Juive*, which incorporates the famous *boulo di gari*, a rat-gnawed globe. The *choir*, which is narrower and lower than the nave and is separated from it by a windowless bay, was decorated by J.Bernus, an artist of the Provençal school, at the turn of the 17&18C.

Chapelle Notre-Dame de Santé: This elegant rococo church was built in 1734–48 by Bishop Inguimbert. The fountain on the adjacent square dates from the same period.

Synagogue: The Jewish community in Carpentras, whose synagogue is mentioned as early as 1367, is one of the '4 holy communities' in France.

The modern building, which contains some lovely rococo boiseries, dates from 1741–3 and and was restored in 1954.

Hôtel-Dieu: This hospital was founded by Bishop d'Inguimbert and built in 1750–1 to the design of A. d'Allemand. It has an elegant rococo façade. On the ground floor is the *pharmacy*, whose faiences, 16&17C mortars, and old cupboards, decorated with monkeys and fantastic landscapes, are definitely worth seeing.

Palais de Justice: Formerly the Bishop's Palace. It was built around 1640 and based on the model of the Palazzo Farnese in Rome.

Porte d'Orange: The second and larger town wall, a massive fortification incorporating 32 towers which was built in the 2nd half of the 14C., was demolished in the 19C. All that survives is the Porte d'Orange, a huge square tower which has battlements and a portal with a pointed arch.

Musée des Beaux-Arts: This

Carpentras, cathedral, S. portal, tympanum

museum, which is also a library, is based on the collection of Bishop d'Inguimbert, which he made available to the public during his own lifetime. Today it contains, in particular, a number of interesting paintings (including Rigaud's 'Portrait of the Abbé de Rancé' and various portraits by J.-S. Duplessis, 1725–1804, who came from Carpentras), a fine *furniture collection* (mainly 18C) which is housed in a nearby rococo building, and Roman and Merovingian objects, which are in the *Musée Lapidaire*.

Also worth seeing: The old *keep*. This is all that is left of the château which was built by the Comtes de Toulouse in the 13C, and which acquired a cast iron bell tower in 1576. The *Hôtel de Ville*, the former Hôtel de la Roque (17C), and the adjacent *Rue des Halles*, which has covered arcades. 17&18C *Houses*.

Environs: Aqueduct (several miles upstream): 800 yards long, this aqueduct was built in 1720–30 and still supplies the town with water.
Aubignan (5 km. NW): A wine-growing town which retains part of its 14C walls. The *belfry*, which has a cast iron bell tower, is 18C.
Beaumes-de-Venise (8 km. NW): A small wine-growing village with caves and a ruined castle. There are *Vizigoth tombs* nearby.
Bédoin (15 km. NE): Charming wine-growing village on the S. slope of Mont Ventoux with 17C church in the Jesuit style which contains a beautiful altarpiece attributed to Mignard.
Château de Tourreau (10 km. NW): Eccentric little country seat built by E.Brun in 1750–70.
Crillon-le-Brave (12.5 km. NE): 15C *château* which has seen many alterations. Interesting Romanesque chapel with 13&14C frescos.
Mazan (7 km. E.): Small wine-growing town which still retains parts of its medieval walls. Of particular interest are the *Gallo-Roman sarcophagi* which were found in the 19C, buried by the

side of an old road. The cemetery chapel of *Notre-Dame de Pareloup* was rebuilt in the 17C and dates originally from the 11C.
Méthamis (15 km. SE): Pretty little village on the edge of the Gorges de la Nesque. Signs of human habitation in the Palaeolithic and Mesolithic periods were discovered nearby.
Modène (10 km. NE): 12C *ruined castle*.
Monteux (4.5 km. SW): The remains of the old, 14C town wall include two beautiful town gates, the *Porte Neuve* and the *Porte d'Avignon*.
Notre-Dame du Moustier (16 km. NE): Romanesque chapel dating from the middle of the 12C.

Cassis
13 Bouches-du-Rhône   p.256☐D 8

Qu'a vist Paris, a pas vist Cassis, a ren vist: Whoever has seen Paris but not Cassis has seen nothing. And it is true that this little town, with its picturesque fishing harbour, defini-

Carpentras, a mansion, 46 Rue des Marins

tely deserves a visit. Over the centuries, the small hamlet which nestled here in the 12C in the shadow of the fortress on the neighbouring hill has developed into a really attractive resort. The feudal lords of Les Baux, so powerful in the 12&13C, then left the place, and their former subjects occupied the fortress in the 14C. Then, in the 17&18C they built an indisputably charming, well arranged town and several houses survive from this period. Some towers and important remains of walls have also survived from the 12C fortress of the seigneurs of Les Baux.

Environs: Calanque d'En-Vau: This cove ('calanque' actually means a deep creek), which is lined by steep, barren cliffs, is said to be the most magnificent in the region and is known as the 'perle des calanques'.

Castellane
04 Alpes-de-Haute-Provence   p.258☐G 5/6

This began as the capital of the Suetri and stood originally on the cliff above the right bank of the Verdon, although now only the ruins of a castle and a Romanesque church survive on this site. The modern town extends along the bottom of the cliff and its appearance is typical of towns in Haute-Provence. Its centre is the Place Marcel-Sauvaire, which has a fountain commemorating the old seigneurs of Castellane. Of the 14C town wall, only a tower and some substantial remains near the church have survived.

Saint-Victor (to the N. of the Place Marcel-Sauvaire): This former parish church was built by monks from the Monastery of Saint-Victor in Marseille towards the end of the 12C. The outside is plain and incorporates two unobtrusive portals on the S. side of the nave. The three-storeyed tower is square and has bell arches and a modern roof. The N. aisle is a later addition. The Romanesque nave, which occupies three bays, supports a ribbed vault, whose ribs and beams are borne by consoles in the form of warriors.

Castellane, panorama, Saint-Victor in foreground

Also worth seeing: Behind the new church there is a footpath which leads (30 minutes' walk) to the chapel of *Notre-Dame du Roc*, which was rebuilt in 1703.

Environs: Barrême (24 km. NW): The 12C chapel of *Notre-Dame de Miséricorde* stands on a rock.
Chapelle Notre-Dame de Valvert (*c.* 15 km. N., left of the road): 12C *chapel*.
Chasteuil (3.5 km. SW): This small mountain village contains a 14C *church* and an old *château*.
Senez (19 km. NW): Known as Sanitium in Roman times. In the 5C the town had its own bishop, by the name of Ursus. The diocese, one of the poorest in France, was dissolved in 1801. The cathedral of *Notre-Dame de l'Assomption* (built 1130–76, consecrated 1242) has a simple exterior. The W. portal has a pointed arch and dates from the 13C; there are remains of a porch. The tower was originally battlemented.t The transept, with its 3 apses, has a flat, round-arched frieze. The interior is simple and well-proportioned and a thorough restoration has preserved the church's Romanesque character.
Trigance (18 km. SW): The ruins of a large *château* with four round corner towers dominate the town.

Cavaillon
84 Vaucluse   p.256□C 5

The modern town is situated between the Durance and Coulon, at the bottom of the rocky Colline Saint-Jacques, or Mont Caveau, which was inhabited as early as the 2nd millennium BC. Later, the Liguri settled in this wild and rocky area, and in the 4C BC the Celtic tribe of the Cavari established the oppidum of *Cabellio* here, which enjoyed a flourishing trade with the Greek colony of Massilia, the modern Marseille. After the Roman conquest of the local Celts, the settlement was moved from the hill top to the plain beneath. Its further history was marked by the same general phases as the other towns of Basse-Provence: the conversion to Christianity, the establishment of a

Trigance (Castellane), castle

bishopric (4C), invasions by the Goths, Franks, and Arabs (5–7C), the Albigensian and Huguenot wars (1223–26 and 1562–98 respectively), famine (1636), and the French Revolution. Today, Cavaillon is thriving and prosperous by virtue of being the 'melon capital', in other words a market for fruit and vegetables.

Roman gate (Place du Clos): This is the only ancient monument in Cavaillon. It consists of two arches dating from the time of Augustus, and originally was probably attached to another building. In any case, the front of the pillars is lavishly decorated with tendrils and sumptuous Corinthian capitals, while the second arch has no decoration at all on the other side.

Saint-Véran (Place Joseph d'Arraud): This used to be the cathedral. Begun in the 12C, it was a beautiful and elegant Romanesque building, but in the following centuries underwent many alterations, inside and out. Of the outer façade, only the five-sided Romanesque apse has remained completely untouched. This clearly shows the Roman influence on the Romanesque of Provence both in architecture and decoration—the wealth of imagination devoted to the ornamentation of the capitals and consoles is most impressive. However, later alterations to the rest of the exterior did more or less decisive harm to its appearance. Thus, the façade was heightened in the 16C, and the octagonal tower standing on a round base was raised an extra storey by the addition of a low roof.

As in so many churches in the Provence, the *interior* stands in semi-darkness. This makes the pointed arches of the tunnel vault above the nave (six bays long) look heavy and take on the appearance of a coping. The opening up of the blind arcades in the wall of the nave (which used to be closed) has not changed this situ-

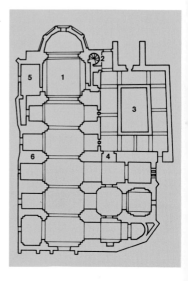

Cavaillon, **Saint-Véran** 1 Dome 2 Bell tower with arches 3 Cloister 4 Entrance to the cloister 5 Chapelle Saint-Véran 6 Buttress

ation, for not much light penetrates inside from the side chapels. More disturbing are the additions of the 19C, like the consoles decorated with reliefs, which do not even suit the severe and spacious layout of the interior. Incidentally, it is worth noting how the bay beneath the dome, which is relatively deep is narrowed to a square by means of arches (as in Avignon and Marseille) and then, above these, is converted, with the help of squinches, into an octagonal drum. This in turn is vaulted by a ribbed octagonal dome of the kind seen frequently in Provence. Immediately adjacent to the bay beneath the dome is the seven-sided *apse* which, since the 17C, has gleamed with its richly gilded wooden panelling. The *Chapelle Saint-Véran*, which dates from the 14C, was also sumptuously furnished in the 17C with an altarpiece by B.Grangier and a painting by

Cavaillon, Saint-Véran, cloister ▷

Cavaillon, Saint-Véran

P.Mignard. The painting of the vault, and the two pictures of the miracles of St.Véran, are by J.Bernus. The *cloister* is as beautiful as ever. It was built at the same time as the church, during the 14C; then, having suffered severe damage during the Wars of Religion in 1562, it was restored in the 17C.

Chapelle du Grand Couvent (Grand'Rue): This was built in the 2nd half of the 17C and has a Louis XIV façade.

Chapelle Saint-Jacques (on Mont Caveau, which incidentally offers a beautiful view over the Durance, the Crau, the Alpilles, and Mont Ventoux). The small Romanesque chapel, which originally only had two bays, was extended in the 16C with the addition of another two bays and again at the beginning of the 17C with

the construction of a relatively deep porch, which gives an elegant appearance to what is otherwise a very simple country chapel.

Synagogue (Rue Raspail): Like the other big towns in the Papal Comtat Venaissin (Avignon, Carpentras, and L'Isle-sur-la-Sorgue), Cavaillon had an important Jewish community, which lived in its own quarter of the town and administered its own affairs. The present synagogue, an extremely elegant rococo building dating from 1772–3, is the third in Cavaillon's history. Its very secular façade has a cast-iron balcony. The room where worship is held, on the first floor, is no less elegant and seems reminiscent of a salon. The ground floor, where the unleavened bread used to be baked, now houses a small Jewish museum which contains the old baking-oven, as well as various objects of worship, including a 17C Tora.

Musée archéologique (Porte d'Avignon): This was established in 1946 in the charming rococo chapel of the *Hospital* which had been built in 1753 by J.H. Mollard. Of particular interest are the prehistoric excavations (including a human skeleton in a foetal position found in the cave of Fonte-Blanco) and the vessels and objects dating from Celtic times.

Also worth seeing: The *Porte d'Avignon*, opposite the museum, is a remnant of the old town wall.

Environs: Gorges de Régalon (13.5 km. SE): A romantic ravine which in places cuts 165 ft. into the rock.
Mollégès (11 km. SW): Small village with pretty old houses on the church square and a Romanesque *cemetery chapel*.
Robion (5.5 km. E.): Remains of old fortifications. At the bottom of the Montagne du Lubéron there are caves which were settled in prehistoric times.

Romanin (14 km. SW): Important gliding centre. Not far away are the ruins of the *Château de Romanin*, which was famous in the Middle Ages for its Cours d'Amour, or courtyards of love.

Châteauvallon

83 Var   p.258□E 8

Centre Culturel et Artistique: This was established in 1964 by the painter and sculptor H.Komatis in association with the journalist G.Paquet. It consisted originally of a single, relatively small open-air stage near a small 17C fort. Today, it comprises a theatre, two open-air stages, and exhibition rooms, as well as offering accommodation and many places where people can meet, so that it has become a meeting point for practitioners in every sphere of art. As well as plays and films, it also presents classical music, jazz, and exhibitions. A short walk takes us to the **Oppidum de la Courtine**—the remains of a Celto-Ligurian settlement where Greek pottery and coins from Marseille have been found.

Cucuron

84 Vaucluse   p.256□D 6

This pretty little village, dominated by the keep of a small castle which is otherwise mostly in ruins, boasts two surrounding walls, both partially preserved. The larger of the two dates from the 16C and is defended by round towers; of the smaller, which dates from the 12C, only the *Tour de l'Horloge* still stands.

Notre-Dame de Beaulieu: This church, part Romanesque, part Gothic, with its barrel-vaulted Romanesque nave, rib-vaulted Gothic apse

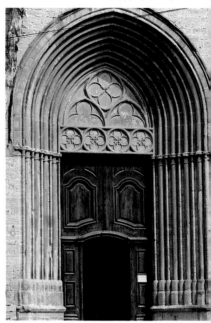

Cucuron, Notre-Dame de Beaulieu, portal

dating from the 14C, and its 14 or 15C Gothic side chapels, admirably succeeds in combining these different styles into a harmonious whole. The tympanum on the 14C Gothic portal, which is decorated with geometrical ornament, is also very beautiful. The *interior* has a baroque high altar (1661), incorporating a marble relief of Christ's Ascension, which deserves attention, as do the pulpit, which has inlays of coloured marble, and a moving painted wooden Ecce Homo dating from the 17C.

Museum (in the 17C Hôtel de Bouliers): Devoted to the life and history of the village; the exhibits include archaeological finds, traditional costumes, and many kinds of hand implements.

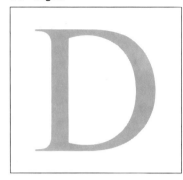

Digne

In antiquity *Dinia*, on the river Bléone, was the main seat of the tribe the Romans called the Bledonii. The original settlement has not been located, and neither Christian nor Roman remains have survived, although Digne was already seat of a bishopric in the 4C. Documents refer to two districts or even to two inde-pendent towns, one in the valley and one on the height: 'le Bourg' or 'Bur-gum' and 'Civitas' or 'Castrum'. The bishop's town was probably on the height, being the older part; Gauls and Romans preferred settlements on heights. Tensions arose in the 13C between the bishop and the towns-people, who demanded administrative representation, as a result of which a consulate was formed to govern the town in 1385. A cathedral was built in the valley, which is traditionally held to have been founded back in the time of Charlemagne (780). However, this information comes from an apocry-phal letter of 1479 and there is no certainty about the matter. In 1437 the market was moved to the height and, following the devastation of the Wars of Religion, the lower town was totally abandoned, the church of the upper town being made the cathedral.

Saint-Jérome (built at the highest point of the town in 1490–1500): The *present cathedral* acquired a splendid façade and flight of steps in the course of its restoration (mid 19C) and was extended to the W. with the addition

Digne, Saint-Jérome, main portal

of a bay. The tower (S. side, 16C) of the basilica, which has a nave and two aisles and chapels along both the flanks, was heightened in the 17C by the addition of a storey with a wrought-iron bell tower.

Notre-Dame du Bourg (on the road to Barcelonnette): The single-aisled basilica and *former cathedral* of Digne is one of the most important architectural monuments in Provence. Existing architectural details date the church back to the 13C; but there are no precise dates of construction. The simple exterior has lavish ornamentation only on the W. front. The sloping gabled roof has been rebuilt. The towers do not rise above the roof because the walls were greatly heightened at a later, unknown, date; the original starting-point of the roof is easily discernible. In the straight end wall of the choir there are 3 beautiful round-arched windows with mouldings. The chapel of Saint-Elzéar was built on to the N. side in 1335. The chapel of Saint-Raymond, built on the W. side of the N. transept back in 1315, was dismantled during the Revolution and there remains only a walled-up columned portal today. N. of the transept are the remains of a built-on house and a chapel of the Pénitents-Blancs (both 16C). Above the round-arched portal in the W. front, with alternating light and dark layers of stone in the piers and archivolts, is a sloping, tiled roof running between the buttresses. A pointed arch spanning the whole breadth of the wall takes the load and encloses an enormous round-arched window with simple tracery, which is flanked on either side by a figure in a pedimented niche (14C). The four-bayed nave has typical Provençal blind arcades along the side walls; its level was raised by over 6 ft. in 1825 due to the dampness of the ground. Stretching out in front of the low choir are the transept arms with pointed arches and a barrel vault. Below the tower (S. side) is a groin-vaulted room, which was probably originally a crypt (Carolingian).

Musée Municipal/town museum (in the former orphanage): Principally Roman and early Christian exhibits; of local importance only.

Digne, Saint-Jérome, detail of façade

Also worth seeing: To the right of the cathedral stands a square *tower* (16C), originally a fortified bell tower, in 1620 it was heightened by the addition of a wrought-iron campanile. On the site of the present prison there once stood a medieval castle. The *Grande Fontaine* (at the end of the Boulevard Gassendi) dates from 1829.

Environs: Courbons (6 km. NW): The cliff-top *church* with Gothic apse and Romanesque nave (14C) dominates the town, some of the houses of which have been destroyed.
Draix (12 km. NE): *Ruins* of a Templar foundation.
La Javie (15 km. NE): *Chapel of Notre-Dame* on the hill above the town.
Le Brusquet (15 km. NE): *Ruins* of the old town. *Chapel of Notre-Dame de Lauzières.*
Malijai (19 km. SW): *Château,* where Napoleon spent the night of 4/5 March, 1815.
Marcoux (6 km. NE): Interesting *Romanesque church.*
Norante (23 km. SE): Ruins of a medieval *castle.*

Tercier (27.5 km. NE): Outside the town are the *ruins of the Cistercian abbey* of Villevieille.
Volonne (25 km. W.): On the left bank of the river of the same name stand a medieval *castle* and a *Romanesque church.*

Draguignan
83 Var   p.258□G 7

The strong position of a Celto-Ligurian town on the Via Appia from Fréjus to Riez led the Romans to build a military post in this area and modern Draguignan is situated at the foot of the Malmont, close to the old town's ruined fortress. The origin of the place name (*Dragonia*) is derived from a legend about the killing of a dragon which once threatened the town. In the 13C it was enclosed by a wall with three gates, and a keep was built on the Horloge hill. In 1535 Draguignan was among the five most important towns in Provence, and its increasing importance and expansion demanded a second wall, which was built in

Digne, Grande Fontaine

1590. From 1797 it was the Préfecture of the Var, until it lost this status to Toulon in 1974.

Notre-Dame-du-Peuple (Rue Notre-Dame-du-Peuple): There is a fine 16C Madonna of the Rosary in the *church*, and also some interesting panelling.

Saint-Michel (1869): This *church* contains two gilded wooden statues of St.Hermentaire, who is said to have saved the town from the dragon in the 5C.

Musée-Bibliothèque (Rue de la République): This dates from the 18C and used to be the summer residence of the bishop of Fréjus; it now houses a collection of coins, sculpture and paintings (Teniers, Parrocel, Van Loo, Mignard etc.); there is also faience from Moustiers.
Attached to the museum is a *library*, which houses a number of valuable manuscripts.

Also worth seeing: The 'Roman gate', part of the town fortifications, is situated in the Place aux Herbes. In 1659 a clock tower, the *Tour de l'Horloge* , which has four corner turrets, was built on the site of the keep, which had been completed under Louis XIV. The *Hôtel de Ville* in the Rue Cisson is housed in a former Franciscan monastery dating from the 18C.

Environs: Bargème (37.5 km NE): This is the highest village in Var, at 3,589 ft., and its *church* has two fine altars (16&17C). There are two 16C *gates*.

Comps-sur-Artuby (32 km. N.): The old town has been partially destroyed, but still has a small, single-aisled 13C *church* with a 15C bell tower, a fine example of the Romanesque-Gothic transitional style.

Eremitage de Saint-Hermentaire (1.5 km. SW): In front of the small Romanesque *chapel* with its Gothic doors are the remains of a Gallo-Roman *bath*.

Figanières (11.5 km. N.): The church of *Saint-Michel* houses a reliquary bust attributed to P.Puget.

Flayosc (7 km. W.): The Romanesque *church* has a 16C Gothic choir and a wrought-iron bell-tower.

La Motte (11 km. SE): The unique old *bardas* in the Rue Aymar are raised stepping stones over the road.

Les-Arcs-sur-Argens (10 km. S.): There is an *aqueduct* still standing from the old Roman Castrum de Arcubus, and *remains of walls* and a square *tower* survive from the old town. The *church* has a *baptistery* with a statue of St.John the Baptist dating from 1638.

Lorgues (13 km. SW): There are some sacred objects from Thoronet housed in the *church* of this typical Provençal village.

Montferrat (15 km. N.): The *church* dates from 1414 and houses a fine 18C altar. There is also the chapel of *Notre-Dame de Beauvoir*.

Notre-Dame de Benva (16 km. W.): The porch of the chapel is decorated with 15C frescos.

Digne, Saint-Jérome, detail of portal

Sainte-Roseline (8 km. S.): Only the chapel still stands from the old 11C *Abbaye de la Celle-Roubaud*, in which the body of St.Roseline de Villeneuve lies in state. There is also a 16C altar and a choir stall (1658).

Trans-en-Provence (4 km. S.): The Belgian inventor A.Knapen built several dramatic *fountains* here.

Embrun
05 Hautes-Alpes   p.254☐G 3

This was originally *Emburodunium*, the capital of the Roman province of Alpes Maritimae. It stands on a rocky spur above the Durance, somewhat to the NW of Mont Saint-Guillaume (8,400 ft.). As early as the 4C it was the seat of an archbishop, which was later transferred to Arles and then brought back to Embrun in Carolingian times. Together with Aix and Arles, it was the centre of one of the three Provençal church provinces, until these were abolished in 1801. Today it presents the appearance of a picturesque old fortified town, with the cathedral and a 12C keep, *La Tour Brune* (reached by a flight of 132 steps), as its main landmarks.

Notre-Dame (end of the 12C/beginning of the 13C): Also known as

◁ *Embrun, Notre-Dame, window in N. wall*

Saint-Etienne. The exact dates of its construction are not known. As a whole, it represents a combination of Provençal Romanesque, Lombard and Gothic styles of architecture. The building is basilican, with a nave and two aisles, but no transept. Outside it is decorated with a continuous frieze of Lombard arcades, with consoles in the form of masks and animals' heads. Only the W. wall has a more complex structure, for it incorporates the tower, which is supported at the bottom by the outside walls and by a pillar in the nave. The upper storeys of the tower begin just above the rounded arches which frame the frieze; they are compact in appearance and were rebuilt in 1825 after having been struck by lightning. The centre of the W. wall (above the early Gothic W. portal) is taken up by a large rose-window, with Gothic style tracery, surrounded by three simple, small round windows. The portal and the window surrounds alike are of alternating grey and yellow stone. The S. wall was modified by the later addition of a sacristy. The N. wall, which retains its original form, is distinguished by a feature of Lombard architecture, namely a large portal with a porch, known as the *Réal*. The outermost marble columns of the porch are borne by two recumbent lions, one of which is grasping a dog in its paws and the other a child, whilst those further into the porch have atlantes. The design of the curling leaves of the capitals was complicated by the fact that they are made of granite. The recessed portal is framed by rounded archivolts; the relief on the tympanum is quite simple and shows Christ surrounded by the symbols of the Evangelists. A depiction of Notre-Dame d'Embrun (or alternatively of the Adoration of the Magi) probably once stood in the porch; it was, in any case, the focus of a famous pilgrimage. The interior of the basilica, which extends over four bays and is 172 ft. long, 76 ft. wide, and 70 ft. high (in the nave),

Embrun, Notre-Dame, lion supporting a pillar

resembles a hall, thanks to the high, pointed arches and the absence of a transept. The Romanesque aisles have barrel vaults and are decorated with blind arcades on the walls, thus contrasting with the virtually plain high walls of the nave, which later acquired a somewhat clumsy groin vault.

Also worth seeing: The former *Archbishop's Palace* and the old *chapterhouse* (13C) on the N. side of the Cathedral.

Environs: Abbaye des Baumes (4 km. N.): *Old Abbey* on the right bank of the Durance (superbly situated).
Savines-le-Lac (10 km. SW): The modern village was built in 1960 near the site of the old one, which had been submerged. It possesses a beautiful modern *church*.

Entrevaux
04 Alpes-de-Haute-Provence   p.258□H 5

This small town, with its 18C fortress preserved intact, stands on the left bank of the Var. The *town wall*, which incorporates three gates, runs around the citadel. In front of the main gate (on the S. side) there is a single-arched bridge over the river which is defended at both ends.

Church (end of 16C): This used to be the cathedral of the diocese of Glandève. It is a late Gothic structure, comprising a single aisle, whose right side is built on to the town wall, which is why the towers were crenellated (one of them is now used as a bell tower). The portal has beautiful door leaves dating from the early 17C and the spacious choir is in the style of Louis XIII.

Environs: Annot (15 km. W.): Old medieval town with crooked streets. The main street begins at the fortified *gate*. Some of the houses in the old town date from the 16&17C, as do the hospital (1656) and the *Hôtel de Ville* (1701).

Le Fugeret (19 km. NW): The 12C church has a beautiful altarpiece.
Pont Saint-Benoît (11.5 km. W.): Medieval *bridge* over the Vaïre.
Vérimande (*c.* 15 km. W): *Chapel* of the Knights Templar.

Eygalières
13 Bouches-du-Rhône   p.256□C 6

This little village is picturesquely situated in the Alpilles. It was known by the Romans as *Aquileria* because of its springs ('aqua' meaning 'water'), and was originally settled in remote antiquity—in fact, this rocky spur was inhabited in Neolithic times. Under the Romans, the aqueduct supplying Arles with water began from here. Today, all that remains from its long past are a few medieval buildings: a 12C *church*, a *tower* which used to be part of the old castle, which has sadly been disfigured by a modern statue of the Virgin Mary, a beautiful 17C *chapel* (Chapelle de Pénitents), and a *Renaissance Hôtel*.

Entrevaux, main gate of the town wall

Entrevaux, church, carved door panels

Eygalières has become known as a colony of writers and painters.

Environs: Chapelle Saint-Sixte (1.5 km. E.): This simple *chapel* stands on an isolated hill which is thickly covered with almond trees and cypresses.

Fayence

83 Var   p.258☐H 6

A small town at the E. end of the plain

of Provence, it offers a beautiful view of the Monts des Maures and the Esterel. In the 14C it was enclosed by a wall incorporating a fortified gate.

Church (15C): This was restored during the 18C, when it underwent some slight alteration. It has a nave and two aisles. The interior contains a fine marble altar.

Also worth seeing: Just outside Fayence is the old monastery chapel of *Notre-Dame des Cyprès* (12C).

Environs: Bargemon (18 km. W.): Four well-preserved *towers* survive from the old town wall. The frescos in the *church* date from the early 17C. The chapel of *Notre-Dame de Montaigu* (1634) contains a relic from Belgium.

Callas (22 km. SW): This typical Provençal village contains a *ruined castle*. Inside the *church* there is a 17C altar.

Callian (9 km. E.): Visitors are not allowed into the 11C *castle*. The church contains a revered relic of St.Maximus.

Entrevaux, panorama

Château de Beauregard (10.5 km. N.): Built in 1570, flanked by round towers.

Mons (13.5 km. N.): The town's landmark is a high, square *tower*. The *church* was built in the 13C.

Montauroux (10.5 km. E.): The 12C chapel of *Saint-Barthélémy* contains wooden panelling dating from 1630, when the chapel was rebuilt.

Notre-Dame de l'Ormeau (3.5 km. W.): The Romanesque *chapel* contains a Renaissance altar with some fine carvings (Tree of Jesse).

Seillans (5.5 km. NW): Remains of the *town wall* and a 13C *gate*. The furnishings of the Romanesque *church* are worth seeing. The castle of *Valmasque* is 3 km. E. of Seillans.

Fontaine-de-Vaucluse

84 Vaucluse   p.256□C 5

This small village stands on a bare and sparsely inhabited limestone plateau. Despite its small size (700 inhabitants), it attracts as many as 800,000 visitors a year, owing its fame, as its name suggests, to its remote and isolated spring ('Vaucluse' comes from the Latin 'Vallis clausa'). In reality, it is probably not a spring at all but more likely an underground river emerging from a subterranean cave, creating in the process an incomparable natural spectacle. The series of caves behind it excited the curiosity of investigators as early as 1878, and since 1955 has frequently attracted Cousteau himself. But the most famous visitor to this isolated spring was Petrarch, who made frequent retreats here between 1337 and 1353, tormented by his hopeless love for Laura. A column still stands on the market place in the village to remind us that a large number of his works were composed here. A small museum has been set up in the house where he is supposed to have lived.

Church of Saint-Véran: Undecorated Romanesque building dating from the first half of the 12C. It has a square tower over the N. transept.

Fontaine-de-Vaucluse, view of the caves

Gânagobie (Forcalquier), cloister

The interior contains blind arcades, in the manner of Provençal Romanesque. The slightly pointed tunnel vault above the single aisle is replaced, in the last bay before the apse, by a transverse tunnel vault.

Environs: Beaucet (13.5 km. N.): Small village with partially-preserved *fortifications*.
Roque-sur-Pernes (11 km. N.): There is a pilgrimage here every 16 May to the *hermitage* of St.Gens, who could tame lions and make it rain.
Saint-Didier (14 km. N.): The old *château* dates from the 15–17C and now accommodates a health centre which practises hydrotherapy. It has beautiful coffered ceilings, a fireplace which was possibly sculpted by Bernus, and frescos which are attributed to Mignard.
Saumane-de-Vaucluse (4 km. NW): Charming little village, well-known for its truffles. It contains a church which was originally Romanesque but has been much altered, and a massive *château*, which was begun in the 15C.

Forcalquier
04 Alpes-de-Haute-Provence   p.256☐E 5

The town is overlooked by a hill which used to be fortified. It was founded in the 7C and during the 11&12C was the principal residence of the Comtes de Forcalquier, a powerful family belonging to the Provençal nobility which ruled Haute-Provence and in 1209 allied itself by marriage to the Comtes de Provence. The attacks made during the 14&16C by the Grandes Compagnies caused severe damage, as also did the Wars of Religion, and the town has never regained its old importance.

Old cathedral: This began as a Romanesque church with a single aisle, but we do not know the exact date of its building. The aisles and the polygonal choir were added in the 13C (the transept was by then already in place). The church which we see today is Gothic and has a rectangular, three-storeyed tower over the crossing dating from the 17C. A Gothic

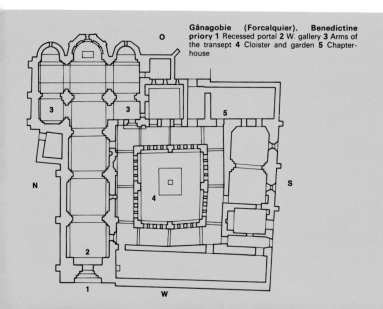

Gânagobie (Forcalquier), Benedictine priory 1 Recessed portal 2 W. gallery 3 Arms of the transept 4 Cloister and garden 5 Chapterhouse

bell tower with a 17C belfry rises above the façade. The windows have rounded arches and are devoid of tracery; they were rebuilt in the 17C. The Gothic portal (13C) at the W. end has a pointed arch and stands beneath a window with a richly moulded round arch, whose tracery bears a great similarity to that of the window in the cathedral in Digne.

Also worth seeing: The exceptionally well restored *former Franciscan convent* (13C) now houses a *museum*. The other small *museum* which is housed in the *Hôtel de Ville* (near the church) is only of local interest. On the Place Saint-Michel there is a *fountain* which has a modern basin, a richly decorated Gothic pinnacle dating from the 15C, and a figure of St.Michael.

Environs: Banon (25 km. NW): This town stands at the foot of a steep cliff and has some remains of its old 15C *town wall*.
Cereste (20 km. SW): *Fortified wall* around the settlement.
Gânagobie (11 km. NE): The *Bene-dictine priory of Notre-Dame du Puy de Gânagobie* stands on a plateau overlooking the Durance valley. This was originally the site of a Celto-Ligurian oppidum and later, in the Middle Ages, of a little town, in addition to the priory. The ruins of the town wall have survived. The priory was founded by Bishop Jean III. of Sisteron (950–65), who owned the hill and built both the priory and the two churches, the priory church and St.John's church, out of his own means. There is no mention of the dates of construction. In its day the priory prospered greatly, but later, with the secularization of 1788, its fate was sealed; the monks were discharged and the buildings and lands were sold off. During the next 100 years the place fell into decay. Restoration work was finally begun in 1891. The church's simple exterior is in keeping with 12C Provençal architecture.
Mane (a few km. S.): Outside the town is the *former priory of Notre-Dame de Salagon*, whose ownership changed continually from the 11C until the Revolution, when it was

Gânagobie, Romanesque portal, tympanum

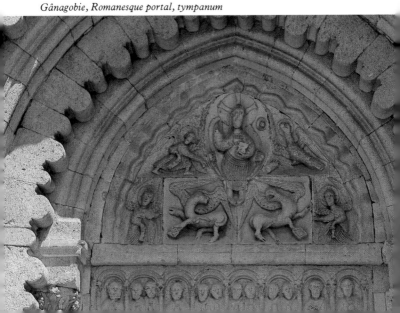

abandoned by the monks. After this the church fell into ruin. Today, the buildings in which the monks used to live (some of them dating from the 15C) stand on land belonging to a farm. The stepped portal, which has columns inset, once contained a painted tympanum. Above it is a restored rose-window (15&16C). On the N. side of the tunnel-vaulted nave, which occupies three bays, has been built a side aisle whose round-arched windows are walled in. A portal with a pointed arch was set into the S. wall during the 14C.

Peyruis (22 km. NE): *Church* dating from the 12&14C.

Sauvan: Several km. to the S. can be seen a *château* which was designed by the architect J.B. Franque. Only the beautiful façade facing the garden was completed.

Fort de Buoux
84 Vaucluse   p.256☐D 6

Fort: The fort takes its name from the little village of Buoux, which has a mere 72 inhabitants and is old enough to contain a tiny church with a 12C Romanesque altar and a cemetery chapel dating from the beginning of the 13C. 550 yards to the N., in the middle of a large and beautifully laid out park, can be seen the old château, dating from the 16&18C, which now houses a holiday home.

Farther along there is a huge overhanging crag with prehistoric graves hewn out of stone, and beyond that a plateau 550 yards long by 33 to 110 yards wide which falls away precipitously and on which the ruins of the old fort stand. This occupies an exceptionally favourable strategic position overlooking the only pass over the Luberon which can be easily traversed. It was built in the 13C, only to be destroyed in the 16C under Louis XIV, when it had become a place of refuge for Protestants. Today one is struck by the wildness and romance of this huge site, now once more overgrown by nature. Behind the W. rampart, which was built in the 16C, is the old fortified square, now covered by rubble and undergrowth, on which the ruins of a 13C

Mane (Forcalquier), panorama

Bonnieux (Fort de Buoux), stone sculpture of lectern on the Place de l'Église

Romanesque *chapel* can still be easily distinguished. There are some more or less identifiable remains of the *old village* round about. A little farther on are the old *stores*, consisting of large spherical holes in the ground, and then the *secret passage*, which used to be concealed, and allowed the inhabitants, when under siege, to descend unseen into the valley and attack the enemy from the rear.

Caves: In the cliff of *Moulin-Clos*, opposite the fort, there are a number of caves which were probably inhabited by early Christian hermits. Many of them had been inhabited in Palaeolithic times.

Environs: Bonnieux (9 km. W.): This is a small market town which retains parts of its old ramparts and has a beautiful old *church*, which in fact looks rather plain from the

outside. It consisted originally of a single aisle, which now has three Romanesque bays supporting a tunnel vault with pointed arches, and two Gothic bays beneath a rib vault, also with pointed arches. The pentagonal choir and the side aisles were built in the 15C.

Saint-Symphorien (2 km. W.): The 11C priory used to belong to the Abbey of Saint-Victor in Marseille. Essentially all that is preserved is the church tower; the vaults and walls of the 11C church having largely collapsed. The slender, elegant square 12C bell tower now rises from the rubble. Only the two uppermost of its four storeys are open to the outside. But, whereas the four walls of the top storey are set off by a cornice and pierced in the usual way by slender double arches, the apertures in the next storey down seem completely out of place. Here, the round-arched

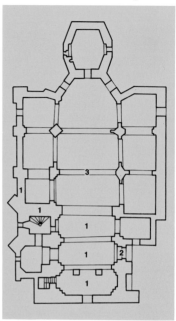

Bonnieux, church tower

Bonnieux, Église Vieille:1 Remains of the old Romanesque church (third quarter of the 12C), consisting of the three E. bays and the N. arm of the former transept **2** Original entrance **3** 15C additions

window is set in a large rectangular niche, with a column standing right in front of its centre. This column, together with the two others which flank the window, support the lintel, above which there are two shell niches filled with various ornaments. The three columns imitate the columns of antiquity, and possess double torus with fluting, swelling shafts and composite capitals; but the lack of an original which might be copied does show in the general design.

Fréjus

83 Var   p.258☐H 7

This site on the coastal plateau was originally occupied by a Celto-Ligurian oppidum. In 49 BC, Julius Caesar founded *Forum Julii* here, and it later expanded to become an important military base on the Via Aurelia. When it became an administrative centre and acquired a naval base, the town flourished, and its population rose to 40,000. During the Middle Ages it lost much of its importance, so that virtually no information has come down to us from Merovingian and Carolingian times. The town was devastated by the Saracens in 940, and the inhabitants fled; but they came back again and built a wall around the city. Bishop Riculfe sponsored the construction of a new cathedral and the reconstruction of the harbour enabled it to become a commercial port, although during the 14C its affairs declined, not least thanks to the ravages of the plague. Fréjus was the seat of a bishop from 374 until 1957, when the diocese was moved to Toulon.

Arènes/Amphitheatre (near the Porte des Gaules): This oval theatre was built by the Romans in the 1 or 2C outside the then town wall. The site is now badly ruined, but the 16 rows of seats which were originally intended to seat 10,000 spectators can still be recognized.

Aqueduct (the remains are in front of the Porte de Rome): This was laid in the 1C BC and was some 30 miles long. On entering the town, it passed over the town wall to the highest point in the town, where there was a reservoir.

Porte des Gaules (SW of the town wall): The gateway is now walled up, but was in antiquity a *town gate*.

Porte d'Orée (S. side): This has been erroneously described as a gate, but is actually a large archway standing on thick pillars, which probably once formed part of the public baths.

Porte de Rome (NE side): It was here that the Via Aurelia entered the town in antiquity. Only a pillar now remains of the original double gate enclosing an inner courtyard.

Roman theatre (NE side): Semicircular theatre, of which only a few rows of seats, as well as the foundations of the orchestra and stage, have been preserved.

Citadels: The Romans built their military base at the NE corner of the harbour, in the area now known as the *Plate-Forme*. Within the walls, which were reinforced by buttresses, were the house of the military commander, a small building housing baths, and store-rooms (called the Grénier de César). The second citadel (SW corner) takes its present name, *Butte Saint-Antoine*, from a 17C chapel of St.Anthony. The strong fort (now ruined) was built between 40 and 14 BC, 33 ft. above the level of the town. In the W. part of the citadel is the *Lanterne d'Auguste*, a hexagonal medieval tower with a small pavilion roof.

Fréjus, cathedral and baptistery

Fréjus, baptistery, capital

Baptistery (left of the cathedral): Small baptismal chapel built in the 5C. 8 monolithic columns define the interior as an octagon. On the lower level, each side contains a niche, corresponding to the 8 windows on the octagonal upper level (these were made by Formigé in 1924). The drum begins above a simple cornice. The baptistery was originally faced with marble and decorated with frescos. In the niches, the mosaic floor has been preserved. An octagonal font of white marble has been recently discovered.

Capitou (N. side of the baptistery): This former palace for the cathedral chapter (built around 1200) almost has the appearance of being fortified. The room on the ground floor has retained its medieval character.

Cathedral (Place J.Formigé): The present church was built around 1200 on top of the foundation walls of two earlier buildings on the same site. It has a square tower above the narthex, with 8 steps leading up to it. Behind the narthex, which has a tunnel vault, there is a beautiful *Renaissance portal* (1530) whose leaves consist of 8 framed coffered panels. The interior gains its effect mainly from its powerful pointed arches and the blind arcades along the side walls.

A connecting bay and recessed, low choir adjoin the three bays of the rib-vaulted nave. A semicircular arch in the W. wall leads into the side aisle, which supports a half-tunnel vault, and is separately dedicated (to Saint-Étienne). The main part of the church, in contrast, is consecrated to the Virgin Mary. There is a sacristy, 42 ft. 7 in. long, adjoining the N. side, and two early Gothic chapels at the W. end. The interior is sparsely decorated with sculpture and there are only a few furnishings to mitigate the austere overall impression: the choir stalls (1441) by F. de Toulon, a 16C wooden crucifix, and a sarcophagus bearing the reclining figures of Bishops Guillaume de Ruffec and Louis de Bouillac.

Cloister: This dates from the 13C and originally consisted of two storeys. The simple vault was replaced in the 14C by a flat, beautifully-carved ceiling with wooden beams, which was

Fréjus, Roman theatre

decorated in the 15C with a painting showing an interesting interpretation of St. John's Apocalypse.

Hôtel de Ville (S. side of the church): This was originally the Bishop's Palace; and the rooms in the cellar were once used as a prison. The massive wall at the back, which dates from the 14C, contains Romanesque windows and is flanked by two square towers. The large assembly room is on the ground floor, with the Salle Synodale directly above it. On the E. side is the Gothic bishop's chapel (14C).

Musée Archéologique (established 1882): The buildings adjoining the cathedral cloister contain, on the first floor, some beautiful Roman objects (notably a mosaic depicting leopards), a collection of ancient lamps, amphorae etc.

Also worth seeing: *La Bastide de Villeneuve* contains the remains of some ancient baths. The so-called *Tourrache* is a 4C mausoleum of which some fragments have been pre-served. The *Church of Saint-François-de-Paule* was built around 1490 in the late Gothic style.

Environs: Auberge des Adrets (15.5 km. NE): This medieval *smugglers' inn* was restored to its original condition in 1898.
La Tour-de-Mare (4 km. N.); Near this town is the *Chapel of Notre-Dame de Jérusalem*. The decoration of its interior was begun in 1963 by J.Cocteau but not completed.
Musée des Troupes de Marine (5 km. N.): Large naval museum with exhibits from past centuries.
Notre-Dame de la Roquette (c. 15 km. NW): Near the ruins of a monastery there is a large 17C *chapel*.
Puget-sur-Argens (5 km. NW): The *church* contains a Roman milestone from the Via Aurelia which is used as a font.
Roquebrune-sur-Argens (12.5 km. W.): Situated on the right bank of the river Argens. We are reminded of its medieval past by the remains of- the *town wall* and a *tower*. The *parish church*, comprising a single aisle with a rib vault, is a late Gothic structure

Fréjus, Arènes, amphitheatre

built in the 16C (with a polygonal choir). The two chapels on the N. side belong to an earlier period of construction, and seem originally to have been the bays of the 13C church which formerly stood on the same site. The baptismal chapel contains a beautiful half-relief figure of St.John the Baptist flanked by two painted figures of saints (1557). An altarpiece depicting the Passion and a Last Judgement also date from the 16C. On leaving the town, there is the Romanesque chapel of *Saint-Pierre* standing on a hill. The simple exterior (with a round-arched portal) was later given a bell arcade. The interior supports a tunnel vault, and the side walls have the usual Provençal blind arcades. The E. end concludes in a connecting bay and apse. The only decoration which stands out is a horizontal cornice at the base of the vault. The *Benedictine monastery of Notre-Dame de Pitié* (1.5 km. SW) has a chapel dating from 1649.

Saint-Raphaël (3 km. E.): The first settlers here were Ligurian. They were followed by the Romans, and

after the Saracen invasion the town passed into the hands of Guillaume I of Provence. The name of San Rafe was first mentioned in a document in 1043 by the monks of Lérins. The Knights Templar fortified the town during the 12&13C, but it did not become more than a little fishing village for a long time, not until the 2nd half of the 19C, in fact, when the writer Alphonse Karr, supported by the mayor, Félix Martin, undertook its development into an important modern resort. The neo-Byzantine church of *Notre-Dame de la Victoire* (1883), on the embankment promenade, dates from that same period. The *Église des Templiers* was built in the 12C on top of the foundations of two earlier churches which had stood on the same site. The Provençal Romanesque church which we see today comprises a single, very broad, aisle, with a main apse and two side chapels at the E. end. Of these, the N. chapel was replaced before 1312 by a slender square watch-tower (also used for signals). The deep blind arcades on the side walls of the nave, which

Fréjus, Porte d'Orée

Fréjus, Hôtel de Ville seen from the rear

Lac de Serre-Ponçon (23 km. E. of Gap), St.-Michel above the submerged town of Ubaye

extends for two bays and has a tunnel vault, convey the impression of side chapels in themselves. A severely-damaged fresco in the left chapel depicts the Baptism of Christ. To the right of the church can be seen a fragment of the Fréjus aqueduct. The former church presbytery has since 1863 housed the *Musée d'Archéologie*, whose principal exhibits are ancient (notably a collection of amphorae), though there are also some later items concerning the history of the town. On a hill to the N. can be seen the chapel of *Notre-Dame de Bon Secours* (17C), which contains modern paintings by Duguy and Fauché.

Gap
05 Hautes-Alpes   p.254☐F 3

Gap is the préfecture of the département of Hautes-Alpes, and is situated

Gap, cathedral

Chorges (Gap), church

on the Luye, a tributary of the Durance.

Cathedral (Town Centre): This was built in 1866–95 and has elements of neo-Gothic style.

Musée Départemental (Avenue de Maréchal Foch): The rooms of the museum include a large variety of exhibits, including the mausoleum of the Connétable de Lesdiguières and the tomb of his wife (17C). Lesdiguières was one of the fiercest Protestant opponents of Catholicism in the 17C.

The museum also includes Bronze Age jewellery, Gallo-Roman, German and Merovingian objects, chests from the Queyras, objects of local folk-art, faiences from Moustiers, and a pennant with which Napoleon honoured the town on his return from Elba.

Also worth seeing: The house (17, Rue de Frence) in which Napoleon spent the night of 5–6 March 1815.

Environs: Chorges (17 km. E.): This village is situated in a wide valley and has a 15C *church*.

Château de Charance (4 km. NW): This was once the residence of the bishop of Gap, and affords a fine view over the town (garden open).

Château des Diguières (35 km. N.): The *ruins* of the old château are situated on the banks of the Drac (S. of La Trinité).

Château de Malmort (47 km. NW): A ruined *Castle* in the wild Soulouise valley.

Notre-Dame de Laus (19 km. SE): A *pilgrimage church* of the Virgin was consecrated here in 1666; according to legend, the Virgin Mary appeared to a shepherd here in 1664.

Saint-Pierre-d'Argençon (40.5 km. SW): This castle dates back to the 14C, although it was rebuilt and extended in the 16&19C.

Serres (42 km. SW): This village is set on a hill washed by the Buech; it has a number of *old houses* from the 15–16C, and a 12C *church*.

Tallard (12 km. S.): This village lies on the right bank of the Durance, and during the Middle Ages was the property of the Counts of Orange. In the 13C they gave it to the Knights of St.John, and in 1322 it was acquired by Arnaud de Trians, a nephew of Pope John XXII. Later, it passed from the Sassenage family (1426) to the Clermonts, and the *castle* to the S. of the town was subsequently extended during the 15&16C. It was severely damaged, first in the Wars of Religion and then by the Duke of Savoy's troops. Finally, in 1957, the town took over the castle ruins for restoration and installed a *museum* in them. The curtain wall, residence and various other buildings including a chapel are still in a bad state of repair. A portal with round arches leads through into an almost square inner courtyard, one side of which had a battlemented wall, and another consisted of houses and the adjacent *chapel*, whose façade shows traces of sumptuous late Gothic. The pointed-arch portal is divided by a pier, and there is a flat shell motif in the tympanum. The ogee arch has a pinnacle with a finial, and there are traceried windows between this and the buttresses which flank it. There is a small domed belfry on the W.side, and the two-bayed interior has a huge window in the straight end wall of the choir. There is an exit from the chapel gallery which leads to the Salle des Gardes, in the upper storey of the residential section; this is a room of 115 × 49 ft. with a row of windows with stone mullions and transoms which open out on to a courtyard. There is a round-arched portal on the ground floor level leading from the courtyard into the residential quarters. The castle has a second courtyard which can be reached through a portal with a pointed arch, but the buildings around it are almost entirely ruinous.

Veynes (26 km. SW): There is a fine

Gordes, panorama

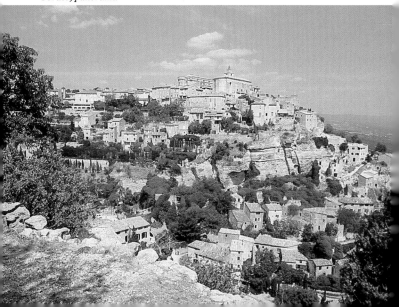

old *Hôtel de Ville*, and a 16C *château* which has been much restored over the years.

Gordes
84 Vaucluse   p.256☐C 5

The church and the fortress are situated, in the manner of a Greek acropolis, on the crest of a terraced spur of the Vaucluse, above rings of encircling and adjoined houses. It was destroyed by the Germans in 1944, but rebuilt by artists such as Vasarely, a pioneer of optical and kinetic art and of the 'alphabet plastique', a new aesthetic language constructed out of simple geometrical shapes and coded colours.

Church: A plain, rather cold classical hall church, with a number of 17C altarpieces.

Castle: This structure was built as a fortress in the 11C, but was extensively altered by B. de Simiane in 1525 and is one of the few Renaissance buildings in the area.

Also worth seeing: There are some restored *old houses*, some of which date from the 16C; there are also remains of the town walls, including the Porte de Savoie. The small *Musée Municipal* is housed in a fine early-13C building and hosts temporary exhibitions. Just *outside the town* is the *Insula Maria*, a rebuilt Roman villa with frescos and mosaics, and the *Village des Bories*, where rustic tools such as threshing flails and ovens are on display. Bories (known in Sardinia as trulli, in Spain as casitas and in Languedoc as capitelles) are common in the Mediterranean: stone huts built to a Stone Age level of sophistication. They have no windows, no mortar and are corbelled to a gradual point at the top; and are still used as stables and tool huts.

Environs: Cabrières d'Avignon (7 km. SW): This was one of the villages which was badly damaged by the Baron of Oppède during the course of the Vaudois uprisings. The *church* and the *château* were rebuilt in the 16C.
Moulin des Bouillons (5 km. S.):

Gordes, Village de Bories

There is a very interesting *glass museum* (Musée de Vitrail), which houses a glass-blowing exhibition, historical documents and a retrospective of the work of F.Duran; there is also a 16C oil mill.

Murs (11.5 km. NE): This is a small village with a heavily restored 15&16C *château*.

Grasse

06 Alpes-Maritimes   p.258☐H 6

Little is known of the historical origin of Grasse, but the etymology of the name may suggest that the town was founded in antiquity by Crassus. It is, however, known that this small hill at the foot of the Roquevignon plateau was already inhabited in Merovingian times, and that by the 10C it was a flourishing town. Its striving for self-government by consuls brought treaties with Pisa (1179) and Genoa (1199), but the struggles betwen the Guelphs and the Ghibellines forced the citizens to side with Raymond Bérenguer IV, the Duke of Provence. The importance of the town was reflected in the fact that it became the seat of the bishop of Antibes in 1243, and the capital of the region in 1388, with Bishop Augustine as ruler. During the Wars of Religion (against the Protestants) and the wars of the Spanish (1707) and Austrian (1746) Succession it was plundered and razed many times, with the result that only the cathedral and the bishop's palace have survived. The walls were torn down in 1536, replaced and burnt down again. In 1644 the diocese was merged with that of Vence, which intensified the rivalry and opposition between the two towns, until in 1791 Grasse regained its own bishop. In 1792 it became the capital of the département of Var. In the Second World War (1944) the local resistance movement succeeded in liberating the city, and today it is one of the centres of the French perfume industry.

Former Bishop's Palace (near the church of Notre-Dame): Now the Hôtel de Ville, it has been rebuilt on

Moulin des Bouillons (Gordes), glass museum

Moulin des Bouillons (Gordes), glass museum

numerous occasions and bears the marks of many different periods. The former bishop's chapel is on two storeys and forms the vestibule. The square tower is 12C and was once part of the well-fortified palace; it is a large building, also on two storeys; its rooms have narrow ground-level windows and the council chamber on the storey above has double- and triple-arched windows on the N. side, which date from the 13C.

Notre-Dame (Place du Petit Puy): This was once the cathedral, and dates from the late 12 or early 13C. The architectural style combines Lombard and early Gothic elements, but the building as a whole remains true to the Romanesque tradition.

The church is a basilica with a nave and two aisles; it does not appear clumsy, despite the sturdy pillars, because the arches and pointed rib vaulting reach right to the top of the nave. The central apse was replaced by a square choir in 1687–90, which houses a 17C painting by S.Bourdon with the theme of the Mystic Mar-
riage of St.Catherine, an Ascension from 1741 by H.Subleyras and Christ Washing the Disciples' Feet by J.H.Fragonard—Fragonard's only surviving religious painting. The right aisle, to which a gallery was added in the 18C, contains three impressive works by Rubens, painted by the artist in 1601 in Rome: 'Crown of Thorns', 'Crucifixion of Christ' and 'Deposition of St.Helena'. The altar of St.Honoratus (late-15C), flanked by St.Clement and St.Lambert, is attributed to L.Bréa. The painted wooden shrine in the sacristy with scenes from the life of St.Honoratus dates from the first half of the 15C and was a gift from the monastery on the Iles de Lérins.

Musée d'Art et d'Histoire de Provence (or *Musée Fragonard*): A museum was established in 1921 in the old Hôtel Cabris, which dates from 1771, at 2 Rue Mirabeau. As well as works by Fragonard, it includes works from the Provençal and Italian schools of the 17C, ethnological items from 17&18C Provence,

Grasse, Notre-Dame, chapel of St.-Sacrement

18C furniture and Moustiers faience. There is a large library attached to the museum.

Villa Fragonard (Boulevard Fragonard): This 18C building was converted into a *museum* in 1976; it houses numerous works by Fragonard as well as several mementoes.

Musée de la Marine (9 Rue Gazan): This former inn contains 18C model ships and documentary material relating to the Duke of Grasse (1722–88).

Also worth seeing: The centre of the modern town is the 17C promenade *Cours Honoré-Cresp*. The Hôpital de Petit-Paris has a small chapel with three 18C paintings by Ch.-J Natoire: 'Adoration of the Magi' and 'Healing of the Plague by St.Roch and St.Germanus'. The old town is spread over a small hill, and its appearance has not altered since the 18C; the streets are narrow and winding and connected by flights of steps. Most of the 18C houses are on the large *Place aux Aires*, near which is the *Chapelle de l'Oratoire* with a 14C façade. Close to the baroque chapel of Saint-Thomas is *Fragonard's birthplace*: 23 Rue Tracastel.

Environs: Auribeau-sur-Siagne (10 km. S.): In the Middle Ages this small village was a dependency of the abbey at Lérins. There is a *gate* from the old wall on a craggy hill. The *church* is 18C and it contains a reliquary shrine from the 5C and a fine chalice from 1563.
Cabris (6 km. W.): The *ruins* of the medieval castle afford a fine view; the *church* dates from 1617 and contains altars in the local folk style and a painting by Murillo. The chapel of *Sainte-Marguerite* was completed in 1500 and houses a fine 16C wooden altarpiece.
Châteauneuf-de-Grasse (6 km. E.): The church of *Saint-Martin* houses a fine 13C altarpiece; the *house of the Marquis Geoffroy du Rouret* was restored in about 1630.
Escragnolles (34 km. NW): The small village's 16C *church* was extended in the 18C; the old *château* dates from 1430.
Le Bar-sur-Loup (9.5 km. NE): The *church* of this typical Provençal village has a 13C nave and a rebuilt 17C choir. The fine leaves of the Gothic portal were carved in the 15C. The back wall of the high altar is decorated with 14 separate panels with scenes from the life of St.James the Great; these are attributed to L.Bréa. There is an unusual 15C painting of the 'Danse Macabre', and at the foot of the bell tower is a 2C Roman tombstone. The towers of the 16C *château* of the Dukes of Grasse look down on the town.
Magagnosc (5 km. NE): The Romanesque chapel of *Saint-Michel*, whose set interior is decorated with modern

wall paintings by Savary, is situated in the midst of fields of flowers.

Mouans-Sartoux (7 km. SE): Two neighbouring towns were merged in 1858. The *church* dates from the 13C but has been gradually altered over the years. The heavily restored *château* dates from the 16C.

Notre-Dame de Valcluse (7.5 km. S.): The *hermitage chapel* dates from the 17C and is situated in an isolated valley; it shows Italian influence.

Opio (7 km. E.): The bishops of Grasse built a *residence* here in the 17C; there is also a 14C *oil press*.

Peymeinade (6 km. SW): The *church* is 18C.

Saint-Arnoux (14 km. NE): 18C *hermitage chapel*.

Saint-Cézaire-sur-Siagne (15 km. W.): This village has maintained its old appearance, with three 14C *towers* and a *town gate* surviving from its old fortifications. The *church* was completed in 1720, and it houses some 17C paintings. The Romanesque *graveyard chapel* is 12&13C and contains the Roman sarcophagus of Julia Sempronia.

Saint-Vallier-de-Thiey (12 km. NW): This village is quite untypical of Provence; it was founded as Castrum Valerii by the Romans. The village and its late-12C Romanesque *church* are surrounded by a medieval *wall*.

Valbonne (9 km. E.): This attractive valley, known to the Romans as Vallis Bona, is the site of a *church* built by Cistercian monks in 1199. The houses are grouped around a central 17C square, which is dominated by a bell tower. 3 km. NE of the town is a plateau which was inhabited from early historical times. As far as we can tell, the Romans used this place from about the 2C BC to the 6C AD as a necropolis.

Gréolières
06 Alpes Maritimes   p.258□H 6

Gréolières is situated at the foot of the Cheiron, looking down over the Loup valley. The derelict old town of Hautes-Gréolières is situated to the N. of the modern town, and to the S. of Basse are the *ruins* of a medieval *castle*.

Church: The church contains a magnificent altar of St.Stephen (1480) by an unknown master of the Provençal school. Other points of interest include a 14C polychrome wooden Madonna and Child from the 14C, a 16C altar wing depicting John the Baptist and a 17C processional cross.

Environs: Andon (15 km. SW): The *church* dates from 1820, and houses an interesting 17C *Christ* of Spanish origin and an 18C font.

Bézaudun-les-Alpes (18 km. E.): In the S. of the village is the chapel of *Notre-Dame du Peuple*, which contains a figure of the Virgin from 1556.

Cipières (5 km. S.): The *church* houses a 15C reliquary of St.Mayeul; in the chapel of *Saint-Claude*, on the road out of town, is a 15C wooden sculpture of the saint and a Deposition from the Cross from the same century, which is painted in the style of a work by Rubens.

Courségoules (12 km. E.): The *church* was built in Provençal style in the 12C, with a squat bell tower. The interior has three bays, a marble altar and an altarpiece which comprises six panels, with John the Baptist standing in between St.Petronillus and St.Gothardus.

Gourdon (c. 15 km. S.): The castle, which was the seat of the Dukes of Provence in the 13–16C, was built on the foundations of a 9&10C Saracen castle. The building was restored in the 17C, and today it houses a small medieval art *museum*.

Le Mas (32.5 km. NW): The 13C *church* houses a 15C reliquary casket with the head of St.Arnulf.

Saint-Auban (27 km. NW): This is a picturesque village situated on the left bank of the Esteron. There are *ruins* of an old *fortress* and a rebuilt *castle*.

Séranon (27 km. SW): The *ruins* of the old village are situated on a cliff. On the road out of Séranon is the 11C chapel of *Notre-Dame de Gratemoine*. On his return from Elba, Napoleon spent a night in the *Château de Groundet*.

Thorenc (15 km. W.): This attractively situated mountain village has a *church* and the fortified *Château des Quatre-Tours*, which was restored in the 16C.

Guillestre
05 Hautes-Alpes   p.254□G/H 2

This small village is situated on a fertile plateau between the Guil and the Chagne, with the Tête de Cugulet rising up above it to a height of 8,300 ft. The village's centre is formed by a beautiful old square. There are only scattered remains of the old fortifications.

Parish church: The original Romanesque building was erected in the late 12 and early 13C, and one of its towers and its W. portal with its open porch still stand. The nave was rebuilt in late Gothic style in the first third of the 16C and the high, square tower has round bell arches; the stone roof and the corner pyramids appear to be more recent. The most remarkable aspect of the W. front is its doorway and porch, a Réal, like that of Embrun, which displays Lombard influence. At the front there are four couchant lions, each supporting a column, above which there are pointed arches and and cross-ribs. The recessed Romanesque portal is framed by slim columns and round arches and the carved door leaves are 16C.

The three bays of the single aisle are only separated by half-columns on the side walls. Despite the late date of its construction, there are no Renaissance elements to be seen, only late Gothic. The choir has rich stellar vaulting. The two-bayed chapel on the N. side of the church was a later addition.

Guillestre, parish church, base of column

Environs: Abriès (31 km. NE): This small summer and winter-sports resort was rebuilt after a fire in 1945; it has a Romanesque *church*.

Aiguilles (26 km. NE): This has a 13C Romanesque *church*, and an *ethnographic museum* for the Queyras district.

Arvieux (21 km. NE): The 16C *church* has a fine porch.

Chapelle de Clausis (38 km. NE): Unique Italian/French *pilgrimage destination* (16 July).

Château-Queyras (18.5 km. NE): 12&14C *castle* on a hill; it was enlarged in the 17C and again in 1840.

Mont-Dauphin (4 km. W.): Vauban built a small *fortress* here in 1693, with pink marble walls enclosing barracks, houses and a small church. It was planned as a garrison, which could also be used for the protection of civilians. There was an exercise hall for use in bad weather.

Saint-Véran (32 km. NE): This is the highest parish in France (6,560–6,760 ft.); it is a small farming community which includes some *old houses* whose single rooms used to function as kitchen, bedroom and stable combined. The 17C *church* has fine furnishings and the remains of a Romanesque porch. The water used to irrigate the surrounding fields flows down a canal on the N. slope which dates back to the 11C.

Ville-Vieille (21 km. NE): A restored 16C *church.*

Hyères

83 Var   p.258☐F 8

In the Middle Ages the Seigneurs de Fos built a fortress on the foundations of the Roman *Nobile Castrum Arearum*, the name of which, *Areis*, became the current name of the town around 1200. Upon his return from the 7th Crusade (1254) St.Louis is supposed to have landed at the harbour of Hyères. His brother, Charles I of Anjou, captured the town after a lengthy siege in 1257, whereupon it lost the independence it had successfully defended for so many years against the Dukes of Provence. Under the rule of Raymond Bérenger V, however, Hyères regained some power. The castle was extended and a Castellan installed, to be replaced in

1523 by a Seneschal of the king. During the Wars of Religion (1579) the town was besieged by Baron de Vins and then, in 1589 and 1596, was captured by the king's troops, after which the walls were torn down. In 1620 the keep on the height was also demolished. During the siege of Toulon (1707) Hyères acquired an Anglo-Dutch garrison.

Saint-Louis (Place de la République): The façade of this simple 13C *church* displays Italian influence. Inside it is Romanesque, with a nave and two aisles; a rib vault; and a straight end wall to the choir.

Saint-Paul (Place Saint-Paul): This single-aisled Gothic *church* (16C) only retains a portal—and that has been altered—from the earlier Romanesque building. It houses a collection of painted votive offerings (17C) and Nativity figures.

Museum: In the town's administrative building there are prehistoric and Gallo-Roman finds, an ornithological collection and a picture gallery.

Hyères, Saint-Louis, portal

Hyères, Commandery of the Knights Templar

Also worth seeing: A few *town gates* (Porte Saint-Paul, Porte de Barruc, Porte du Fenouillet) testify to the town's medieval past. In the garden of the Comtesse de Noailles there is a villa, the *Château Saint-Bernard*. The 13C chapel of *Saint-Blaise* belonged to the former *Templar Commandery*. In the S. of the town lies the *Jardin Exotique Riquier*.

Environs: Bormes-les-Mimosas (22 km. E.): A town with a turbulent history: note the 16C chapel of *Saint-François*; the 18C church of *Saint-Trophime* is richly furnished inside; standing on a rocky height is the chapel of *Notre-Dame de Constance* (12C).
Bormettes (11 km. E.): The *château* was built to plans by the painter H.Vernet.
Cap Bénat (29 km. SE): *Château du*

Cap Bénat and *Château de Retz*, both dating from the 17C.
Collobrières (33 km. NE): The 12C *church* was enlarged in the 16C.
Costebelle (3 km. S.): The chapel of *Notre-Dame de Consolation* was dedicated to St.Michael in the 11C. After its destruction in 1944 the new building was supervised by the architect Vaillant.
Fort de Brégançon (13 km. SE): The *fortress* (summer residence of the French president) dates in its present form from the time of Louis XIV.
Giens (10 km. S.): In the W. of the peninsula is the old *château* of the Pontevès.
L'Almanarre (5.5 km. S.): Within the ancient town walls of the Greek colony of Olbia are the early Romanesque chapel of *Saint-Pierre* and the ruins of a 13C *Cistercian chapel.*
Le Lavandou (23 km. E.): The town takes its name from lavender. In the town centre stand the *Hôtel de Ville* and the church of *Saint-Louis* (1857).

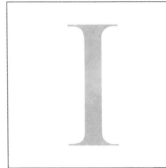

Iles d'Hyères (I)
83 Var   p.285□F/G 9

The Greeks named this group of islands off the coast of Hyères the Stoechades, because of their straight alignment; in the Renaissance they were called the 'Iles d'Or', because of

their beauty; their present name dates from their affiliation to Hyères.
The first settlers were probably Phoenicians. The Romans followed and in the 5C the monks of Lérins with a priory. Mariners, fishermen andb traders inhabited the islands and were subjected to constant attacks by pirates and Saracens (7–16C). Jeanne, Countess of Provence, inherited the islands from J.de Galbert in 1348. Francis I also settled the Knights of St.John here. In 1531 the castle on Porquerolles was rebuilt and a new one built on Port-Cros. Richelieu had the Tour de l'Eminence and the fortresses of Etissac and Port-Martin built in 1634. But even these could not protect the islands from plunder and attack during the War of the Spanish Succession (18C). In Napoleonic times and in the two World Wars the islands were again the scene of military actions.
The largest and most populous of the islands, Porquerolles, lies to the W., followed by Port-Cros with the little Ile de Bagaud and finally the bare Ile du Levant.

Ile Saint-Honorat (Iles de Lérins), gate

Ile de Bagaud: This 110-acre island is uninhabited and has been designated a *national park*, which can only be visited with a guide.

Ile du Levant: Ancient Hypea is a rocky island with a surface area of some 2,500 acres. At *Héliopolis* (W.) is the old *Fort Napoléon* (prohibited military zone).

Ile de Porquerolles: With an area of 3,100 acres Porquerolles is the largest of the islands. Near the harbour of the town of *Porquerolles* stands the church of *Sainte-Anne* (1850), containing a Christ's suffering, carved in walnut by the soldier J.Vaugier in 1868.
Further fortresses occupy strategic points on the island: 16C *Fort de l'Alicastre* (5 km. NE); *Fort du Bon-Renaud* (NW); *Fort du Grand-Langoustier* (ruins, 5.5 km. W.); *Fort de la Repentance* (2.5 km. NE).

Ile de Port-Cros: There is a *national park* with unique European flora and fauna on the 1,150-acre island.
NE of the harbour of *Port-Cros* is the 19C *Fort de l'Eminence*. In the N. is the *Fort de l'Estissac*, built under Richelieu in 1634, and the *Fort du Moulin* (16&17C), which was built under Francis I. Rebuilt in 1841 after its destruction by the English.

Iles de Lérins (I)
06 Alpes-Maritimes   p.258☐I 7

These two islands, some 800 yards apart, lie just over half a mile S. of Cannes/Cap de la Croisette. The ancient historians Pliny and Strabo report that this area was populated from the earliest of times and the Romans built villas, constructed arsenals and fortified the islands. The name is reputedly derived from a temple dedicated to Lero, a hero who was worshipped as a god.

Ile Saint-Honorat: Towards the end of the 4C or at the start of the 5C St.Honoratus and his companion Caprais came to this little 150 acre island, which, according to the legend, was beset by a plague of snakes. The saint freed the island of this evil, whereupon numerous followers flocked to him. Around 410 he built a *monastery* here, which in the 6C was a famous centre of Christianity and produced a series of important bishops. In 660 the order established by St.Honoratus was replaced by that of St.Benedict. At about the same time a cloister was commissioned by the canonized Abbot Aygulf. Around 690 the island is supposed to have accommodated 3,700 monks, but their number was decimated by the constant onslaughts of the Saracens (730–950). In 732 the monastery buildings were badly damaged and 500 monks slain. Under Pippin the Short the monastery was rebuilt by St.Eleuterius and in 1073 Abbot Aldebert II had a massive keep built. Nevertheless, plundering pirates managed to capture the island in 1180. In 1400 the tower, now extended into a castle, found itself in the hands of Genoese corsairs, who were driven off with the help of Provençal knights. In 1464 the monastery's decline began when it began to be held in commendam. In the following centuries the island was subjected to constant attacks by the Spanish (1524, 1526 and 1635) and Austrians (1746), with the result that monastic life could only be continued with difficulty. Added to this came the endeavours of the French kings to have the monastery secularized by the Pope, so that they could develop the island as a strategically important military base. This aim was finally fulfilled in 1788 with the dissolution of the monastery. In 1791 the island came into the possession of the Alziary de Roquefort, but in 1859 it was bought back by the Bishop of Fréjus, Monseigneur Jordany. In 1870 Cistercian monks arrived, repaired a part of the buildings and still inhabit the

Ile Saint-Honorat (Iles de Lérins), Chapelle de la Trinité

island today. Of the original 7 chapels only 3 are still standing, while 2 others (Saint-Pierre and Saint-Porcaire) are identified.

In the W. of the island is the small *Chapelle Saint-Caprais*, named after the companion of St.Honoratus.

The *Chapelle Saint-Sauveur* (W. of the monastery) was built in early Romanesque style in the 8C. The unembellished, octagonal, centrally-planned building looks like a baptistery. It has a main apse to the E. and 6 semicircular niches. A flat dome vaults the chapel, which was restored in the 17C.

The *Chapelle de la Trinité* (8C) in the E. of the island, rebuilt by J.Formigé in 1938, is dedicated to the Holy Trinity, symbolized by the triple conch form. The barrel-vaulted nave is entered through a rectangular portal and extends for two bays to a Byzantine-style pendentive dome over the crossing. The altar base dates from the 6/7C. Arranged around the chapel are remains of monks' cells and of the cloister.

The best-preserved building stands right on the cliffs of the S. coast.

Work began under Aldebert II in 1073 on the *Château Saint-Honorat*, which was intended as a place of refuge. The strong walls of dressed stone are battlemented. The little entrance gate (N.) is positioned some 13 ft. above the ground, so that the ladder could be drawn up in times of danger. The inner court was simultaneously used as a cloister with a two-tiered arcade. In the windowless ground floor, used for storing provisions, there are 6 (7 ft. 5in.) columns. The upper storey looks very charming, its close-set white marble columns allegedly being a gift from the Genoese following their siege of 1400. Of the badly damaged buildings one can still identify the refectory (S. wing) and the large Romanesque dormitory. A spiral staircase built in the N. wall in 1439 leads to the 2nd storey, where, in the Chapelle Sainte-Croix (SE) the relics of St.Honoratus were preserved. The 3rd storey, where the sacristy, library and archive room apparently once were, is destroyed, as are the servants' and soldiers' quarters on the 4th storey.

The actual *monastery* (N. of the

Ile Saint-Honorat (Iles de Lérins), monastery

Isle-sur-la-Sorgue, Hôtel-Dieu

a relief with Christ and the 12 Apostles.

Ile Sainte-Marguerite: This largely wooded, 530 acre island owes its name to the sister of St.Honoratus, who settled here with a small community of Christians. The monks of the smaller island also came here occasionally to lead the contemplative life of a hermit. Queen Jeanne gave the island to Bertrand de Grasse in 1351, but the monks bought it back in the 15C. In 1617 the region was acquired by Claude de Lorraine, Duke of Chevreuse, and a year later it passed to the Duke of Guise. Richelieu occupied the island in the name of the king and built a fortress, which, however, did not stand up to the attacks of the Spanish (1635); although the French recaptured this important strategic position after a couple of years. In 1685 the fort became a French state prison. In the 18C the fort was seized in turn by the Austrians, Piedmontese and English, but they were all driven off.
Fort Royal (to the N., above the harbour), restored in 1971, was built in 1635 at the behest of Richelieu. The complex was extended by the Spanish and then to plans by Vauban. A W. gate leads into the large inner court, on the right side of which stand the officers' house and a 17C chapel. Installed on the left is the small *Musée de la Mer*.

castle), behind battlemented walls, was rebuilt in 1869. Architectural fragments of the old Romanesque buildings are displayed in a small museum, which also contains records of the lives of St.Honoratus and St.Benedict and an altarpiece in fragmentary form, attributed to L.Bréa. The only parts left standing of the simple old monastery buildings are the chapterhouse (E. side), the refectory (S. side) and the cloister (closed), parts of whose walls date from 660, as well as the barrel vault of 1073. The monastery church was built in 1880 on the site of the 12C Romanesque one. In the porch of the building, which has a nave and two aisles, there are figures of saints. The façade was designed by Viollet-le-Duc. In the right arm of the transept there is a funerary chapel (10C). The sacristy contains an early Christian sarcophagus (5C), the upper side of which has

Isle-sur-la-Sorgue
84 Vaucluse   p.256☐C 5

Intersected and surrounded by 5 arms of the Sorgue, the 'Venice of the Comtat' was dominated by mill wheels in the Middle Ages. Silk-weaving mills, dye works, paper mills, corn and oil mills abounded in the pre-Industrial Revolution industrial town, which today, with its weaving mills, jam and biscuit factories and distilleries, makes a comparatively rural impression.

Parish church: Although still late Gothic in its spatial arrangement and vaulting, the church is a model example of Provençal baroque decoration. Nevertheless, parts of the preceding church had to be incorporated into the building begun in 1647: The free-standing bell tower of 1460, the rectangular choir, rebuilt in 1499, with adjoining polygonal apse (Gothic rib vaulting) and two side chapels with transverse barrel vaults. To these the architect F.R. de la Valfenière of Avignon added six bays with Gothic rib vaulting. The *façade*, however, leaves no doubt as to the date of construction. The clear articulation of the two storeys, divided by a high entablature, through semi-columns and pilasters clearly shows it to be a creation of the baroque.

Even more obviously baroque is the exceedingly lavish *interior decoration* with its carved wooden facing in the form of niches, panelling, columns and pilasters. The display of magnificence is overwhelming. Particularly impressive are: the *Gloria* with God the Father and Son, the Virgin Mary and angels borne on clouds (26 figures altogether), which is attributed to the Florentine Angloglio, the *12 Apostles* on their high pedestals in front of the pillars, the 22 *semi-relief figures* in the spandrels by J.Péru (1688) and the *high altar* with the massive altarpiece and large figures of saints.

Hôtel-Dieu (Place de la Juiverie): Built between 1749 and 1757 by the brothers Brun to designs by J.B. Franques, the Hôtel-Dieu is distinguished by beautifully made wrought-iron bannisters and an elegant chapel.

Also worth seeing: *Renaissance house* (Rue Ledru-Rollin); 16C *mansion* (Rue Carnot).

Environs: Velleron (7 km. NNW): 2 old *mansions*.

La Barben
13 Bouches-du-Rhône   p.256☐C 6

Château: This building was first mentioned in 1063. Originally belonging to the Marseille monastery of Saint-Victor, in the 15C the fortress passed to King René, who sold it to the powerful de Forbin family. In the 17&18C the castle, which had already been rebuilt in the 14C, was turned into a country house, but without losing its defensive character. The complex still seems fortress-like today with machicolations around nearly all parts of the building and its many towers and turrets, some round, some square. Closer inspection reveals the castle to be a veritable omnium-gatherum of medieval architectural elements, Renaissance forms and the French baroque, the classicism of the 17C.

Environs: Pélissanne (2 km. W.): Beautiful 17C *belfry*.
Sainte-Anne-de-Goiron (15 km. NE): 12C Romanesque *church* with Gothic chapels added on like a transept. Beautiful view.

La Ciotat
13 Bouches-du-Rhône   p.256☐D/E 8

La Ciotat (la cité, the city) dates back

to a Greek colony and was originally merely the harbour of the trading station of *Citharista* (Ceyreste), founded by the Phocaeans of Marseille. It was not until 1429 that it became self-governing: it was then ruled by a judge and a governor nominated by the Abbot of Saint-Victor in Marseille and by 3 consuls elected by the people. Within a century this brought the town a certain prosperity through shipbuilding, coastal shipping and the export of wine. In the 19C development began with the building of docks and dry docks, which was to make La Ciotat the second most important harbour in France after Saint-Nazaire. Today, however, in spite of the building of the 'Grande forme' for tankers over 300,000 tons and the overall modernization of the installations, the future of the town, 75% of whose working population is employed in the shipping industry, is uncertain due to the world-wide shipping crisis.

Fortunately the town attracts countless tourists in the summer, thanks to its beautiful sunny beaches, and a luxury resort with palm-lined avenues and smart villas and boutiques has developed next to the Old Town with its narrow streets.

Church: Near the old harbour, it was begun in 1626 and contains an interesting 17C *Descent from the Cross* and an 18C image of the Virgin protecting La Ciotat from the plague (1720).

Also worth seeing: The 16C *Chapelle des Pénitents Noirs* (Place Esquiros) and the *Chapelle des Pénitents Bleus* from the start of the 17C (Esplanade de la Passe), as well as the *Musée Ciotaden* (Rue des Poilus) with documents on the town's history.

Environs: Cap de l'Aigle (S.): The cape is due to become a national park because of its rich flora.
Ceyreste (5 km. NE): Citharista, the mother-town long since outgrown by La Ciotat, now has only 2,037 inhabi-

tants. Its medieval remains include a small Romanesque *church* (nave and aisle) and remnants of the *town walls*.
Figuerolles (SW): Pretty rocky inlet. Beautiful panoramic view from the *Chapelle Notre-Dame de la Garde*.

La Tour
06 Alpes-Maritimes   p.258☐I 5

Chapelle des Pénitents Blancs: The simple exterior of the chapel contrasts with the *frescos* in the choir (straight end-wall) and in the bay before it. According to an inscription the paintings were executed in 1491 by two artists from Nice: C.Brevesi and G.Nadale. A Last Judgement covers the E. wall, with—as is customary—Christ in a mandorla presiding in the middle, flanked by the Virgin Mary and John the Baptist interceding for the Dead Souls. Below this scene are angels sounding the trumpet-call to judgement. On the left are the Damned being taken to Hell by the Devil, on the right Peter receives the Blessed into Heaven. The contrast between Heaven and Hell is emphasized by depictions of the Virtues (N. side) and Vices (S. side) on the lower part of the side walls, recognizable from their inscriptions, attributes or gestures. Above these are scenes from the Passion of Christ, reading from the top left of the N. side to the bottom right on the S. side. The scenes start with the Entry into Jerusalem and end with the women at Christ's tomb. The stiffness and dignity with which the figures are portrayed is a product of the late Gothic tradition. The individual scenes have architectural frames, but no landscape backgrounds. Separate from the Passion and the Last Judgement is the depiction below the latter of the Virgin between St.Bernard, the founder of the Alpine hospice and St.Brigid of Kildare, the patron saint of cattle.

Environs: Clans (18.5 km. NW):

The Romanesque *church*, which was partly altered in the 18C, has the oldest frescos in the region. The hunting scenes from the 12C and the depiction of the Virgin and St.Peter are still somewhat clumsy, but painted in a gracefully naive way. The *Chapelle Saint-Michel* dates from the 16C, as do the frescos within. 1 km. outside the town stands the *Chapelle Saint-Antoine*, which is painted inside with scenes from the Life of St.Anthony (16C).

Massoins (*c*. 22 km. W.): Ruins of the *Château de la Salette*.

Villars-sur-Var (28 km. W.): Inside the *church* are a wooden statue (1524) of John the Baptist by M.Danvers and 2 altarpieces from the School of Nice. One shows the Angel of the Annunciation appearing to the Virgin Mary (16C); the second has 4 saints: Francis of Assisi, Clare, Honorius and Lucy.

Le Luc-en-Provence
83 Var   p.258□F/G 7

This town dates back to a fortress, which was built near a Celtic foundation (Fouriette) in the 10C. Le Luc-en-Provence was one of the 3 towns in Provence, where the Protestants could freely practise their worship according to the Edict of Nantes. Today the little town is known for its thermal baths, but the very busy by-pass robs it of its charm. The Old Town is picturesque with its twisting alleys and *ruined castle*. A *town gate* from the old walls (13&14C) is now a bell tower.

Bell tower (on the right by the entrance to the town): This hexagonal tower dating from 1517 is a relic of a Romanesque church.

Church: Belonging to a former Carmelite convent, the building dates from the 15&16C. The E. end has a five-sided apse; inside there is a beautiful pew (*c*. 1800) and 17C organs.

Environs: Astros (12.5 km. NE): Of the former foundation of the Knights of Malta there now remains only the *Chapelle Saint-Lambert*. In the district of Avens there is an under-

Le Luc-en-Provence, church, portal

Le Luc-en-Provence, bell tower

ground chapel of *Saint-Michel*, which reputedly dates from the time of the Christian persecutions under Diocletian.

Flassans-sur-Issole (9 km. SW): At the foot of a mountain, where Flatus Sanus of the Romans once stood, are the *ruins* of the old town.

Gonfaron (10 km. S.): The *church* has an old clock tower. 3 km. outside the village is the *pilgrimage chapel of Notre-Dame du Figuier*.

Le Cannet-des-Maures (2 km. E.): Known to the Romans as Voconii, it now has a 10C Romanesque *church*. A beautiful wrought-iron *bell tower* dates from the 12C.

Notre-Dame des Anges (26 km. S.): The early Romanesque *chapel* (enlarged in the 19C) is now a popular pilgrimage shrine.

Pignans (16 km. SW): The *church* has paintings from Spanish and Italian schools and a 17C grille.

Puget-Ville (24 km. SW): Of the small medieval town there now remains only a *tower*. The chapel of *Sainte-Philomène* is 14C.

Taradeau (15 km. NE): In the town there is an Romanesque *church*; just outside is a medieval *watch tower*.

Thoronet (15.5 km. NW): Thoronet is one of Provence's three Cistercian abbeys along with Sénanque and Silvacane. Raymond Bérenger III, Duke of Provence, gave the region to the monks of Mazan, who built a *monastery* near Tourtour in 1136. In about 1160 it was moved to its present isolated position and by the end of the century whole buildings had been completed thanks to lavish donations. The strict discipline of the order was eased in the 14C and abandoned altogether in the 15C. As a result the church choir acquired a baroque facing of marble and stucco and windows were opened in the nave. Nevertheless, the buildings all betray the ascetic attitude of the order, which expresses itself in the lack of any decoration and in purity of line. In 1791 the monastery was dissolved and sold. In 1851 it was inherited by the State and from 1873 was restored to its medieval form.

The simple church of *Sainte-Marie* (at the highest point) was built in 1160–80, with an entirely plain exterior; apart from the W. front, which has window openings and portals for the two side aisles. At the E. end is a small, square, stone bell tower. Saddle and shed-roofs lie directly above the vaults of the basilica, which has a nave, two aisles and a projecting transept (slit windows) with two chapels attached to each arm. These are bounded on the outside by a continuous straight wall. Nave and transept have a pointed barrel vault, the weight of which is taken by the half-barrels of the aisles. The high walls are windowless and the only decoration is a cornice and cube capitals. The N. transept leads to the 10 ft. long sacristy, which has a barrel vault and is at a lower level than the church.

Further down the slope lies the two-storeyed Romanesque *cloister*, which is the largest of its kind in Provence (121 ft. long E. walk). It has a trapezoid ground plan and barrel-vaulted walks opening on to the garden through round arches, each of which frames two smaller arches supported by a column. On the N. side is a hexagonal lavatory with a modern fountain basin. Grouped around the convent (after 1160) are the *monks' buildings*. Directly adjoining the transept in the E. corner is a small library (armarium), where the Holy Scripture and the literature of the order were kept. To the left of this is the most richly decorated room in the abbey, the twin-aisled chapterhouse, with stone steps and three round-arched windows on the E. wall. The rib vault was added after 1200. Adjoining to the N. is the parlatorium, a narrow, barrel-vaulted room leading to the monks' garden. A covered staircase leads to the upper floor, where there is a large dormitory (92 ft. × 26 ft.). Above the sacristy lie the former archives and the treasury and above them the sacristan's room. Adjoining this is the barrel-vaulted room for the abbot (later for the prior). In the N. of the abbey one can make out the refectory, the kitchens and the caldarium. A granary was built along the W. side around 1200. Blind arcades on the W. wall support a pointed-arch vault. Also from the early 13C is the locatarium (NW), the former abbot's house. On the ground floor is a three-bayed refectory. The barrel-vaulted dormitory on the upper floor has a door in the N. wall, behind which were once the latrines. In the NW corner of the abbey is the old guesthouse.

Thoronet (Le Luc-en-Provence), monastery

Les Baux-de-Provence

13 Bouches-du-Rhône   p.256☐B 6

Now a small, semi-ruinous mountain village with 367 inhabitants, dominated by a massive castle, in the Middle Ages Les Baux-de-Provence was a proud, independent town, defying even kings. The cornerstone of this development was laid by the Counts of Les Baux, an important family of Provençal nobles, which in the 10C chose the *c.* 1,000 yard-long and 220 yard-wide spur of the Antilles called Les Baux as their main seat. (French bau, Provençal baou means 'escarpment' and occurs in other southern place-names.) Thus the rock, which had earlier been a Celtic settlement, and had indeed been occupied in Neolithic times, entered history—a history marked by war, but also by prosperity. As early as the start of the 12C the town was involved in a 100-year war against the Catalan Counts of Barcelona. The territory in dispute was Provence, which the last male descendant of the line, Gilbert, Comte de Provence, had

left to one of his daughters, who was married to the Count of Barcelona, while the daughter married to Raymond des Baux received nothing. In spite of this war, however, the town enjoyed an economic and cultural heyday in the 12&13C. Troubadours sang the beauty of the ladies of the court and the population rose to an impressive 4000. Guillaume des Baux, under whom Provence was finally lost to Les Baux, was compensated for this loss by the title of King of Arles. In 1399 Les Baux-de-Provence fell to Provence, together with the 'Terres Baussenques', its other lands and some 80 castles of the Counts of Les Baux. The last Count of Les Baux, who had lived as a robber baron, highwayman and blackmailer, was driven out in disgrace. In 1481 the town passed to France with Provence. When it rebelled against this its castle was pulled down and the town reduced to a minor barony. Just 50 years later, however, its resurgence began under the Constable A. de Montmorency. The castle was rebuilt, churches erected and beautiful palaces and private houses built in the style of the Renaissance and French classicism. Les Baux enjoyed a new heyday but in 1631, however, when it sided with Gaston d'Orléans against Richelieu, the castle was blown up once and for all and the inhabitants gradually dispersed.

Castle: Of the once mighty castle there now remain only a few sections: the Tour Sarrazine, the Chapelle Sainte-Catherine, the keep and the Tour Paravelle, and even these are more or less in ruins. Very little survives of the living apartments adjoining the keep to the W., the main building between the keep and the chapel of Sainte-Catherine and the fortress wall, which, doubled by a parapet walk, stretched from the keep to the Tour Sarrazine. Of the *Cha-*

◁ *Thoronet (Le Luc-en-Provence), cloister*

pelle Sainte-Catherine, originally Romanesque, but heavily restored in the 16C, there remains only a bay with late Gothic vaulting. The least damaged is the *keep,* a massive rectangular building from the 13C, which rises sheer up from the rock on two sides and has a cistern cut out of the rock. This relatively wide tower was originally divided into 3 bays by two partition walls and pierced by unusually large windows on the precipitous and inaccessible E. side. In the lower room the springs of a rib vault can still be seen. Outside, on the rock supporting the tower, there is a bas-relief with three life-size figures, the Trémaié or three Holy Marys.

Saint-Vincent (parish church since 1481): This Romanesque building from the 2nd half of the 12C, partly cut into the rock on the S. side, originally had a nave and an aisle and two bays. In the 16C it was extended with the addition of interconnected Gothic chapels, which act as an aisle. At the start of the 17C an extra bay was added. Also from the 16C are the galleries and the 'dead man's lantern', a slender, domed side turret with four windows. The glass in the dome over the choir, a gift from the Prince of Monaco, whose son bears the title of Marquis des Baux, is by M.Ingrand.

Chapelle des Pénitents Blancs: This mid-17C chapel, very simple but for its baroque portal, was painted with large frescos by Y.Brayer in the course of the renovation of 1974.

Chapelle Saint-Blaise: Only the outer walls and the round-arched portal of the W. front remain of this Romanesque chapel.

Museums
Musée d'Art Moderne (in the Hôtel de Manville, Rue du Château): Also housed in the building are the mayor's office and an information bureau. Behind the beautiful Renaissance façade of 1572 works by major con-

temporary painters are annually exhibited in association with the board of the Musées de France or the Pompidou Centre.

Musée d'Archéologie Régionale: This museum is housed in the Hôtel des Porcelet, an appealing house of 1569, the ground floor vaults of which are painted with 17C frescos.

Musée Lapidaire et d'Archéologie (in the elegant Manoir de la Tour de Brau, 14&15C): The beautiful Great Hall with its Gothic arches and vaulting is principally devoted to remains of the castle, while the archaeological department includes the reconstruction of pre-Christian urn tombs, as well as burial objects from the 1&2C BC.

The most interesting museum is the **village** itself with its many houses from the 15, 16&17C, some of which are hewn out of the rock; the old town gate, the *Porte Eyguière* with its parapet walk on the upper platform; the large paved area for collecting water; the enormous *cisterns* cut into the rock; the remains of an old *windmill* and the partly-preserved *castle graveyard* with tombs cut into the rock.

Environs: Alpilles: A 15 mile long and 4–5 mile wide limestone massif, much lauded for its beautiful scenery with wild, jagged peaks and deep-cleft ravines, in the heart of which lies Les Baux-de-Provence.
Aupiho (wrongly transcribed as Opiés in French): At 1,617 ft. the highest point of the Alpilles.
Carrières: Numerous quarries, some abandoned and used as wine cellars (can be visited on application).
Cathédrales d'Images: A series of vast subterranean chambers, 33–9 ft. high, which serve as the backdrop for a unique audiovisual drama. With the aid of over 30 projectors the *Image totale*, after an idea by A.Plécy, is created as an image freed from its frame and incorporating the visitor.

Grottes des Fées: Subterranean cave-passage, over 656 ft. long, in which human bones and tools from prehistoric times were discovered.
Mouriès (10 km. SE): With an annual production of between 60,000 and 250,000 litres, this is the most important oil-producing village in France. Just before the village is *Mas de Brau*, a typical Provençal farmstead.
Pavillon de la Reine Jeanne (in Vallon de la Fontaine): A small, lavishly decorated Renaissance pavilion (1566–81), built by a Baroness des Baux, which F.Mistral had copied for his tomb.
Plateau des Bringasses: A Celto-Ligurian oppidum with a double defensive wall, surrounded by a fosse hewn out of the rock.
Quartier de la Vayède: Remains of a Celto-Ligurian wall and two cemeteries, one from pre-Roman times with urns, the other Gallo-Roman, with tombs cut into the rock.
Val d'Enfer: Wild gorge with numerous caves, which served as shelters for humans in prehistoric times.

Les Saintes-Maries-de-la-Mer
13 Bouches-du-Rhône   p.256☐A 7

One of the main attractions for any visitor to the Camargue, a paradise of nature, is its famous capital, Les Saintes-Maries-de-la-Mer. Van Gogh was captivated by its magic and painted many of his pictures here, intoxicated by the power of a merciless sun.
Situated by the sea, to the E. of Grau d'Orgon, in the S. of the Camargue, the town is reached by somewhat uneven roads. These twist their way from Aigues-Mortes, Saint-Gilles or Arles through the largely uninhabitable, reedy marshes of the Camargue with their isolated huts, past herds of bulls and paddocks and flocks of pink and white flamingoes to the once poor

fishing village, which today is condemned to a veritable pseudo existence under the onslaught of tourism. Once the stream of obtrusively loud visitors has finally ebbed, however, and one can ignore the camping sites and fake cabanes, then this brave little fortress, in the middle of a desert under a relentless, blazing sun, washed by the sea, occasionally buffeted by the Mistral and threatened by the shifting waters behind, becomes visible once more.

It is a town whose history has been as hard as its environment. For centuries fishermen clung to a meagre existence, mistrusted by the other peoples of Provence, as their poverty often had to be supplemented by robbery or scavenging. Constantly raided by pirates, particularly Saracens, they turned their church into a fortress with a defensive tower, where they could shelter with their families in times of danger. In those days it was still several miles from the sea, which has since moved threateningly closer and the ramparts, which protect the town from the sea, are now fortress-like. Its settlement has been documented since Roman times. In the 10C Count Guillaume is supposed to have driven out the Saracens, built a fortified church on the site of a 6C reliquary chapel and helped fishermen and shepherds settle. In the 2nd half of the 14C Queen Jeanne had a watch installed in the church tower to report any threat to the whole of the region.

For many years the legend persisted that around AD 40 Mary the mother of St. James the Less, sister of the Virgin Mary, Mary Salome, mother of the Apostles James and John, Lazarus, his sisters Martha and Mary Magdalene, together with Maximinus and Sidonius and Sarah, the dark-skinned servant of the two Marys, were cast adrift by the Jews in a sailless and rudderless boat. Contrary to expectations this boat did not, according to the legend, sink, but miraculously bore its occupants to the south coast of France, past the cliffs in front of Les Saintes-Maries-de-la-Mer, where it landed. Martha is supposed to have gone to Tarascon to announce the advent of Christendom, Maximinus and Sidonius to Aix, Lazarus to

Les-Saintes-Maries-de-la-Mer, cabane

Marseille and Mary Magdalene to the holy grotto of Sainte-Baume. The other two Marys, however, stayed where they had landed with their servant Sarah and later died there. In 1448 King René instigated a search for the relics of the saints, which reputedly were indeed discovered here and ceremoniously placed in reliquaries. From then on there began a stream of pilgrims, which did not abate for centuries. The church had to be enlarged and the name of the place, which had been Notre-Dame-de-la-Mer since the 11C, was finally recorded as Les Saintes-Maries-de-la-Mer in the 18C, although it had already been in common usage amongst the people long before. In 1794, during an attack on the church, the relics were saved and in 1797 placed in new reliquaries in the chapel above the choir.

Church: The bell tower with its 5 bells and 3 gables can be seen from afar, gleaming white in the sun against the deep-blue sky above long, winswept sand dunes. The architecture of

the church is unique, serving as it originally did as a pilgrimage church, a castle offering shelter and a fortified tower simultaneously. From the outside its fortress-like character predominates. The now single-aisled

Les-Saintes-Maries-de-la-Mer, church

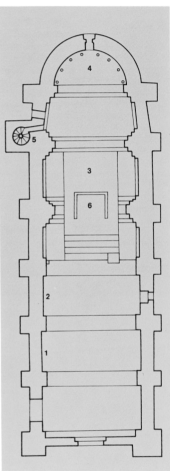

Les Saintes-Maries-de-la-Mer, church 1 Pre-Christian altar-stone **2** Figures of the Virgin Mary and Mary Magdalene in the boat **3** Crypt **4** 12C choir surrounded by columns **5** Staircase to the battlements **6** Well (behind the wrought-iron grille) used in the Middle Ages by people who had sought sanctuary in the church

church was built in the last third of the 12C. In the 15C a further two W. bays were added to the existing three to accommodate the increasing numbers of pilgrims. A crypt was installed in the E. in the 14&15C, resulting in one of the E. bays lying above the other and the alteration of the steps. At the same time the bell tower was built above the choir. The battlement walk on the church, which provides a good all-round view, and the fortified SW tower are 12C.

The dark medieval *interior* and the alterations connected with the addition of the crypt combine to obscure the beautiful *capitals* of the columns in the apse. These are obviously the work of masters who had worked on the cloister of Saint-Trophime in Arles and in the cathedral of Nîmes. In a niche in the third bay on the left, surrounded by ex-votos, is the much-photographed *boat* with the two Marys, which is carried to the beach during the procession. The niche in the preceding bay contains a pre-Christian altar stone, which originally served the cult of Mithras. The chapel (St-Michel) above the choir contains the reliquaries of the two Marys but is closed. Just once a year, during the pilgrimage at the end of May, the reliquaries are lowered on flower-festooned ropes and shown to the people. In the *crypt*, where the bones of St. Sarah are revered, is her statue, adorned with costly materials and jewels.

Annually on the 24 and 25 of May, the feast of Mary the mother of St. James the Great, an unusual *pilgrimage* is held, which draws gypsies from all over Europe to celebrate their patron saint, Sarah. They arrive in their caravans, ignoring the passing streams of tourists, and celebrate their festival in total devotion with hundreds of yard-long candles in the church, as the reliquaries of the two Marys are lowered from the upper chapel. They then carry the statue of St. Sarah amidst dancing and singing to the beach. The men lift the statue up high and then wade into the sea up to their chests and the priest, after making a speech, blesses the sea and the fishermen. Arlesian women in

Les-Saintes-Maries-de-la-Mer, church, the Virgin Mary and Mary Magdalene in the boat

their beautiful costumes lead the procession on, while mounted guardians keep order. On the following day the boat with the two Marys is carried in a procession to the sea. The festival ends with dancing and a turbulent gypsy feast on the beach.

Museum Baroncelli: In the old Hôtel de Ville, between the church and the beach, amidst former fishermen's houses, cafés, stalls and flat-roofed holiday homes, is the museum. This was endowed by the friend of Mistral, Falco de Baroncelli, a lover of the Camargue who raised bulls and horses here and helped to preserve the region. There are stuffed specimens of birds native to the Camargue and examples of the region's furniture, tools and horsemen's accoutrements.

Environs: 2 km. N. of Les Saintes-Maries-de-la-Mer on the N570 is the waxworks museum, the **Musée du Boumian,** which depicts scenes from everyday life in the Camargue. 2.5 km. further along the same road, on the right, is a most interesting **Ornithological Park,** a remarkably

large zoological garden displaying the birds of the Camargue, some free, some in cages, some in aviaries.

Le Thor
84 Vaucluse   p.256□C 5

This market town on a tributary of the Sorgue, prosperous through the growing of grapes, has retained two important monuments from its past: a 14C *town gate*, which was later turned into a clock tower crowned by a wrought-iron belfry; and the *church*, which has been little altered over the centuries.

Church: This is one of the most beautiful examples of Provençal Romanesque: A single-aisled, massive building like a gabled house, supported by strong buttresses, with typical round arcades on the apse and corners accentuated by pilasters. Typical too are the classically inspired W. and S. portals (the N. side, as is common practice owing to the mistral, is entirely without doors or

Les-Saintes-Maries-de-la-Mer, church   *Le Thor, church, portal*

windows). Based on Roman triumphal arches, flanked by columns, surmounted by a gable and embellished with antique decorative forms (egg-and-dart moulding, toothed frieze, wavy ribbon-decoration). *Inside* there are characteristic blind arcades on the walls, as well as rectangular pilasters and an octagonal dome borne on squinches above a rhomboid bay—another recurring feature of Provençal Romanesque. Equally typical are the small reliefs of the symbols of the Evangelists on the squinches. Another standard feature is the way the half-domed apse opens directly off the domed bay through a Gothic arch. A new feature, however, at least for a building of this breadth, is the groin vault, which, unlike the barrel vault, does not extend over all the bays, resulting in a marked change in the structure of the interior.

The rather unsuccessful octagonal crown on the *tower*—an octagonal drum formed by cutting the corners off the square cross-section of the tower—was not added until 1834.

Château de Fontségugne (half a mile N.): In 1854 the 'Félibrige', a group of writers under Frédéric Mistral, was formed here with the aim of preserving Provençal literature and customs.

Environs: Grotte de Thouzon (2.5 km. N.): 755 ft. long cave with curious sinter formations.

Levens
06 Alpes-Maritimes   p.258□I 5

The old village was built, probably for strategic reasons, on a sparsely covered, rounded mountain top, providing a wonderful view of the valley where the gorges of the Var and the Vésubie meet.

Church: The core of the building is Gothic (13C), but in the 17C a classical stucco facing was added. Inside there is a 'Holy Family' (1860) by Vannetto.

Also worth seeing: The wall paintings in the *Mairie* were executed in

Le Thor, church, details of portal

Le Thor, town gate

naive style by Dussour in 1958. On private ground in the SE of the village (Quartier de la Madone) is the former church of *Sainte-Marie*. The building is now used for other purposes and is totally altered inside, but it retains its importance as one of the few early Romanesque religious buildings surviving in Provence. The original building had a nave and two aisles, the E. aisle having 3 apses. The flat arcades and the use of pilaster strips is typical of the early Romanesque. Below the choir, only partly below ground, is a *crypt* of two bays, divided by pillars into a nave and two aisles with an apse. The groin vault has monolithic pillars at the four corners. These are linked by arches built of pink and grey stone. Three narrow round arches (W.) lead into a small, barrel vaulted room.

Environs: Berre-des-Alpes (28 km. SE): The *church* has a painted 15C Madonna and Child in the *church*. In the 18C the sister of the politician Mirabeau, the Marquise de Cabris, lived in the *château*, which is now in ruins.

Châteauneuf-de-Contes (17 km. SE): The *church*, first mentioned in 1109, has recently been shown to have been built as early as the mid 11C, making it one of the earliest Romanesque churches in Provence showing Lombard influence. Its exterior has undergone several alterations in the course of time. Two chapels were added in the 17C and in the 19C the bell tower and the sacristy. Inside, it retained its Romanesque character, despite baroque furnishing. The small, single-aisled church has the typical articulation of pilasters and blind arcades at the W. end and the same arrangement is to be found on the outside of the choir wall. The addition of 3 powerful buttresses in the 17C rather marred the overall concept, particularly as they provide no real support. Inside, the apse retains its original structure: a half-dome above 7 tall, shallow niches. The nave probably once had a timber ceiling.

Coaraze (29.5 km. E.): According to legend the town derives its name from 'Coua rasa' (cut-off tail). The inhabitants of Coaraze are supposed to have lured the Devil here and by means of a trick to have cut off his tail. Another legend says that the local inhabitants, unlike the Gauls, wore their hair cut short in the Ligurian fashion. The beautiful mountain village has a 17C *church* with baroque decoration, and side chapels flanking the bays of the nave. At the entrance to the village is the chapel of *Saint-Sébastien* with 16C frescos. In the village there are several *sundials*, one of which was made by Jean Cocteau.

Contes (21 km. SE): In the Old Town there is the chapel of *Saint-Joseph*. This has beautiful liturgical pieces, which once belonged to the brothers of the Pénitent order. The

Lourmarin, panorama

16C *church* acquired a bell tower in the 19C. The Magdalene altar (16C) is attributed to F.Bréa. The furnishing also includes an altar of the rosary (1667) and other items from the 16&17C, including a monstrance, a liturgical vestment and a tabernacle. The beautiful *fountain* in front of the church dates from 1587.

La Roquette-sur-Var (6 km. SW): This beautifully situated village is mainly of interest for the chapel of *Notre-Dame del Bosco*, which was painted in 1526 by A. de Cella. Only ruins remain of the old *château*.

Saint-Blaise (9 km. S.): Picturesque *ruins* on a wooded rock in the S. of the village. The Cistercian monastery of *Notre-Dame de la Paix* outside the village was built by M.Bret in 1932.

Saut-des-Français (8.5 km. N.): There is a beautiful view from this village, where in 1793 French soldiers were made to leap from the crag in the Peasants' War. A small *cross* commemorates this dreadful deed.

Tourrette-Levens (10 km. S.): Nestling in a green hollow, this little town still retains its old *walls* and a tall medieval **tower**. The *church* is 17C.

Les Traverses (1 km. S.): Near the village is the little chapel of *Sainte-Pétronille*.

Utelle (22 km. N.): The Gothic church of *Saint-Véran* acquired a new vault and stucco decoration in the 17C. A Gothic porch and a portal, on the leaves (1524) of which are carved scenes from the life of St. Veranus, lead into the church, which has a nave and two aisles and contains an interesting late-15C Annunciation from the school of Nice. From the same school came the artist who carved the back of the high altar: scenes from the Passion frame the figure of St.Veranus. The *Chapelle des Pénitents Blancs* contains a carved altarpiece based on a Descent from the Cross by Rubens. 6 km. from Utelle is the shrine of *Madone d'Utelle*, founded in 850.

Lourmarin
84 Vaucluse   p.256☐D 6

This little village, praised by poets and the adopted home of Albert Camus, who is also buried here, has a beautiful Renaissance château, to which the Académie des Sciences of Aix annually invites writers, scientists and researchers to a seminar on Provence.

Château: Little remains of the *Château vieux*, the predecessor of the present château, which was built as a fortified residence on the site of an even older watch-tower in 1495–1525. The surviving sections include the tower with its waterspouts, the old steps and remains of the front. All the rest belongs to the *Château neuf*, built in 1542. This again is fortified, although the fact is not immediately apparent. Behind the attic wall concealing the roof, for example, there is a sentry walk with embrasures, which runs around the whole house. The largely plain château owes its aesthetic quality to its clear articulation: the cornices running around the building like narrow ribbons on the one hand and the verticals formed by the large windows with their pilaster-like frames on the other.
Today, as ever, there is a major puzzle posed by a sgraffito in one of the rooms, the meaning of which no-one can solve: a small sailing boat surrounded by mysterious birds with human faces. The locals believe it to have come from the gypsies, who once used to stop here on their way to Saintes-Maries-de-la-Mer   and wanted to avenge their expulsion from the castle with a curse.

Also worth seeing: Small 15&16C *church* with a beautiful 15C font.

Environs: Rognes (14 km. S.): The *church* (1610) of this village, which became famous for its stone quarries, has an extremely impressive series of wooden altarpieces dating from the end of the 15C to the 18C.
Vaugines (5 km. NE): Pretty little village at the foot of the Luberon with a 13C Romanesque *church* (11C apse, modern side chapels) and a small Renaissance *château*.

Maillane
13 Bouches-du-Rhône   p.256☐B 6

This small market town near Saint-Rémy has risen to fame as the birthplace of the celebrated Provençal poet, Frédéric Mistral (1830–1914), the son of a prosperous farming family, who spent most of his life here. Together with some other Provençal poets, he founded the 'Félibrige', which dedicated itself to creating a literary Provençal language. He also published the 'Trésor du félibrige', which was a comprehensive Provençal-French dictionary, and celebrated his homeland in novels, narrative verse, and poetry. In 1904 he was awarded the Nobel Prize, which he used to found the Museon Arlaten (see Arles).

Mistral's house: This was built for Mistral when he was married. It was

Malaucène, church

left unchanged after his death and now forms the *Museon Mistral*, which those interested in the poet's background may visit.

Also worth seeing: Mistral's *tomb* in the local cemetery. It is modelled on the Pavillon de la Reine Jeanne near Les-Baux-de-Provence, and is also adorned with symbolic sculptures.

Environs: Notre-Dame-du-Pieux-Zèle (4.5 km., on the road S. from Eyragues): Pretty chapel with a 12C apse and a small Romanesque tympanum on the classical portal. The name is a distortion of 'Notre-Dame des Pucelles' ('virgins').

Malaucène

84 Vaucluse   p.256☐C 4

Charming village with narrow streets and twisting lanes, lying at the foot of Mont Ventoux.

Church: Malaucène can boast a church founded by Charlemagne. However, the present Romanesque structure—which from the S. side would not immediately be recognized as a place of worship—was built as a fortified church by Clement V in the 14C. Its appearance from the outside is severe and cold. The round-arched windows of the nave have no tracery and are set unusually high; and the rectangular panels in the upper storey, which look like walled-up windows, are actually walls containing embrasures. The W. portal is protected by machicolations, and the roof is strikingly strong. The *interior* is marked by the transition from the pointed tunnel vault of the nave to the transverse tunnel and rib vaults of the side chapels.

Also worth seeing: The beautiful 16C *Maison du Centenaire* (Place Picardie); the old *belfry* with its cast-iron bell-frame; the remains of the *town gates*, and finally the *fountains, wash-houses and chapels*.

Environs: Prieuré de Sainte-Madeleine (9 km. SE): This priory was mentioned as early as the 10C and has one of the oldest and most typical of Provençal *chapels* (dating from the middle of the 11C).
Suzette (9 km. SW): Small village beautifully situated in the *Dentelles de Montmirail*, a bizarre chain of crags (whence the name, which is derived from *mons mirabilis*).

Manosque
04 Alpes-de-Haute-Provence   p.256☐E 6

The foundations of this town were laid by the Comtes de Forcalquier, who built a castle, which was later taken over by the Knights of St.John. The threat posed by the 'Grandes Compagnies' during the 14C necessit-

Manosque, Porte Saunerie

ated the building of a town wall, of which only some sections and two gates survive. The Place du Terreau now stands on the site once occupied by the buildings put up by the Order of St.John. A baptistery, now no longer extant, was built to serve the three parish churches (Saint-Sauveur, Notre-Dame, and Saint-Etienne), even though Manosque was never the seat of a bishop.

Notre-Dame: This began as a Romanesque church with a single aisle, side chapels were added in the 16C. On the W. front, the rose-window, framed by an astragal moulding, has retained its original form; but the portal itself is now Renaissance. The blind arcades on the nave walls and the tunnel vault were part of the original church (whose date of construction is unknown). Inside, the blind arcades were later opened up to lead into the side chapels, a rib vault was added and there is a Gothic polygonal apse.

Saint-Sauveur: No details are available concerning the building of this church, although it is known to have originally been single-aisled. It has a plain exterior, and the apex of the gable of the W. façade, with its typical Provençal proportions, is simple. A rose-window surrounded by a moulding, similar to the two rose-windows in the side aisles (17C) has been set above the 14C portal, which has a pointed arch. The Romanesque façade was altered by the addition of the side aisles in the 17C. The square tower on the S. side dates from the 15/16C and is divided into storeys. The interior has lost its original Romanesque character (for example, the blind arcades were opened up), and only the choir and transept have retained their medieval form. The crossing has an octagonal dome supported by squinches. The five-sided apse, which has striking, slender columns, is vaulted by a ribbed half-dome.

Porte Saunerie: This magnificent 14C gate was once the S. entrance to the town. It resembles a tower and straddles a narrow, round-arched passageway. There are embrasures in the walls, and the gate is topped by machicolations and battlements. The central section, supported by two arches and pierced by two double windows, is more recent.

Porte Soubeyran (14C): This was the N. gate and closely resembles the S. gate, except that it has lost its fortified appearance with the removal of the crenellated machicolations. Instead it has acquired a terrace and a clock-tower with an iron belfry.

Also worth seeing: Opposite the church of Notre-Dame is an 18C *nobleman's house* which today houses the Hôtel de Ville. There is a *war memorial* by Sartorio and a *memorial to the Resistance* on the Place du Terreau.

Environs: Gréoux-les-Bains (14 km. SE): An old *castle* stands above this little town on the right bank of the Verdon. 4 km. upstream, on the

left bank, can be seen the 15C *Château Cardache* and a *Romanesque chapel*.

Marseille

13 Bouches-du-Rhône   p.256☐D 8

Marseille is the second largest city in France and the largest port on the Mediterranean; and, just as it was once Asia's gateway to the West, so now it is the West's gateway to Asia. It was founded around 600 BC as a trading colony by Greeks from the Ionian settlement of Phocaea in Asia Minor, and first began to prosper in the 2nd half of the 6C BC. After the destruction of Phocaea by the Persian Emperor, Cyrus the Great (545/40 BC this Greek settlement on Ligurian territory, known as *Massilia*, was swollen by emigrants and took over the role of its old metropolis. Trading points and military bases were established all along the W. Mediterranean coast, and the city state soon acquired an international standing. Its rivals on the international scene were the

Marseille, view of the city from on board ship

Carthaginians and Etruscans, and it allied itself to Rome. In the 2C BC, Massilia invoked the assistance of the Romans against the Saluvii, its inland neighbours and trading partners, who had declined to look on passively at the extension of Massilia's power into the hinterland. The Romans came promptly to the aid of the ally which in 390 BC had paid part of their ransom to the Gauls, and set up garrisons in the interior.

A golden period now began but then the city made a mistake which had serious consequences. In the struggle between Caesar and Pompey, it supported the wrong side, for which it paid for by losing not only its temples, walls, and vast hinterland, but also its political and economic supremacy: Caesar did everything to promote Arles and Narbonne in its place, and even established a new port called Forum Julii (Fréjus). Forced now to

accept a minor role, Marseille remembered its Greek heritage and made a name for itself as a university town.

With time, however, this Greek city acquired a Roman character, thus establishing the basis for a recovery. However, it could not regain its old status as a self-ruling state, in spite of all its struggles for independence (against the Frankish mayor of the palace, Charles Martel, in 714; against the Comtes de Provence in the 12&13C, who were charged with administering the region; and later against the Revolutionary government). It did indeed succeed, in the 1st half of the 17C, in once again sending its own diplomatic envoys to Asia Minor and the Near and Middle East, but in 1660 the King's armies destroyed its ambitious dreams.

In general, though, from the 2 or 3C onwards, Marseille shared the history of the other large towns of Provence: it was converted to Christianity and then became the seat of a bishop quite early on; during the 5&6C it was attacked by Visigoths, Ostrogoths, Burgundians and Franks; later on it

Marseille, Old Cathedral of 'La Major': 1 Nave 2 Domed crossing 3 Choir 4 Apse 5 Transept 6 Side apses (1-6: 12C) 7 Side chapels (13/14C)

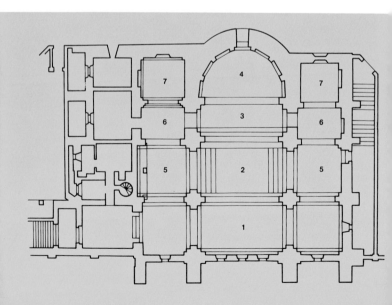

was besieged by the Saracens and Normans; and in 1481 it became part of France. However, the crisis which resulted from the end of the Crusades and the loss of the ports in the Levant was unique to Marseille.

Old Cathedral 'La Major' (Place de la Major): The name 'Major' implies that, when the original early Christian cathedral stood here, there was also another church dedicated to the Virgin in Marseille.

In 1852, the old cathedral was very nearly demolished in its entirety as a worthless medieval relic, in order to make way for the new cathedral; but after the Second World War it was restored as far as possible to its original appearance, and is now considered by 20C art historians to be one of the most beautiful Romanesque churches in Provence. It was built around the middle of the 12C on the site of the early Christian cathedral, which had been rebuilt in the 11C but had since become too small for the greatly increased population. During the following centuries, the new cathedral itself had to be expanded continually.

The existing church consists of a nave and two aisles, each comprising a single bay, and a transept which does not extend beyond the line of the two side aisles, and is flanked by a small rectangular tower. The unusually narrow bay of the choir adjoins the crossing, followed by a polygonal apse which is flanked by two square chapels. There are also two side apses, one to the S. and the other to the N.

Interior: The nave and side aisles support slightly pointed tunnel vaults running lengthways, as did the transept originally; later, though, the S. arm was given a transverse tunnel vault. The two side chapels were added later; that on the S. side (13C) has a groin vault, while the 14C N. chapel, supports typically Gothic vaulting on pointed arches. The apse has Provençal blind arcades and is vaulted by a half-dome. A half-dome supported by squinches also connects the side apses with the lower side chapels. The *dome* over the crossing is a small architectural masterpiece. As in

New cathedral of Sainte-Marie-Majeur

Notre-Dame de la Garde

the cathedral in Avignon, the rectangular bay of the crossing is converted into a square by a series of arches rising above each other; squinches then turn the square into an octagon, from which an octagonal, ribbed dome rises.

New Cathedral of Sainte-Marie-Majeur: This neo-Byzantine church was built in 1852–93 and was greatly admired when it was completed. It is actually the largest cathedral built in France since the Middle Ages (it is 460 ft. long and its dome is 197 ft. high). The W. façade, depicting the Coronation of the Virgin, is correspondingly massive. Though many of its details are Romanesque, its ground plan, comprising a Latin cross with an ambulatory and radiating chapels, is Gothic. Inside the cathedral, note the four large figures of the Evangelists by Botinelly (1937), beneath the central dome, the 16C crucifix in the nave, and the church treasure (a small ivory reliquary dating from the 12C).

Saint-Victor (Place Saint-Victor): During the Middle Ages this was one of the richest and most influential abbeys in Provence, as well as one of the oldest. It was built around 410–15 on the site of the Roman cemetery and above the relics of St.Victor, the martyr. Its architectural style was based on Palestinian and Egyptian monastic buildings. Soon, like Les Alyscamps in Arles, it became famous as a burial-place, and everyone wanted to be buried next to the canonized Roman officer who had been martyred in Marseille. The abbey flourished; its possessions stretched as far afield as Spain and Syria; and the sculptors of Marseille prospered too. The new building was begun in 1005 and finished in 1047; in the 13C a Romanesque church was erected which incorporated the early Christian basilica of Notre-Dame. During the 14C, under Pope Urban V, a fortified church with battlements and towers was built at the E. end (the architect was the ecclesiastical chamberlain Pons de l'Orme, later to be Abbot of Montmajour). During the 18C, following the secularization ordered by Clement XII in 1738, the abbey was converted by Louis XV, in 1751,

View of Notre-Dame de la Garde from the old harbour

into a convent for the nobility. During the Revolution the buildings were declared national property, but the church was again allowed to be used for worship in 1804. It was restored in 1895, and is used today as a parish church.

From the outside, this Romanesque church, with its strong towers and battlements, looks much more like a fortress than a place of worship. The walls have slits but are otherwise bare and devoid of ornament. Indeed, the church really was part of the fortifications on this site in the 14C. When the choir and transept were extended in 1363, the adjoining wall was demolished, and in its place a bell tower was erected in the style of a keep, and the gap which remained was closed by the massive choir walls, supported by four projecting buttresses. At the same time, the tower over the porch, which was older, was fortified and a chapel, whose roof was also used for defensive purposes, erected between the two towers—the 'Grandes Compagnies', the great scourge of the 14C, brought terror even to Marseille. Thus it is that one's first impressions of Saint-Victor, even today, are determined by the events of the 14C, next to which the 13C Romanesque church seems to pale into insignificance. All that remains of the early Christian church that once occupied this site are the lower part of the tower above the porch and the N. outer wall.

Interior: The porch in the Tour d'Isarn and the recessed portal (both dating from the 11C) lead into the basilica, comprising a nave and two aisles and consisting of four bays, which was built in the 1st half of the 13C. Behind the choir, which is separated from the crossing by a deep arch, there is a five-sided apse. All in all, it is a severe, massive, plain interior, whose windowless walls are perfectly in keeping with the outside. Inside the powerful walls, which are over 10 ft. thick, there are spiral stairways leading up to the parapet walk on the roof. The nave has a pointed tunnel vault, while the two side aisles have an early Gothic ribbed vault.

Crypt: However, by far the most interesting part of the church is the crypt, with its labyrinth of catacombs and chapels. A staircase leads down

Old harbour

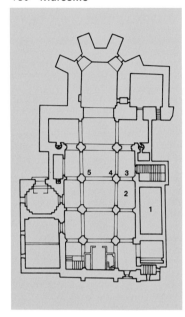

Marseille, Saint-Victor: 1 Atrium **2** Early Christian basilica of Notre-Dame-de-Confession **3** Catacomb chapel **4** Catacomb tunnel containing early Christian graves **5** Old cemetery

from the S. side aisle to the atrium, dating from the 5C, whose columns were removed at the beginning of the 19C and placed on the public squares of Marseille. The adjacent early Christian basilica, comprising a nave and two aisles, was also much altered by being built over in the 13C. Today, the nave's apse is missing, and the nave itself, which originally pointed towards the harbour, is aligned along an E.-W. axis. To this end, the low left aisle was opened into the nave through a large arch, while the arcades of the right aisle were walled in, thus separating it from the nave; and the altar was placed against this new wall. One passes through what used to be the right aisle but which is now a passage to the so-called *catacomb chapel*, which resembles a cave and has been carved out of the rock; it was here that the relics of St.Victor are said to have reposed originally. From here the *catacomb tunnel*, containing early Christian graves, leads to the old cemetery. (Some graves were also found beneath the floor of the nave, dug into the rock). At the end of this

Hôtel de Ville

passage there is a cave, at whose entrance can be seen a column carved from the rock and depicting the head of a man together with an abbot's crook; next to it there is a niche in the rock, which is known as the 'seat of St.Lazarus'. Legend has it that the same Lazarus whom Christ resurrected from the dead came to the Provence with his sisters and St.Maximinus and Mary Magdalene and lived for some time in a catacomb in the cemetery at Marseille. The other chapels, some of which were only discovered in the 18C, are all older. Some, like the *Andreas Chapel* and the *Isarn Chapel*, date from the 11C, but most were built in the 13C as the substructure of the upper church.

Notre-Dame de la Garde: This neo-Byzantine church dominates the city from its position on a 530 ft. high limestone spur, and is indeed one of Marseille's landmarks. Its tower is 148 ft. high and is crowned by a 10 ft. high statue of the Virgin. The church was consecrated in 1864 and stands on the site originally occupied by the

famous chapel of the same name, which was built in 1214. The red, white, and green marble of the interior is impressive.

Notre-Dame-des-Accoules (Place du Mazeau): All that remains is the Gothic bell tower. Next to it is the *Cour des Accoules* which contains a *Calvary chapel*, a 19C domed, circular building, and replicas of the Chapels to the Virgin in Lourdes and of the grotto of Mary Magdalene in Sainte-Baume, with the Stations of the Cross in a crypt beneath and a Calvary above it.

Notre-Dame-du-Mont-Carmel (Rue Mery F. Eboué): Late Gothic nave dating from the 16C with apse; the façade was rebuilt in the 17C. Beautiful wood panelling.

Saint-Cannat (Place des Prêcheurs): 16C Dominican church whose choir and apse are Renaissance. Famous for its large *organ*, which was built by Isnard in 1742. The marble high altar, which is by the school of P.Puget, is one of the most beautiful baro-

Bourse

Château du Pharo

que altars in Provence. There is also a fine wrought-iron grille in front of the baptismal chapel (1739).

Saint-Ferréol (Rue Joliette): This single-aisled church is typical of Provençal Gothic, but was extensively altered in the 19C. The façade was rebuilt at the end of the 19C in neo-Renaissance style.

Saint-Laurent (Rue Saint-Laurent): This small Romanesque sailors' church, whose peculiar traditions include fish sacrifices, stands on a historic site, occupied first by a pagan temple, then a temple to Apollo, and later by the 'Château Babon', which was a place of refuge built by Bishop Babo in 850, principally to protect the local population from attack by the Saracens. It incorporated a church of Saint-Laurent, over which the church

we see today was built in the 12C. It comprises a nave and two aisles, with a main apse and two side-apses. The octagonal bell tower was added in 1664.

Chapel of Notre-Dame-Étoile-de-la-Mer (S. of Saint-Laurent): Fishermen's church comprising a single aisle and dating from the beginning of the 17C. The choir and the dome, which is supported by squinches, are older.

Saint-Maurice (Boulevard Romain Rolland/Boulevard Icart): Modern church built in 1961.

Saint-Théodore-des-Chartreux (Rue des Dominicaines): This 17C basilica, with a nave and two aisles, originally formed part of a huge monastery possessing two cloisters

Palais Longchamp

(which have not survived) and monks' cells arranged around a courtyard with a columned portico.

Saint-Vincent-de-Paul or **Eglise des Réformés** (Rue Adolphe Thiers): Large neo-Gothic church (1849–90).

Cité Radieuse or **Unité d'Habitation** (Boulevard Michelet/Point du Prado): Modern residential block designed by Le Corbusier and built in 1947–51.

Port: The old harbour, or Vieux Port, of Marseille, which has been made famous far beyond the borders of France by the writings of Blaise Cendrars and Marcel Pagnol, is still the heart of the city, though it has lost its old position as economic centre, and is used nowadays only by fishing-boats and yachts. The development of steam navigation, together with the opening of the Suez Canal and the establishment of a French colonial empire, doubtless made the construction of a new port unavoidable. This was begun in 1840, and today (despite its destruction by the Germans in World War 2) its quays have a total length of some 17 miles and its waters occupy 600 acres. But the fame of the old, natural harbour remains undiminished. Its entrance is still guarded by two forts, the *Tour Saint-Jean*, or *Tour du Roi René*, a square tower built by King René in 1448–52, around which a fort was built in 1644, and the *Fort Saint-Nicolas* (1665–8), which has star-shaped out-works.

Château d'If: This stands on a rocky island in front of the harbour and was built around 1524 by Francis I. Later, it was used for many years as a state prison, in which capacity it was made notorious by Alexandre Dumas in 'The Count of Monte-Cristo'. The fort is square and gleaming white and is flanked on three sides by round towers. The sea-wall was added in the late 16C.

Château du Pharo: This magnificent building stands on a hill from where it towers impressively over the harbour. It was built for Napoleon III and is now used by the local legislature.

Hôtel-Dieu (Place Daviel): This simple building dates originally from 1188 and was rebuilt in 1692 according to plans approved by Mansart.

Hôtel de Ville (Quai du Port): This elegant baroque building, which was completed in 1674, betrays clear Genoese inspiration, consisting of a central section with a projecting cornice linking the two wings; which are crowned by pediments and cornices.

Vieille Charité (Esplanade de la Charité): This is a splendid three-storeyed baroque building with beautiful arcaded galleries with semicircular arches. It was designed by P.Puget, who was himself born in a house only a few yards away (Rue de la Charité/Rue Puits-du-Denier).

Museums
Musée Borély or **Musée Archéologique** (in the Château Borély): This elegant, early neoclassical building was built by Clérisseau and Brun in 1776–8. The large park, which includes English and French gardens as well as a botanical garden, was only laid out in the 19C.

The archaeological collection is principally famous for its *Egyptian section*, which is the third finest in France (after those in the Louvre and the Strasbourg museum). The granite statue of a prince, which has been in France since 1570, and a stone sacrificial table, are particularly beautiful. Also of great interest, however, are the reliefs, clay figures, and stele from the Far East and the Greek and Roman worlds, as well as the *Musée Lapidaire*, which is devoted to local archaeological discoveries.

Fort Saint-Jean

Musée Cantini: Housed in the Hôtel Montgrand, once the residence of the Governor of Provence, who was also the son-in-law of Mme. de Sévigné, the famous letter-writer; its last owner, the sculptor J.Cantini, bequeathed it to the city together with a number of collections. It contains beautiful Marseille and Provençal faience, as well as carpets, Renaissance furniture, Provençal furniture, Greek pottery, and French and German porcelain dating from the 18C.

Musée des Beaux Arts (Palais Longchamp; Boulevard Longchamp-/Place Bernex): Founded by the Consulate in 1800. It was filled with works of art taken by Bonaparte's armies or confiscated by the Revolutionary government. Since 1869 it has been housed in the Palais Longchamp, which had been built seven years earlier by H.Espérandieu to the design of the sculptor Bartholdi, and which provides a fitting background for a fine art collection. The two wings of the museum, which are in Italian Renaissance style, are linked by a semicircular Ionic colonnade, at whose centre is a splendid fountain decked with sculptures, itself a splendid work of art. The exhibition contains a wide selection of paintings ranging from the 15–19C, as well as Provençal paintings from the 17–20C.

Musée d'Histoire Naturelle (right wing of the Palais Longchamp): Interesting natural history collections. The basement contains a fine aquarium, and there is a zoo behind the Palais.

Musée des Docks Romains (on the excavation site): This shows part of the Roman docks as well as Roman store-rooms, which take the form of a number of large clay vessels, some up to 6 ft. 6 in. high, which have been sunk into the earth, and used to contain oil, grain, and wine.

Musée du Vieux-Marseille (in the Maison Diamantée, a beautiful Renaissance building with diamond-shaped stones on its façade and a Renaissance staircase which might be one of the exhibits): Provençal furni-

Vieille Charité

ture, Marseille engravings from various centuries, beautiful faience dating from the 17&18C, when Marseille was an important centre for their production, and similar items.

Musée Grobet-Labadié (opposite the Musée des Beaux-Arts): Fine collection of furniture, paintings, and tapestries.

Musée de la Marine (in the Bourse; Canebière/Rue de la République): The museum is housed in an impressive and elegant building which was erected in 1852–60 and is typical of the Deuxième Empire. Very informative about the history of Marseille, with charts and many models of ships.

Also worth seeing: The famous *Canebière*, which is the city's artery, and along whose lower part some houses by E.J. Brun can be seen. *Théâtre antique* (E. of the church of Saint-Laurent) and *Palais de Justice* (1743, on the Place Daviel). Old houses: the *Hôtel de Cabre* (Grand' Rue/Rue Bonneterie) dates from

1535 and is probably the oldest house in Marseille to have been preserved.

Environs: Aubagne (17.5 km. E.): The old town still contains some remains of the old walls and a 14C church (17C vault with pointed arches). But despite being the birthplace of Marcel Pagnol and the headquarters of the Foreign Legion, the town is now no more than a dormitory suburb of Marseille.
Auriol (30.5 km. NE): Small industrial town containing the ruins of an old *château*, a 17 or 18C *belfry* and the remains of the old *fortifications*, including a clock-tower built in 1564.
Ensuès-la-Redonne (20.5 km. NW): Small wine-growing town.
Gémenos (22.5 km. E.): Old *château* (built around 1700).
L'Estaque (9.5 km. NW): Today this is a monotonous industrial suburb of Marseille, but in the 2nd half of the 19C and the beginning of the 20C it attracted such famous painters as Cézanne and Braque to stay here frequently.
Madrague-de-Gignac (24.5 km. NW): Pretty little cove.

Jardin des Vestiges, excavations

Château d'If

Massif de la Marseilleveyre: Rising to 1,526 ft. and offering both walks and climbs. Since the 14C it has been known as *Masselha veyra*, which may derive from the Latin *vigilia*. In fact, there was a watch post on the summit even before Roman times.

Massif de Puget: In parts quite a wild mountain range with steep crags, like the impressive *Falaises du Devanson*, which afford a superb view.

Morgiou (12 km. SE): Cove with fishermen's huts, overlooked by the ruins of a small 17C *fort*.

Niolon (18.5 km. NW): Pretty cove.

La Redonne (24.5 km. NW): Beautifully situated cove.

Roquevaire (26.5 km. NW): Once famous for its apricots and figs. 1.5 km. SE, near the hamlet of Lascours, is the entrance to the *Rato-Pennados caves*, which are on three levels and house innumerable bats.

Saint-Jean-de-Garguier (22 km. E.): This is an old place of pilgrimage whose *chapel* contains a collection of beautiful votive pictures painted between 1500 and 1914. 18C *château*.

Saint-Julien-les-Martigues (35 km. NW): The *chapel*, just before the small town, contains a Gallo-Roman bas-relief (6 ft. 6 in. × 13 ft.) which may have depicted the hunt of Hippolytus and which without any doubt originally belonged to a mausoleum.

Saint-Pons-de-Gémenos (in the Parc Départemental de Saint-Pons; 25.5 km. E.): All that remains today of the Cistercian convent, which was built in 1205 and abandoned in 1407, apart from the remains of the chapterhouse and the much restored hospice, is the Romanesque *church*, a long, narrow structure with a single aisle, which is in fact the S. aisle of a much larger church which was never completed.

Sausset-les-Pins (31 km. NW): Small old fishing harbour. Popular weekend resort.

Sormiou (12 km. SE): This is the largest of the many coves, with a small fishing harbour as well.

Martigues

13 Bouches-du-Rhône   p.256☐C 7

Perhaps founded under the Romans.

In the Middle Ages, the settlement on the Etang de Berre consisted of three independent market towns: Jonquières, Ile, and Ferrières. They all had their own administration, church, and town walls, and it was only in 1581 that they were amalgamated by Henry III to form Martigues (the name derives from 'mouartaigues', which in the old Marseillais dialect meant 'dead waters'). The town prospered in the 17C, only to decline when the plague of 1727 carried off a third of its inhabitants and drove another third into emigration. It took Martigues two hundred years to recover from these events; but today, thanks to its industry, it is back on the road to becoming a flourishing community.

What used to be the three old market towns are now quarters of Martigues, separated by canals. In *Ferrières*, the *Musée du Vieux-Martigues* (opposite the 17C church) documents the town's history with the help of objects excavated locally, arts and crafts, religious art, and so on.

In the quarter of *Ile*, the *Église de la Madeleine*, a 17C church with a Corinthian façade, and the beautiful 17C Hôtel de Ville, are particularly worth seeing.

Environs: Couronne (9 km. S.): Small hamlet whose quarries were exploited in Roman times and now supply huge cement factories.

Lavéra (5 km. W.): Oil port supplying the Rhône valley, Alsace, Switzerland, and West Germany (Karlsruhe). On a promontory stands the *Fort de Bouc*, a tower built by the people of Marseille in the 13C and surrounded by a wall in the 17C by Vauban, the military architect. It is used today as a lighthouse.

Marignane (15.5 km. E.): Industrial town whose population has grown five-fold since 1963. Despite this, its narrow, winding alleys and streets have largely survived. The *church* was built in the 13C and contains a beautiful gilded high altar dating from the end of the 16C.

M.-Ponteau (9 km. SW): Thermal power station with a capacity of 6 thousand million kwh.

Port-de-Bouc (6 km. W.): Oldest industrial town in the region. Since

Marseille, Jardin des Vestiges, excavations of ancient city

1899 it has been the site of a large ship yard, the Chantiers de Provence.

Menton
06 Alpes-Maritimes   p.258□K6

Blessed by a favourable climate, the region was settled as far back as prehistoric times. The modern name of the town was first mentioned in documents in 1261 and derives from Mont d'Othon. A small community began to develop here in the 12C and ownership changed several times over the centuries. In 1157 it was given by its then owner, Guido Guerra, the Duke of Ventimiglia, to Guillaume Vento of Genoa; then, in the 13C, it passed into the hands of Charles of Anjou. During the struggles between the Guelphs and Ghibellines (1346) Menton returned briefly to the Vento family. Then it was acquired by Charles Grimaldi, Prince of Monaco. In 1524 it was bombarded by Andrea Doria, after which, together with Monaco, it came under the control of Charles V. It was only in 1641 that it once more became a protectorate of France, in accordance with the provisions of the Treaty of Péronne of that year. In 1792 it was attached to the department of Alpes-Maritimes. The Treaty of Paris (1814) once more gave Menton to the Grimaldis, but it broke away from Monaco in 1848 on the initiative of Charles Trenca and became a free town, accepting Sardinia's protection. After a referendum in 1860, it was annexed once more to France. A year later, Charles III of Monaco sold his rights to Menton and Roquebrune to Napoleon III for 4 million gold francs. During World War 2, the town was occupied by the Italians and later by the Germans, before being freed by the French in 1945.

The old part of the town, which stands on a rocky hill to the NE and centres on the Place Saint-Michel, still retains its medieval appearance, and comprises a labyrinth of alleys, streets, steps, and dark passages.

Chapelle de la Conception (to the W. of Place Saint-Michel): This was the chapel of the Pénitents Blancs,

Roquebrune (Menton), panorama

and was built in 1687. There is a tall bell tower on the N. side. The vertical pillars and niches containing figures, balanced by the horizontal entablature, form a harmonious façade. The interior is small and has baroque furnishings as well as 14 large figures of saints which date from the 18C.

La Miséricorde (Rue du Général-Gallieni): This was the *chapel* of the Pénitents Noirs, built in the 17C just beneath the old town, on the site once occupied by a Capuchin monastery. The building we see today has been much restored. There is a painting on the choir ceiling.

Saint-Michel (in the S. corner of the Place Saint-Michel): Steps lead up to the *church*, which was built between 1619 and 1675 by Prince Honoré II. The façade was added in 1817. Its three doors are separated from each other by double columns mounted on plinths, and each is surmounted by a niche containing a statue. On the upper storey the columns frame the windows and the triangular pediment is overtopped by two bell towers. The

Menton, Saint-Michel

interior takes the form of a columned basilica whose rich and colourful decoration is reminiscent of Nice Cathedral. To the right of the choir there is an altarpiece (1565) by A.Manchello, which represents Sts.Peter, Michael, and John the Baptist. An Adoration of the Shepherds and the Crucifixion date from the 17C and 18C respectively. The marble statue of the Madonna and Child was sculpted by a Genoese pupil of Puget. The choir vault is decorated with a fresco of St.Michael which dates from 1888.

Hôtel de Ville (Rue de la République): This was built in 1860 in the Italian style of the 17C.

Musée Jean Cocteau: This is housed in a late medieval bastion near the pier and exhibits works by the famous writer and painter, as well as mosaics which were executed to his design.

Musée de Peinture (in the W. quarter): In 1715 the *Palais Carnolès* was built as a summer residence for Antoine I, Prince of Monaco. Between 1860 and 1960 it was used as a casino (the interior was decorated in 1820), and today it is a *picture gallery* formed from the collection of Wakefield Mori. It includes paintings from the Italian (14–16C), Dutch, Flemish, and French (16&17C) schools, as well as the École de Paris of the 20C.

Musée Régional (Rue Lorédan-Larchey): This contains a small collection of modern paintings, in addition to its prehistoric exhibits and items illustrating local history and folklore.

Also worth seeing: The *Rue Longue* was the main street of the old town as early as the Middle Ages. *No. 45* is the Maison Paretti, which has a monumental staircase dating from 1645. *No. 123* was built as a residence for the Princes of Monaco. *No. 129* has a beautiful lintel (1543). The *Rue de*

Bréa also contains several *old houses* including the Maison de Monléon at *No. 1*, where Pope Pius VII stayed in 1814. General Bréa was born at *No. 2*, and Napoleon lived for a short time during 1796 at *No 3*. A marvellous view can be gained from the *old cemetery*, which is laid out above the old town in four rising terraces, one for each of the community's religions.

Environs: L'Annonciade (5.5 km. N.): On a terrace lined with cypresses and eucalyptuses stands a *Capuchin monastery*, whose present building dates from the 17C and was extended in the 19C. The chapel, which was completed in 1703, contains the relics of St.Fortunatus as well as the burial chapel of the Monléon family, who bought back the monastery from foreign owners in 1808.

Castellar (7 km. N.): This little town extends along a plateau beneath the summit of Mt.Orméa, whence it dominates the valleys of the Fossan and the Careï. Picturesque streets with vaulted passages.

Castillon (15 km. N.): This village was destroyed during World War 2 and then rebuilt after 1945. A few miles away are the *ruins* of Vieux Castillon, which was destroyed by an earthquake in 1887.

Garavan: The E. quarter of Menton extending up to the French-Italian border constitutes a small town in itself, with beautiful houses and villas on the Bay of Garavan, which contains a large harbour. The 17C chapel of *Saint-Jacques* is at No. 31, Quai Bonaparte. At the end of the Boulevard Saint-Jacques is the remarkable *Jardin Botanique Exotique*, where numerous tropical and Mediterranean plants are grown.

Gorbio (8 km. NW): This old town is laid out on a hill in terraces and the houses are connected to each other by arches. The *church* was completed in 1683 and the chapel of *Saint-Lazare* dates from the 12C. The old *Lascaris castle* is now a ruin.

Notre-Dame de la Menour (*c.* 26 km. NW): A staircase and bridge lead to the *chapel*, which has a fine Renaissance façade.

Peille (23 km. NW): Situated above a gorge, at a height of 2,067 ft. Its small community was once adminis-

Menton, Chapelle de la Conception, detail of façade

tered by consuls; in the 13C it was the seat of the governor of the judicial district of Nice and in 1258, it was attached by Charles of Anjou to the district of Vintimille-Val de Lantosque. When the inhabitants refused to pay high church taxes to the Bishop of Nice and attacked the Château de Drap, they found themselves excommunicated by him. The ruins of the medieval *castle* dominate the town, which also possesses numerous Gothic houses—the old consul's residence of the Dukes of Provence (Place du Mont-Agel) being an outstanding example. The *church* has a Romanesque aisle (12C) and a Gothic aisle (13C) as well as a tall, Lombard belltower.

Roquebrune (4 km. SW): The old town extends along a spur of the mountainside. Some of its narrow, winding streets are still vaulted. The *castle*, which was heavily restored in 1970–1, was built by a Duke of Vintimille, supposedly in the 10C. It was rebuilt and altered in the 12&13C and new buildings were erected connecting the two square towers to either side, thus forming a courtyard. The older tower is nearly 100 ft. high.

Roquebrune-Cap-Martin (5.5 km. SW): This is the new quarter of Roquebrune and its beautiful streets and houses extend down the peninsula. The church of *Saint-Martin du Cap* was built in 1974 by the architect J.Pace and decorated by P.Leroy. To the left of the church, on private land, are the remains of the Roman settlement of *Lumone*, which date from the 1C BC. The *triumphal arch* on the E. coast of the Cape is also Roman. 800,000 year-old animal bones were discovered in the *Grotte du Vallonet* (no admittance) and it constitutes one of the oldest such sites in Europe. The Swiss architect Le Corbusier (1887–1965) is buried in the cemetery. The chapel of *Notre-Dame du Bon Voyage* is situated in the Cabbé quarter.

Saint-Agnès (11 km. NW): This magnificently situated village contains the ruins of a *castle* allegedly built by a Saracen whose love for a Christian girl led him to embrace her faith.

Monaco, Principality of

p.258□K 6

This area of what is now the Côte d'Azur was inhabited in prehistoric times. The Phoenicians built a temple here which the Greeks later took over and dedicated to Hercules. This explains why the Romans called the place *Portus Herculis Monoeci*, from which its modern name derives. The region was devastated by Goths, Lombards, and Saracens in turn. Then, in 1191, the powerful Republic of Genoa acquired it by treaty from Frederick I. In 1215 a citadel was built here which was captured by François Grimaldi towards the end of the 13C. The Grimaldis were driven out by the Genoese, but they returned in the 14C under Carlo I and proceeded to annex Menton (1346) and Roquebrune (1355) to their independent principality. The struggle with Genoa continued into the 16C, but the Monégasques emerged victorious. During the 16&17C Monaco was under the protection of Spain, and from 1641 under that of France. When the Grimaldi family had no male successor, its heiress married into a Norman family, the Matignons, whose descendants rule today.

In 1793, Monaco (under the old name of *Fort-Hercule*) was annexed to the department of Alpes-Maritimes, but with Talleyrand's support the principality managed to regain its sovereignty. In 1815 it became a protectorate of Sardinia. Menton and Roquebrune proclaimed their independence from Monaco in 1848 because of taxes, whereupon its ruler sold them to Napoleon III for 4 million gold francs. This dried up one of the principality's main sources of income, so a gambling casino for tourists was established, 60% of whose

Monaco, panorama

income went to the principality. This is still the basis of its prosperity.

Today Monaco extends over an area of 473 acres along the slopes of the Tête-de-Chien down to the coast. It is extremely densely populated, and offers the sharp contrast of picturesque old houses and ultra-modern skyscrapers which seem to shoot out of the earth like mushrooms. It consists of four districts: Monaco Ville, La Condamine, Monte-Carlo and Fontvieille.

Monaco Ville: This is the old town, and is situated on a spur of rock 213 ft. high which runs down into the sea. A wall whose appearance has not changed since the 16C surrounds the district's narrow alleys and colourful façades, as well as the *Fort Antoine*, which was built by Vauban in 1709, and the Prince's Palace. The stairway, known as the *Rampe Major* (1714),

led up to three *gates* (16&18C) and could be controlled from the *Saillant de l'Oreillon* (1708). All that remains now of the *citadel* built in 1215 by Franco di Castello is the *Tour de Serravalle* and a part of the E. façade. Work on the *castle* began in the middle of the 17C, under Honoré II; during the following years it was rebuilt and extended. The chapel of *Saint-Jean Baptiste* was built in 1656. This is a large building containing a number of sumptuously decorated rooms (reception room, throne room, etc.) which one may visit. The *Musée Napoléonien et des Archives Historiques du Palais* was installed in the SW wing in 1970. It exhibits mementoes of Napoleon and historical documents concerning the principality. Near the castle is the neo-Romanesque *Cathedral*, which was built of white stone in 1875–84 on the site where the 13C church of Saint-Nicolas had once stood. The interior contains two masterpieces by L.Bréa, an altarpiece (1500) in 18 parts which depicts scenes from the life of St.Nicholas, and a wonderful Pietà (1505) which is flanked by the figures of Sts.Stephen and James the Elder, themselves the product of the Nice school (16C). The choir vault is decorated with a mosaic by Facchina which was executed in 1886 in the Byzantine style. Other sacred buildings here include the *Chapelle de la Miséricorde* (1646) and the *Chapelle de la Paix*. The Avenue Saint-Martin contains the *Musée Archéologique*, which has an interesting collection illustrating ancient civilizations.

La Condamine (between Monaco and Monte Carlo): This is situated beneath the old town and on the square-shaped *harbour* which was constructed in 1901 at the behest of Prince Albert I. The church of *Sainte-Dévote* (Place Sainte-Dévote) was built on the foundation walls of an 11C chapel. It is dedicated to a Corsican martyr of the 3C.

Monte-Carlo (NE of Monaco): This fashionable town sprang up in the 19C at the foot of Mont-Agel. The famous *casino* was built in 1878–9 to the design of the architect Ch. Garnier. Garnier also designed the villa which now houses the *Musée National de Monaco* (Avenue de la Princesse-Grace). Among other things, this contains the world's most important collection of dolls and automata (18&19C), which was bequeathed to the principality by Madeleine de Galéa.

Fontvieille (W.): The large *Jardin Exotique* was designed by the landscape architect L.Notari and laid out above the modern industrial quarter of Monaco in 1912. It contains countless exotic tropical plants. Beneath the garden are the *Grottes de l'Observatoire*. The *Musée d'Anthropologie Préhistorique* (between the Jardin Exotique and the Parc Princesse-Antoinette) was established in 1904 by Albert I.

Montmajour

13 Bouches-du-Rhône   p. 256☐B 6

The Abbey of Montmajour was built on a rock in the middle of marshland, and could once only be reached by boat. The area was drained by the monks themselves, a significant achievement which they completed in the 17C.

We know little of the early history of this rock, though it was inhabited in the Celto-Roman period and indeed, it appears, before that. We do know for certain that there was a cemetery here in the 10C, during the reign of King Conrad of Arles. Probably, during the course of time, hermits settled here to work as grave-diggers (there are hermits' cells in the chapel of St.Peter). In any case, a monastery was founded here in the 10C. Its monks followed the rule of St.Benedict without actually joining the order. Being much favoured by the Archbishops of Arles, and chosen by the Comtes de Provence to be their burial-place, it soon acquired an exceptional reputation. This fame was further increased by its extraordinary commitment to the renewal of the monastic life. But it was above all the celebrated 'Pardon de Montmajour', an indulgence which was famous far and wide throughout the Middle Ages, that drew swarms of pilgrims here.

During the 14C, the monastery, already rich, became a prebend of the Holy See, so that its revenue was sent to Rome, and in the 16&17C it became a commendam which the Kings of France granted as an apanage. In these circumstances, it is hardly surprising that monastic discipline declined, so that in the 17C reform proved unavoidable. This was accompanied by the renovation of the buildings, parts of which had collapsed. These measures, however, only temporarily delayed its long-term decline.

In 1786 the Abbot, Cardinal Rohan, who had been involved in the affair of the diamond necklace, was deposed, and the abbey, which now numbered 11 monks, was dissolved by the King. During the Revolution it was declared national property and sold; its new owners proceeded to plunder it, selling off wall panellings, floors, and beams. Finally, Réattu, a painter from Arles, bought the keep, and then in 1838 the town of Arles bought the abbey and church, in order to save what was left.

Church: The present building was erected between 1140 and 1160/70 on the site of an earlier church, which had been completed in 1060/70. Although originally planned to have five bays, a supposedly temporary W. wall was built after only two bays had been completed, and this still stands today. The only later extensions are the funerary chapel which was built on to the N. arm of the transept in the 14C and the sacristy and treasury which were added to the N. side of the nave (15C). The cloister, which was begun at the same time as the church, was completed in 1375, as were the monks' living quarters.

Exterior: There is a particularly impressive view from the E., from the Les Baux road. The bare, steep walls, as massive and strong as those of a medieval fortress, are lightened only by a few window-slits. It is only when one looks more closely that one sees, beside the conspicuous keep, the outlines of a church, notably its polygonal choir and powerful transept. The N. and W. sides are equally bare, though not quite so impressive. The W. end (originally meant to be temporary) has a door which is framed by two columns but otherwise undecorated and stands beneath a Romanesque arch.

Interior: The interior, which is entered through the crypt, perfectly matches the monumental scale of the outside. Indeed, one is so overwhelmed by its massive dimensions that one feels incapable of taking in their layout at first glance. The vaults

Montmajour

of the crypt extend along the whole area of the upper church, and are supported by walls on one side and carved out of the rock on the other, S. side—the first purpose of the nave, transept and choir of the crypt being to level out the site. In fact, after a while one sees that the interior is composed of a nave (10 ft. wide, barrel-vaulted, and flanked on the N. side by a narrower passage which turns into an ambulatory), transept, and choir and ambulatory with radiating chapels. The effect is very subterranean, and the interior is lit by windows in the apses which are virtually slits. A gentle staircase leads up to the *upper church*, which is also heavy and almost without decoration, and achieves its effect mainly through the weight of the stone and the beautiful clear architectural proportions, especially of the blind arcades on the outer walls, which emphasize the Romanesque structure, the historiated pillars, which introduce rhythm and movement, and the powerful, slightly pointed tunnel vault of the nave, which unites the other elements. For the rest, the structure is the same as that of the lower church. The rib vault of the crossing is later (13C); the chapel prolonging the N. arm of the transept, which contains Gothic tombs, dates from the 14C; and the sacristy and archive on the N. side of the nave date from the 15C.

The *cloister* adjoins the S. side of the church. After the Saint-Trophime cloister in Arles, it is one of the most beautiful in the whole of Provence. In fact, the two have much in common, both architecturally and in terms of sculptural decoration. For example, it is easy to see how the arcades have been modelled on the cloister in Arles. Again, there is the same alternation between broad intermediate piers and groups of 3 or 4 double columns. However, the intermediate piers here are considerably wider than those in Arles, and the walls, unlike those in Arles, are smooth. This ambitious and successful solution was made possible by the invention, inspired by ancient architecture, of a type of arch which spans the space between the piers and draws the weight of the vault on to the intermediate and corner piers, thus making it possible to do without the pilasters.

In this way, the rectangular ribs of the round barrel vault were able to be spring directly from the cornice, which is only supported by consoles. This device, in turn, gives greater weight to the consoles, which are

Montmajour, Cloister The cloister is richly decorated with sculptures depicting classical, Christian, and medieval motifs, including Biblical stories and local legends; there are some fine bearded heads and many animals and mythical beasts. **1** Head of Tantalus **2** Temptation of Jesus **3** The four Evangelists (14C) **4** St.Peter with Papal crown and keys **5** Burial of a monk **6** Pentecost, outpouring of the Holy Spirit **7** Annunciation **8** Supper in the house of Simon of Bethany (Mary Magdalene kisses Jesus' feet) **9** Coronation of the Virgin Mary **10** Knight with lance and shield doing battle with a chimaera **11** Knight in chain mail doing battle with a lion **12** Two crowned heads: the Queen of Sheba and King Solomon **13** The famous Tarasque of Tarascon, who is just about to swallow a man **14** Tarasque biting an unfortunate person's head off **15** and **16** The heads depicted here could be symbols of the moon, the mistral, fire, and the sun

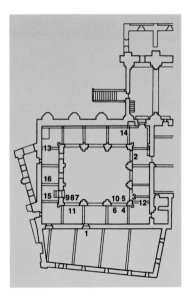

decorated with animals' heads, masks, and mythical creatures, and it was frequently imitated in Provence in the years which followed.

The *chapterhouse*, which occupies three bays and has been partly carved out of the rock, adjoins the E. walk. Like the *refectory*, to which it lies at right angles, it has been much misused over the centuries.

The *keep* was built in 1369 by Abbot Pons de l'Orme and is a rectangular tower 85 ft. high, punctuated by a few openings which resemble embrasures, and topped by machicolations. Like many fortifications built in Provence in the 14C, its construction was principally motivated by the fear of the 'Grandes Compagnies', as the marauding mercenaries of Charles V called themselves. The high-ceilinged room inside, which has a rib vault, could once have been divided into three rooms by means of raftered ceilings. From the platform there is a beautiful view of the abbey and surroundings. At the bottom of the tower, the graves which were cut into the rock can still be seen.

To the SE of the keep, a staircase leads down the steep rock to the *Chapelle Saint-Pierre*, part of which has also been carved into the rock. It dates from earliest days of the abbey, probably from the first half of the 11C. The entrance to the chapel is reached through a doorway in the abbey wall, which leads to a slope and then the chapel itself. Its S. side is supported by massive buttresses dating from a later period (15C). The chapel comprises two aisles and is only 31 ft. 6 in. long by 8 ft. 10 in. wide. A tunnel-vaulted rectangular porch has been set in front of it. The main part of the interior is also tunnel-vaulted, and leads into a recessed choir and then a semicircular apse, which is also recessed, creating a dynamic effect. Even more interesting, though, are the 12 *capitals*, which are decorated with acanthus leaves, palmettes, and guilloche ornaments (a form of decoration which had been known to the Merovingians), whose wealth of invention is quite startling. In fact, each one of the 12 capitals has been decorated differently—only in Venasque can one find a similar profusion.

From the S. wall, a narrow passage leads into the *Hermitage* and to a niche in the rock which is known as 'St.Trophimus's confessional'.

The *Chapelle Sainte-Croix*, which stands 220 yards to the E., outside the abbey walls, dates from the end of the 12C. It was used as a cemetery chapel. There are even tombs in the passage connecting the chapel with the abbey, part of which runs underground. The shape of the chapel is most unusual in that it resembles a quatrefoil; this was allegedly chosen so that the chapel could contain a part of the True Cross which the monks were said to have in their possession. In reality, the scholars are still guessing at the function of the main part of the interior and the four apses. The *façade* of this beautiful building is striking principally for the clear, sharply drawn lines which—apart from the buttresses, roofs, and gables—are all that relieve

Montmajour, Chapelle Sainte-Croix

the nearly windowless walls. The four semicircular apses form sharp edges where they abut each other, and the square central part of the building, which has a triangular pediment on all four sides, also reveals sharp edges as it rises between them. It is crowned by a lantern which is pierced by round arches on all four sides and capped by a small spire. A torch for the dead used to burn in this lantern, as was also the custom in the church of Saint-Honorat in Arles. An inscription on the lintel of the rectangular portal in the W. porch names Charlemagne as responsible for the endowment.

Baroque buildings: After the Romanesque W. part of the abbey, which contained a library, kitchen, cellar, and a second dormitory, had collapsed in 1703, work was begun on the massive complex of buildings whose ruins are today so impressive. The architects were P. Mignard and, after the fire of 1726, J.-B. Franque from Avignon.

Environs: Butte du Castellet (2 km. NE): The remains of a *castle* of the Comtes de Provence stand on farmland here; among them is the apse of the Chapelle Sainte-Croix du Castellet. Far more interesting, though, are the megalithic monuments in this area, known as *Hypogées* or *Allées couvertes*. These are underground rows of dolmen-like graves, the rows being up to 213 ft. long and, in some places, entirely carved out of the rock. Some of the flat stones have drawings carved on them which have been interpreted as maps of the heavens; and from these the monuments can be dated to the Bronze Age (roughly 2,000 years before Christ).

Fontvieille (4.5 km. NE): This pretty, prosperous market town does very well out of its stone quarries (which have been worked since the 15C), from bauxite, and from the stream of tourists lured here by Daudet's mill.

Le Moulin de Daudet (S. of Fontvieille): This was supposed to be where Daudet wrote his celebrated 'Lettres de mon moulin', although in fact he is known to have written them

Nice, Préfecture

in Paris. Today the mill contains a small *museum* which exhibits various of Daudet's manuscripts, engravings, caricatures, and published books, as well as other items.

Mornas
84 Vaucluse   p.256□B 4

This attractive village nestles at the bottom of a sharply descending limestone plateau. It still retains its fortified gates, and may itself be described, in the true sense of the word, as the gateway to Provence. On the top of the crag stand the ruins of a 12C *castle* of the Comtes de Provence, which was extended during the centuries which followed by Papal vassals. But, however big it became, it was still only one section of the entire system of fortifications, which included the whole plateau. As a Catholic stronghold during the Wars of Religion, it was the scene of appalling bloodshed, then of a no less bloody revenge: Protestants and Catholics both

seemed to find the rock a suitable spot for hurling each other off.

Notre-Dame du Val Romigier: This 12C church has a single aisle which extends for two bays. Its three apses directly abut the tower (above the dome of the crossing) and the wall of the transept; there is no intervening choir. The narrow *interior* features the two-tiered blind arcades which are typical of Romanesque architecture in Provence.

Nice
06 Alpes Maritimes   p.258□I 6

The coastal area around Nice is known to have been inhabited for 400,000 years, thanks to its favourable situation. Around 600 BC Greeks from the city of Phocaea settled here and founded a colony which may have been called *Nikaia*. Ligurians were also settled in the part of Nice now called Cimiez, and in the 5C BC the Greeks built fortifications. In about 120 BC the Romans settled on the hill now occupied by Cimiez, where they established the administrative and military capital of the Province of Alpes Maritimae, known to them as *Cemenelum*.
Nice acquired a bishop in the 4C and Cimiez in the 5C, though the former was subordinate to the Archbishop of

Aix and the latter to the Bishop of Embrun. In 465 the resultant rivalries between the two persuaded Pope Hilarius to merge them into a single diocese based in Nice, though there are no references to it until the 6C.

In order to assert its political independence from Provence, Nice concluded an alliance with Pisa against Genoa in the 12C. In 1388, it refused to recognize the authority of the Duke of Provence, Louis d'Anjou, and placed itself under the protection of the Counts of Savoy. During the war between Francis I and Charles V (1524), the former laid claim to Nice, but then Pope Paul III, who was mediating between the two, arranged a cease-fire (1538), thus ending their long quarrel. But it did not hold for long. In 1543 the town was besieged by French and Turkish troops who nonetheless failed to capture the citadel.

During the War of the Spanish Succession, Nice was occupied, and the citadel was taken by Marshal Berwick (1706), who proceeded to raze the fortress. This left the town exposed to attack from its enemies, and the struggle to control it began anew. In 1720 the Count of Savoy became King of Sardinia, and Nice now passed into his hands for several decades. In 1792, the town was annexed to France at its own request. It was occupied by imperial troops in 1800 but then managed to expel them; then in 1814 it reverted to Sardinia. Union with France was finally brought about by another plebiscite in 1860. Now that it could develop in conditions of peace, the town rapidly began to prosper; and for this the English visitors who made Nice their favourite winter resort were not least responsible. The town expressed its gratitude by calling the long promenade along the harbour after them (Promenade des Anglais). Today, Nice is the prefecture of its department as well as being an internationally famous sporting centre and holiday resort and, not least, an important cultural and artistic centre—with the École de Nice and its rich tradition.

Château: The old *citadel* was never rebuilt after its destruction in 1706.

Nice (Cimiez), Franciscan monastery

Its site on the promontory is now occupied by a large park and a massive 16C bastion, which is known as the *Tour Bellanda* and now houses the *Musée Naval* (the exhibits include models of ships, navigational instruments, and seascapes).

Chapelle de la Miséricorde (Place Pierre-Gautier): This chapel, which used to belong to the old Theatine monastery, may justly be described as a masterpiece of baroque art. Inspired by Italian models, it was built in 1736 by B.Vittone and was the centre of the Pénitents Noirs brotherhood. The portal in the beautiful two-storeyed façade leads into an oval interior which is roofed by a shallow dome and surrounded by chapels. Its gold and stucco ornament is extremely sumptuous.

Chapelle de l'Annonciation (Rue de la Poissonerie): This small chapel (also known as Saint-Jaume) was built towards the end of the 17C. The furnishings are Italian baroque in style; indeed, the influence of Guarini cannot be mistaken.

Saint-François-de-Paule (Rue Saint-François-de-Paule): The church was built in 1733–50 by Guarini, in Italian baroque style. It comprises a single aisle with rectangular chapels. The furnishing of the interior has a more secular than sacred appearance. There are rococo galleries on both sides of the choir.

Saint-Jacques (Rue Droite): This former Jesuit chapel was built in the 17C on the model of the Geschapel in Rome. The simple façade contrasts with the rich furnishings of the interior.

Cathedral of Sainte-Réparate (Place Rosetti): The old cathedral, built near the citadel in the 12C, was abandoned in favour of this new one, which was built in 1650 by J.-A. Guibera and dedicated to St.Reparata, a 3C martyr. It has a two-storeyed façade and consists of a nave and two aisles. The nave, which extends four bays, is tunnel-vaulted. An ambulatory runs above the entablature of the pilasters. The choir contains beautiful stalls and a 17C marble altar. The sac-

Nice (Cimiez), cemetery

Nice, Cathedral

risty acquired its superb wood panelling in the 18C.

Cimiez (N. district of Nice): *Cemenelum* was occupied by the Romans for about 500 years. The dimensions of the necropolis and of the town itself, which has been partly excavated, give some idea of the importance which Cemenelum had in ancient times. It was nonetheless abandoned during the 6C. The Roman amphitheatre (1&3C) can still be seen, but it has lost its original appearance, having been quarried for stones in the Middle Ages. The *baths* are the largest to have survived in France. They probably consisted of two separate baths for men and women. The frigidarium of the N. bath survives to its full height (33 ft.). Traces of the *early Christian basilica* and the *baptistery* can still be seen on the site of the baths. The *Villa des Arènes* was built in the 17C between the theatre and the baths. Its ground floor today houses the *Musée Archéologique*, which exhibits all kinds of archaeological discoveries documenting life in Cemenelum from the 5C BC to the 5C AD. The first floor of the Villa contains the *Musée Henri Matisse*, which has some impressive paintings by the artist illustrating the various periods in his creative life. *Musée National du Message Biblique Marc Chagall* (Avenue du Docteur-Ménard): This was specially built in 1972 to house 17 great works by Chagall. There are also gouaches, lithographs, sculptures, and 200 sketches. The *church* of the simple 17C *Franciscan monastery* was built and extended in various stages from the 14–19C. The porch and the vault of the church were painted by the Venetian artist Giacomeli in 1859. There is a large and important altarpiece by L.Bréa (1475) of the Pietà, with Sts.Martin and Catherine on its wings. A second altar (1512) by Bréa depicts the Crucifixion. 1681 saw the installation of the beautiful wooden panelling in the sacristy. The former *Benedictine monastery of Saint-Pons* is now a military hospital. The oval interior of its church is richly furnished and has a chapel (on the N. side) which is supposed to contain the remains of the marble sarcophagus in which St.Pons was buried in the 8C.

Nice, Place Masséna

Musée Jules Chéret (Avenue des Baumettes): The exhibition includes works by such famous French painters as Van Loo, Chagall and Braque, and also by Picasso, as well as paintings by Italian and Flemish artists.

Musée Masséna (Promenade des Anglais): This is housed in a 19C villa and contains numerous books, pieces of faience, furniture, ornaments and objects connected with folklore.

Musée de Terra-Amata (Boulevard Canot): This documents the prehistory of the region with an exhibition of finds 400,000 years old.

Musée du Vieux-Logis (Avenue Saint-Barthélemy): This old oil mill now provides the setting for the reconstruction of a bourgeois Gothic and Renaissance house (15&16C).

Palais Lascaris (Rue Droite): Built in the 17C in Genoese style. The staircase was painted by Carloni.

Also worth seeing: The old town consists of a maze of alleys, steps and houses behind the large old squares (Garibaldi, Masséna, Cours Saleya). The 17C baroque church of *Saint-Augustin* contains a Pietà by L.Bréa. The *former Senate building* (Place Charles-Félix) dates from the beginning of the 18C and is in the form of a Genoese palace. On the Cours Saleya is the *Musée de Malacologie*, which displays exotic and Mediterranean molluscs. On the Boulevard Risso can be seen the *Musée d'Histoire Naturelle* (whose exhibits include fish species of the Mediterranean). *Préfecture* (former palace of the Kings of Sardinia; early-17C).

Environs: Aspremont (12 km. N.): This small village stands beneath the mountain of the same name. The church, which has no windows, was built in the 13C. The choir and aisles were rebuilt in the 16C.

Beaulieu-sur-Mer (10 km. NE): The *Villa Kerylos*, built in classical Greek style, houses a collection of Greek works of art.

Drap (9.5 km. NE): This was enfeoffed in 1067 to the Bishop of

Eze (Nice)

Nice, who then built a castle here, of which some ruins are all that survive today.

Eze (11 km. NE): Eze became a county in the late 16C. A town wall was built which was however destroyed in 1706. The town itself has retained its medieval appearance (14C gate). The *Chapelle des Pénitents Blancs* (1306) is richly furnished, containing, among other items, a Spanish crucifix dating from 1258, and a 16C Crucifixion by the Bréa school. Outside Eze can be seen the medieval *Château de Madrid* and a 17C chapel of *St.Michael*.

Falicon (10 km. N.): This village, which clings to a crag, has a *church* dating from 1621.

Fort du Mont Alban (4.5 km. SE): The *fort* was built on a hill in 1577 for military purposes.

Madone de Laghet (15 km. NE): This is perhaps the best known *pilgrimage chapel* in the region, and was built in the 17C. The Carmelite monks built a *monastery* here whose church and cloister, both in the classical style, contain many ex votos.

Peillon (*c.* 18 km. NE): It was in this interesting little medieval town that the Brothers of the Pénitents Blancs built the chapel of *Notre-Dame de la Madone des Douleurs* in the 15&16C. In the late 15C the choir was painted with tempera on dry plaster (attributed to J.Canavesio). The painting depicts scenes from the Passion and the Mourning of Christ. The *church* (18C) contains a Madonna of the rosary (1639) and an 18C crucifix.

Saint-André (7 km. N.): The *château*, built on a hill in the 18C, was frescoed by Van Loo. Nearby is the large *limestone cave of Saint-André*.

Saint-Jean-Cap-Ferrat (*c.* 10 km. E.): It was in this former fishing village that the King of Sardinia had a *chapel* built in 1821 on the foundation walls of a burial sanctuary. Near it there is a *watch-tower* 43 ft. high, which dates from the 18C. Not far from here is the **Musée Ile-de-France**, which has an extensive collection of paintings, tapestries, porcelain, etc.

La Trinité (8 km. NE): The small *church* was built in the early 17C in baroque style.

La Turbie (18 km. NE): It was here,

La Turbie (Nice)

La Turbie (Nice), Alpium Tropaea

in the foothills of the Tête-de-Chien range, that the Romans founded Alpis Summa, which remained the frontier between Cisalpine and Transalpine Gaul until the Middle Ages. The *Alpium Tropaea (Trophée des Alpes)* was erected in 7/6 BC as a symbol of Roman power and of the conquest of the Alpine peoples by Julius Caesar and Augustus. It was originally 151 ft. high, and was set up on the highest point of the pass in order to be seen from afar. A huge plinth supported 24 Doric columns on which rested a stepped pyramid; and upon this base there stood a colossal statue of Augustus. In the 12C, the monument was turned into a keep by the Guelphs. A failed attempt to blow it up (1705), and the plundering of its stone, left it so much damaged that it required extensive restoration, which was carried out by J.Formigé at the beginning of this century.

Villefranche-sur-Mer (6 km. E.): This terraced medieval town extends along the shore of a large bay. The

citadel was built by Provana towards the end of the 16C. The small chapel of *Saint-Pierre* was painted by Cocteau in 1964.

Notre-Dame-d'Aubune
84 Vaucluse   p.256☐C 4

The beautiful old chapel stands halfway up a steep hill which is supposed to have been inhabited in pre-Christian and early Christian times. During the time of the ancient Greeks, the trade road from Marseille to Vaison/Lyon passed along its base. Under the Romans, the populace descended into the more fertile plain, as also happened in many similar geographical locations, only to return to the mountain in search of refuge when the invasions of the Goths began.

Chapel: Some experts believe that this was built during the second quarter of the 12C, while others maintain that the building technique employed in the construction of its walls, the low arms of the transept,

Notre-Dame-d'Aubune, Chapel 1 Nave **2** Transept **3** Apses **4** Tower **5** Porch **6** N. aisle

Notre-Dame-d'Aubune, chapel

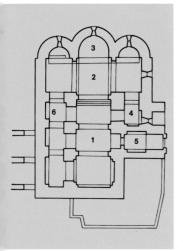

and the juxtaposition of the apses, all features characteristic of early Romanesque, mean that it should be dated to the 9 or 10C. The *tower* is dated by these two schools of thought to the last third of the 12C or the 11 or 12C respectively. Whatever the truth, it reveals a sure mastery of ancient form. During the Wars of Religion, the interior was badly damaged and for a time the church was even used as a stable. It is entered through a tunnel-vaulted porch by the tower and inside it is decorated with wall paintings in naive popular style which date from various periods. The structure originally comprised a single aisle of three bays, but it was enlarged and given a N. aisle at the beginning of the 17C.

Environs: Gigondas (7.5 km. N.): This famous wine-growing town, which has numerous wine cellars, was mentioned by Pliny. Remains of the medieval *ramparts* and *fortress*.
Plateau des Sarrazins: On the grey rocks behind the chapel of N.-D.-d'A. can be seen the ruins of the cha-

pel of *Saint-Hilaire*, which date from the 6/7C. The old oppidum was resettled in the 3C but destroyed in the 8C by Charles Martel because its inhabitants had formed an alliance with the Saracens to protect their independence.
Sablet (12 km. N.): Typical Provençal village with concentric streets and a *church* dating from the 12&14C.
Séguret (14 km. N.): Extremely attractive village which contains the ruins of a fortified *castle*. It is a kind of artists' colony which mounts exhibitions and small theatre festivals in the summer. The old *Porte Reynier* (12C), the *Fontaine des Mascarons* (17C), and the 12C *church*, are also very beautiful.
Vacqueyras (3.5 km. NW): Remains of the old *fortifications* and of the *castle*.

Notre-Dame de Lumières
84 Vaucluse   p.256□C/D 5

This is now a famous Provençal pil-

Pont Julien (Notre-Dame de Lumières)

grimage town. It first began to attract attention at the beginning of the 17C, when mysterious lights were seen near the Chapel of Our Lady in the Limergue valley. When an old farmer really was miraculously healed here in 1661, the chapel became sought out by large numbers of pilgrims; and as the number of miracle cures continued to increase thereafter, so the stream of pilgrims has been uninterrupted to the present day.

Pilgrimage church: After the first miracle, a new and larger church was built (1663–9) over the old Romanesque chapel, which now serves as a crypt. Apart from Our Lady of the Lights, a black Virgin dating from the 16 or 17C, and a 17C Pietà, it is also worth seeing the extremely interesting collection of ex votos in a right side-chapel, which exhibit numerous examples of naive art.

Environs: Goult (1 km. NE): This village (present population: 1,052) was once famous for its glass-works. It contains a classically Romanesque *parish church* dating from the middle of the 12C, which is now in severe need of restoration. It originally had a single aisle comprising three bays of unequal length. The effect which it achieves is due largely to its severity and balance.
Pont Julien (6.5 km. E.): One of the best preserved Roman bridges in France. It has 3 arches and is 223 ft. long, 14 ft. wide and 46 ft. high. 1 km. up the Calavon is the small 13C fortress of *Roqueture*, which contains a chapel that has been carved out of the rock.
Saint-Pantaléon (4.5 km. NW): This tiny village, with a mere 88 inhabitants, contains a small Romanesque *church* which, unusually, is wider than it is long. It comprises a nave and two aisles, the nave consisting of one bay, a choir bay, and a semicircular apse. The interior, which contains a beautiful marble altar table, achieves a captivating effect through its successful, geometrical arrangement.

Notre-Dame du Groseau
84 Vaucluse   p.256☐C 4

The lovely countryside which surrounds the source of the Groseau seems, from all appearances, to have been considered sacred in antiquity, a status which it regained in the 7C, when it became the site of an abbey. A Papal palace which has since disappeared was built here in the 14C.

Chapelle Notre-Dame: This small Romanesque chapel is all that remains of the former abbey church (and indeed of the abbey). It consists of a tunnel-vaulted narthex and a nearly square interior, which has a semicircular apse with a half-dome at the E. end and a side-chapel (possibly a side-apse) on the S. side with a transverse tunnel vault, which was added later in the 12C. The main part of the interior could be the last, domed bay, of the

Notre-Dame du Groseau, Chapelle Notre-Dame

single-aisled church which had previously stood on the same site.

Noves
13 Bouches-du-Rhône   p.256☐B/C 5

The fertile countryside in which this little town is set has made it a prosperous centre for the fruit and vegetable growing industries. The settlement of this site began with a Celtic oppidum situated on a ford of the Durance; this became the *Nauda* of the Gauls and, later, the Roman *Noues*. It developed into a busy market in fairly early times, as is attested by the discovery here of coins and ceramics dating from the 6C BC onwards, from which may be inferred a commerce with the Greeks of Massalia (Marseille), and also by the excavation of a famous pre-Roman sculpture called the 'Tarasque of Noves'. A castrum seems to have been built on the hill overlooking the river fairly early, and this was rebuilt and strengthened by the erection of a keep at the beginning of the 14C by Pope John XXII, who, as Bis-

hop of Avignon, owned the town. However, the whole site was razed in 1611/12 on the orders of the Duke of Guise, though a considerable part of the town wall (which had also been rebuilt in the 14C to hold off the 'Grandes Compagnies'), including two square gate-towers, did survive.

Saint-Baudile: This is a beautiful old church dating from the second half of the 12C. The outside staircase which leads up to the tower was added in the 15C. The staircase by the nave leads to a sort of parapet walk in the walls, which allowed sentries to be posted between the buttresses in times of danger. The W. and N. sides of this Romanesque church were unfortunately almost completely built over in the years which followed. The *interior* originally consisted of a single aisle of four bays, to which in the 15C two side-aisles were added, giving it a broad, cavernous appearance; it is as dark as most churches in Provence.

Noves, Saint-Baudile 1 Nave dating from the second half of the 12C **2** Bay beneath octagonal dome **3** 15C Gothic side aisles

Noves, Saint-Baudile

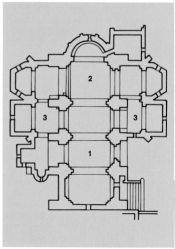

Environs: Bonpas (on the other side of the river): Until the bridge was built in 1166, this was known as 'malus passus' because of the difficult crossing of the Durance at this point; but after that, its name was changed to 'Bonpas', and the bridge was entrusted to a brotherhood for protection. This brotherhood was dissolved by the Carthusians in 1320. All that has been preserved of the Carthusian monastery, the *Chartreuse de Bonpas*, are a beautiful little Romanesque chapel dating from the beginning of the 13C with a crypt which has been carved out of the rock, and a residential building dating from the 17C. The remains of the medieval *fortifications* are also most interesting.

Caumont-sur-Durance (4.5 km. NE): Romanesque *chapel* dating from the 11C with a crypt carved out of the rock. Remains of the village *fortifications*.

Châteaurenard (4.5 km. W.): This small old town is today, with Cavaillon, the largest centre in Provence for the export of early fruit and vege-tables; it dispatches several trainloads daily of cauliflowers, tomatoes, lettuces, apples, plums, and peaches to northern France, Belgium, and Germany. There are still some most impressive ruins of the once mighty *castle* of the Counts of Provence (14&15C) on the hill above the town, despite the fact that two of the original four massive, rectangular towers were destroyed in the Revolution.

Orgon (15 km. SE): Small market town wedged between two hills. It has a Gothic *church* dating from 1325 which has a single aisle (the side-chapels were added in the 17C), remains of the old *fortified wall*, including a 14C *gate*, and a *Renaissance house*. During his journey to exile in Elba, Napoleon is said to have been pulled out of his coach by the inhabitants of this place and forced to watch them as they burnt his effigy. From the hill to the S., on which the ruins of a medieval castle can still be seen, there is an overwhelming view over the Alpilles, Durance and Luberon.

Bonpas (Noves), Chartreuse de Bonpas

Bonpas (Noves), Chartreuse de Bonpas

Ollioules
83 Var   p.258☐E 8

The coast is so densely populated in these parts that Ollioules is virtually a suburb of Toulon. On the hill to the N. are the remains of the Oppidum de la Courtine.

Church: This was built in Provençal Romanesque style and has a single aisle. Its furnishings include a painting by Bonnegrâce (the martyrdom of St.Lawrence). The door leaves of the portal are 18C.

Also worth seeing: A castle was built here by the Vicomtes de Marseille in the 13C but it has since been destroyed. Some old *arcaded houses* can be seen in the town centre.

Environs: Bandol (10 km. W.): The *church* contains several sculptures (17&18C).
Évenos (3 km. N.): The old town is dominated by the ruins of a *castle* (10&11C) and by the *Fort de Pipaudon*.
La Cadière-d'Azur (16 km. NW): The *church* dates from the 16C. The two *Penitents' chapels* contain 18C liturgical objects.
Le Beausset (9 km. NW): The Romanesque chapel of *Notre-Dame de Beauvoir* contains a collection of ex-votos which is worth seeing.

L'Ile de Bendor (this side of Bandol): The *Musée Universel des Vins et Spiritueux* has a collection of wine bottles from 52 countries.
Saint-Cyr-sur-Mer (16 km. W.): On the other side of the railway track can be seen the simple *Château des Beaumelles* (17&18C).
Sanary-sur-Mer (6 km. SW): There is a 75 ft. medieval *tower* on the quay. A 17C *chapel* stands on a spur of rock.

Oppède-le-Vieux
84 Vaucluse   p.256☐C 6

This was abandoned by its inhabitants at the beginning of this century for the more fertile hamlet of Poulivets on the plain; and, once left to itself, the beautiful old village began to fall into decay. The *castle ruins* on the steep cliffs which dominate the town and its church (which was rebuilt in the 16C) still remind us of its former splendour. The castle was originally ceded to the Pope by Raymond VI of Toulouse, who built it. Subsequently, it passed into the hands of the lords of Les Baux, and later still came into the ownership of the Meynier family, raised by the Pope to the status of barons, who gave the village a tragic notoriety in the 16C.

Environs: Lacoste (10.5 km. E.): This is a small mountain village surrounded by stone quarries. It has a pretty belfry dating from 1620. The *castle*, whose massive ruins still look down on the village, was the home of the notorious Marquis de Sade (1740–1814) who lived here, entangled in every kind of dispute with neighbouring families and with the organs of justice, from 1771 until his flight and again from 1774 until his arrest in 1778.
Ménerbes (4.5 km. E.): It was in this old fortified town that the Calvinists withstood the Catholic troops from

Orange, Arc de Triomphe

1573–9. An old secret passage, running to the N. from a vault near the town hall (which has a fine wrought-iron belfry) still survives. It is also worth seeing the 14C *church* and the *castle*, which was rebuilt in the 16C. There are *dolmens* beneath the village.

Mérindol (27.5 km. SE): This small village, though unimportant in itself, has become part of French history thanks to the 'Arrêt de Mérindol'. This was an edict by the Parliament of Aix which decreed that the Vaudois villages should be destroyed and the members of the sect burnt to death. Although its implementation was at once suspended by Francis I, it was seen by the Baron of Oppède-le-Vieux as a means of enlarging his property, and in 1545 he had a number of villages, including Mérindol, destroyed and their inhabitants massacred.

Orange
84 Vaucluse   p.256☐B 4

The Romans founded *Colonia Julia Firma Secundanorum Arausio* in 36 BC at the foot of the hill of Saint-Eutrope, which itself had been inhabited in Celtic times. Its fate was broadly similar to that of the other large towns in Provence, for it prospered under the Romans, was converted early to Christianity, became a bishopric in the 4C, and then was plundered and devastated by barbarians, being destroyed by the Visigoths in 412. But Orange did have a particular history thereafter, which began when it was made a county by a certain Guillaume au Court, (also called Courb Nez on account of his short or crooked nose), a legendary figure who is said to have been the nephew of Charlemagne and was made famous by a Chanson de Geste. The county later became a principality and passed through the hands of various noble houses to Holland and then England, whose king bequeathed it to the King of Prussia in 1702. It was he who ceded it officially to the King of France in 1713. This explains how it came to be destroyed, and its walls razed, by a French King (Louis XIV) in 1673, after the Dutch War. It also suffered greatly from having been a stronghold of the Reformation.

Arc de Triomphe (on the N7, the 2,000 year old Via Agrippa, in the N. part of the town): Though known as a triumphal arch, this might more correctly be termed a monument to the foundation of the town, for triumphal processions were permitted only in Rome. It has finally been dated, after long debate, to the years 26–1 BC. It was converted by Raymond des Baux into a castle with a crenellated tower and glacis, and only restored to its original form in the 18–20C. Despite this period of misuse, it is today the best preserved Roman arch-

way in the whole of France. Overall it is 27 ft. 7 in. deep, 58 ft. 5 in. high, 64 ft. 2 in. wide, and comprises three arched gateways, each of different size and all with richly decorated coffered ceilings, which lead into the Via Agrippa and the town itself. Each of the four sides has four fluted Corinthian half-columns, which give unity to the whole. There is nonetheless a difference, in that the half-columns on the two narrow sides are supported by a continuous base course, whereas those on the long sides stand separately, each on its own high pedestal. The architrave runs uninterrupted around the whole structure. Above it is a frieze of figures, whose central part incorporates the pediment, and above that there is another frieze. The wide central block of this upper frieze depicts the tumultuous scene of a cavalry battle, while the two side sections of the lower frieze depict parts of ships and their equipment, giving the impression that they have been assembled as booty, thus symbolizing, perhaps, Rome's mastery of the sea. In exactly the same way, the helmets, shields, swords, lances,

Orange, Arc de Triomphe, details

saddles, and harnesses, representing Celtic weaponry, which are depicted on the parts of the walls above the low side arches, are meant to celebrate Rome's supremacy over the Gauls.

Ancient theatre: This is one of the biggest and best preserved theatres in the Roman world, even though it was used for a time as a fort and then as a stone-quarry, like the one at Arles. Its *outer façade*, which is 340 ft. long and 125 ft. high, was described by Louis XIV as 'the most beautiful wall in my kingdom', and the impression which it makes today is as great as ever.

The *cavea*, which is a semicircle 338 ft. in diameter, has been partly cut into the hill, and comprises concentric terraced rows of seats, supported by cross-walls and intersected by vaulted passages, divided by walkways into sections of 20, 9 and 5 rows of seats. The three tiers of the orchestra had marble seats for guests of honour, senators, and other persons of high rank. Altogether, the theatre could hold 10,000 people. Access was provided by radial stairways. The topmost tier broadened out into a sort of platform for a colonnade.

The *stage* (42 ft. 7 in. × 200 ft.) was separated from the auditorium by a wall decorated with columns and pilasters and enclosed on the other three sides by the *scenae frons*. This wall, which survives to its full height, was once faced with marble. The section of it behind the stage was decorated like a façade, with portals, niches containing figures, and arches flanked by columns, and was doubtless quite magnificent in Roman times. The statue in the large niche above the tall central portal has been assiduously reassembled from fragments and probably represents the Emperor Augustus. The stage was once covered with a gently sloping wooden roof, and the auditorium too could be protected from the heat and rain, at least in part, by numerous small triangular awnings. The technical equipment itself left nothing to be desired. For instance, the set could be curtained off with the help of machines beneath the stage (the trench into which the curtain was lowered is some 2 ft. 4 in. wide and

can still be seen behind the wall between the stage and auditorium).

Forum, Gymnasium, or Circus: The function and purpose of this second large semicircle, next to the theatre, have always been disputed. Even today it cannot conclusively be proved whether this formed part of the gymnasium, the forum, or the circus. All we know for certain is that its walls extended for a good 220 yards the other side of what is now the Rue du Pontillac towards the Arc de Triomphe. (There are still some remains of the W. wall which are up to 52 ft. high). The central building in the semicircle could have been the foundation wall of a theatre which was later abandoned when the main theatre was constructed (this theory is based on the various foundations which have been discovered here). However, the more probable interpretation is that what we see here are the fragments of the podium of a temple, which the traditions of Roman town planning would have placed in a straight line with a second temple and the town's capitol. Now,

archaeologists have indeed discovered the remains of a second temple half-way up the hill of Saint-Eutrope, in the S. part of the town, and, on its summit, traces of three temples standing parallel to each other and probablyk dedicated to the Capitoline deities, Jupiter, Juno, and Minerva, which are thus reminiscent of the Capitol in Rome. However, the construction here by William the Silent, Prince of Orange and Count of Nassau, of a fort (later destroyed by Louis XIV) which incorporated the theatre has rendered any archaeological investigation very difficult.

Musée Municipal (opposite the forum on the Rue du Pontillac): This is a good place to conclude a visit to the Roman town. The museum has three sections. The first is the *Musée Lapidaire*, which contains sarcophagi, fragments of friezes, etc., and the extremely interesting fragments of the Roman land register for Arausio, which was carved on a marble tablet and shows the plan for the settlement of plots, affording an insight into Rome's colonial policy. The other two

Orange, Arc de Triomphe, detail

sections are the *Musée du Vieil Orange* and the *Section de Peinture*.

Former cathedral of Notre-Dame: This dates from the 12C and was originally Romanesque, but it was severely damaged in the Wars of Religion and has now largely lost its medieval appearance. Only the transept, which supports a dome borne by squinches above the crossing, and the apse have survived from the original Romanesque structure; the nave, which has a tunnel vault, and the side-chapels date from the 16C. Finally, to crown it all, walls were put up in the 19C to separate the arms of the transept and the apse from the crossing.

Environs: Caderousse (6 km. SW): This is an unusual village which used to be under permanent threat from the river Rhône, until its inhabitants built a dyke around it. During times of flood, the two gates in the dyke were closed and any cracks were plugged with manure. The Romanesque *church* has a beautiful late Gothic chapel dating from the 16C in the best Flamboyant style.

Orange, ancient theatre, the Emperor Augustus

Orange, Arc de Triomphe, detail

Camaret-sur-Aigues (6 km. NE): Two fortified medieval *town gates*—the *Porte de l'Horloge*, which was restored and fitted with a wrought-iron belfry in 1750, is outstanding. It is flanked by two round towers.

Châteauneuf-du-Pape: (16.5 km. S.): Famous for its strong, full-bodied red wines. Its *castle*, the Châteauneuf, today only a ruin, was used in the 14C as the summer residence of the Avignon Popes.

Courthézon (9 km. SE): This is a large market town which became well known because of the 'Cours d'Amour' which the troubadour Raimbaud d'Orange held in his castle here.

Saint-Cécile-les-Vignes (18 km. NE): Well-known wine-growing district. A Calvinist assembly was held here in 1563.

Sérignan-du-Comtat (10 km. NE): Ruins of the *castle* of Diane de Poitiers, destroyed by the Huguenots in the 16C. The famous French entomologist J.H. Fabre lived here from 1879 until 1915; there is a small *museum* in his old house, L'Harmas.

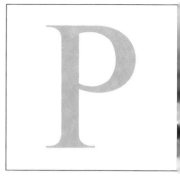

Pernes-les-Fontaines
84 Vaucluse   p.256□C 5

Capital of the Comtat from 968 to 1320, this now rather insignificant country town owes its name to its 33 fountains.

Parish church of Notre-Dame: This was not included within the town during the building and rebuilding of the town walls in the 14&16C

Orange, ancient theatre

but it does date back to the 12C, and the apse, a remnant from an earlier building, actually dates from the 11C. A particularly interesting feature of this heavy, massive-looking building is the masterly use of antique elements, as in the Romanesque S. porch, in the extremely carefully executed regular masonry and in the beautiful *carved decoration* (leaves, acanthus, rosettes).

Château: Only the late medieval *keep* remains from the 11–13C castle of the Counts of Toulouse. Since the construction of the town clock in 1486 it has served as the *Tour de l'Horloge* and in 1765 a wrought-iron belfry was added.

Fortifications: Of the old system all that survive are remnants of the ramparts with a parapet walk (14C) and all three town gates: the beautiful *Porte Notre-Dame*, flanked by two powerful semicircular towers with embrasures for small cannon and machicolations (1548) in the NE, the *Porte Saint-Gilles* (14C) in the SE and the *Porte Villeneuve*, which is also flanked by two round, machicolated towers (1550).

Hôtel de Ville (Rue Brancas): The town hall is housed in the former town palace of the Dukes of Brancas, a stylish, classical building of the 17C with a pretty inner court and various wall paintings.

Tour Ferrande (Rue Gambetta): Free-standing, square residential tower from the start of the 13C, the sole remnant of the old hospice of the Knights of St.John, containing beautiful *wall paintings* dating from 1275 on the 2nd and 3rd storeys, which deal equally with religious and secular themes.

Also worth seeing: *Hôtel d'Anselm* (near the Hôtel de Ville) with a charming late Gothic façade; and many elegant fountains, such as the *Fontaine du Gigot* (Rue Gambetta) and the *Fontaine du Cormoran* (by the Porte Notre-Dame), many of which date from the 18C.

Pernes-les-Fontaines, castle, Tour de l'Horloge

Puget-Théniers

06 Alpes-Maritimes   p.258☐H 5

Puget-Théniers stands at the mouth of the Roudoule gorge, at the point where the river joins the Var. In the heart of the Old Town there are old houses and a gate from the medieval town walls. The town is dominated by a height, upon which stand the ruins of the *Château des Grimaldi.*

Church (Old Town): The early-13C Romanesque church was altered in the 17C. It contains 18C wooden carvings depicting the Crucifixion, Burial and Resurrection of Christ. A beautiful altarpiece from 1525 is striking with its rich but well-matched colours.

Also worth seeing: *Monument,* built by Maillol and symbolically entitled 'L'Action enchaînée', to the revolutionary Louis-Auguste Blanqui (1805–81), who was born in Puget-Théniers.

Environs: Aiglun (28 km. S.): A small village set in beautiful countryside amidst olive groves overlooking the Cheiron, with the church of *Saint-Raphaël,* which contains a few interesting sculptures.
Ascros (17 km. SE): This little village provides a panoramic view over the valleys of the Var and the Esteron. The ruins of the *Château des Grimaldi* stand out. Just outside the village is the chapel of *Sainte Baume.*
Briançonnet (33 km. SW): The façade and bell tower of the beautiful Romanesque *church* were recently rebuilt. Inside the church, as an altarpiece, is a miraculous image of the Virgin Mary (1513) attributed to L.Bréa.
Cuebris (29 km. SE): The settlers of Cuebris founded their village in a gully. There is a *fountain* of 1841 in a small square. The *church* was fortified as a means of defence. On a rocky height above the village stands a medieval *castle.*
Daluis (21.5 km. NW): This village stands on a 2,650 ft. high spur with the ruins of an old *castle.* From the village a footpath (50 minutes) leads

Puget-Théniers, panorama

to the *Grotte du Chat*, the largest cave in the Alpes-Maritimes region. The dried-up bed of a subterranean river extends a total of 790 yards.

Gars (32 km. SW): This little village lies in desolate countryside at the foot of the mountain chain of the same name. In the graveyard of the Romanesque *church* there are Roman inscriptions.

La Croix-sur-Roudoule (6.5 km. NW): The church of this village, which lies in a ravine-scored area, has an altarpiece by F.Bréa, preserved in fragments, with images of Sts.Catherine, Michael and John the Baptist.

Lieuche (18.5 km. NE): The *church* contains an interesting altarpiece of 1479. The Annunciation is thought to be by L.Bréa.

La Penne (10 km. SE): This settlement dominating the Chanan valley is commanded by the *church* and a *tower*.

Roquesteron (25.5 km. SE): This little town has the air of a small regional capital. In 1388 the town, which straddles both banks of the Esteron, was divided into two and from then on the river formed the border between Provence and Savoy. The Treaty of Turin (1760) reaffirmed this division and the two towns continued to exist side by side. The older and smaller *Roquesteron-Grasse* lies on the right bank in the shelter of a crag, upon which stands a small fortified church from the 12C. There are still some remnants of the medieval *rampart*.

The settlement on the left bank of the Esteron, *Roquesteron-Puget*, did not flourish until the 18C, when it grew into the larger of the two towns with its own *church*, Saint-Arige (1816). 1.5 km. W. of Roquesteron stands the chapel of *Notre-Dame d'Entrevignes*, built in the late 12C, which was painted throughout in 1536. The frescos depict scenes from the Life of the Virgin Mary.

Sigale (20 km. S.): The Garcia peak towers over the Riolon and Esteron valleys. Gothic houses and two fortified *gates* (14&15C) round off the medieval appearance of the town. A *fountain* dates from 1583. Iron arches surmount the more recently built *tower*.

Touët-sur-Var (10 km. E.): This town lies at the foot of a near-vertical limestone cliff. A maze of little streets and covered galleries link the terraced houses. The *church* was built above a mountain stream, which can be seen through a trap-door inside the church.

Toudon (28.5 km. SE): Todon was partly destroyed by landslides in 1619 and 1644. The little chapel of *Saint-Jean*, built in 1032, was thoroughly restored in 1960. The wall paintings inside are the work of L.Depagne.

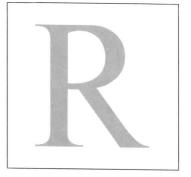

Riez

04 Alpes-de-Haute-Provence   p.258☐F 6

Sited at the confluence of the Auvestre and the Colostre, Riez was already settled in antiquity and was probably the principal seat of the Albici. The Romans founded the colony of *Julia Augusta Apollinaris Reiorum* here—it was known as Reia Apollinaris for short.

From the 5C up until 1790 Riez was the seat of a bishop, making it one of the earliest dioceses in Gaul. A council was held here under Archbishop Hilarius of Arles in 439 and the first cathedral appears to have been built under Bishop Maxime (433–52). The height, to which the town was moved in the Middle Ages for security reasons, was also named after him (Saint-Maxime). A new cathedral was built on this height. From the 13C, by which time the population had already returned to the river meadow, the church of Notre-Dame de la Sed (next to the baptistery) was used as parish church and referred to as such in documents of 1274. A new cathedral in the valley was not mentioned in documents until the 16C.

After 1354 the valley settlement was enclosed by walls, the towers of which, however, were not completed until 1424, by which time the town's heyday had already passed, although it remained a bishop's seat. The population steadily declined, the town on the height was destroyed and the chapel of Saint-Maxime (nave completely rebuilt in the 19C) is all that remains of the cathedral there.

Roman columns (on the road to Allemagne-en-Provence, on the right bank of the Colostre): The group of 4 Corinthian columns (monoliths) are now considered to be the remains of an ancient temple (pantheon), whose front faced S. Although the foundations and the steps to the pronaos have been partly excavated, the exact proportions of the temple can not be determined. The columns themselves are 19 ft. 4 in. high and are made of grey granite with white marble bases and architraves. The Corinthian capitals and the architrave with its reliefs can be dated to the 1C, but to whom the temple was dedicated cannot be ascertained.

Baptistery (on the right along the road to Allemagne-en-Provence): The smallest early Christian baptistery in Provence (30 ft. 4 in. × 27 ft. 7 in.), it is also one of the earliest Christian religious buildings in France (late 4/early 5C).

The almost square exterior proves to be octagonal inside with side niches (marked similarity with the baptistery in Fréjus). The walls are of small rubble stone, but are strengthened at the corners with ashlars, which also

Riez, ramparts and clock-tower

surround the portal and the round-arched windows. The building is surmounted by a more recent, octagonal drum with a tent roof. There used to be a lantern supported by columns. Eight free-standing columns of antique origin (39 ft. high) mark out the inner octagon, in the middle of which stands an octagonal font. The space between the columns and side walls forms an ambulatory. In early Christian times there was also a 13 ft. wide ambulatory around the building. The grey-blue granite shafts of the columns have Corinthian capitals and twisted slabs. Vaulting these is a dome, rebuilt in the 12C, the ribs of which give it the appearance of a domical vault and it is relieved by the somewhat flattened quarter barrels of the ambulatory vaulting.

A door in a screen leads to a small *excavation museum*, where early Christian sculptural and architectural fragments, tomb stele, mosaic remains etc. are exhibited.

In front of the chapel one can see the excavated remains of an early Christian *church* (5C). Built on the foundations of a Roman temple, the building (apse discernible) was destroyed in the 15C.

Also worth seeing: On the main street of the old town there are still a few old houses to be seen: *Hôtel de Mazan* (No. 12), with a beautiful flight of steps; interesting *Renaissance house* (No. 27) from 1598. The Grand-d'Rue starts at the *Porte Ayguière* (13&14C), in front of which stands a *fountain* with an antique column. The street ends in the W. at the *Porte Saint-Sols* (14C). To the right of this are remains of the old walls and the *clock tower*. Also near the gate stands the modern parish *church*, which incorporates Gothic elements from the preceding building; bell tower (16&17C). On the height of Saint-Maxime stands a small *chapel*, which was rebuilt in 1857. Six antique Corinthian columns form an ambulatory in the Romanesque apse. As was customary in Provence, a building was added on to the chapel (to the S.), which provided shelter for pilgrims.

Environs: Aiguines (15 km. SE): The large square *château*, flanked by

Riez, Rue des Quatre Coins, portal

corner turrets, has a glazed tile roof. Also of interest are the chapel of *Saint-Pierre* and, opposite the town hall, the 18C *Hôtel des Consuls d'Aiguines*.

Allemagne-en-Provence (8 km. SW): The *castle* was built in austere, sober style by the Castellane family around 1500. Two inner courts are surrounded by a rectangular building with towers. A battlemented 14C keep dominates the castle. A poor restoration was undertaken in the 19C.

Esparron-de-Verdon (*c.* 15 km. SW): Occupying a commanding position above the Verdon, the *château* belonged to the Castellane family from the 13–18C. The most striking feature is the overwhelming, square keep (13C), which is all that remains of the medieval castle. Adjoining this is a residential section. A spiral staircase (possibly 15C) leads into the courtyard.

La Palud-sur-Verdon (35 km. E.): Church of *Notre-Dame de Vauvert* (12C) with a beautiful Romanesque bell tower. The *château* (17&18C) is in a poor state of repair.

Moustiers-Sainte-Marie (15 km. NE): Its position at the entrance of a gorge makes this one of the most interesting villages in France. The houses are built in tiers one above the other in a very confined space; and the streets are steep and narrow. A mountain torrent, the Rioul, and the Maire divide the village in two but the halves are linked by several bridges. The emblem of the village is the *Cadeno* (La Chaîne de l'Étoile), a 745 ft. long chain suspended over the valley (at a height of 500 ft.), in the middle of which hangs a gilded star. According to legend, a certain baron from the Blacas family donated the chain of the Virgin Mary in fulfilment of a vow upon his return from the 7th Crusade (1249). The name of the place is derived from *Castrum Monasterium* (mentioned in 1084). As early as 435 St.Maximus arrived here with a few monks from the island monastery of Lérins, built a chapel to the Virgin Mary and lived in grottoes. The Saracen threat compelled the monks to leave the place, but they returned in 1052 and founded a priory. A settlement grew up, which Raymond Bérenger V, Count of Provence, made an

Moustiers-Sainte-Marie (Riez)

administrative centre for 18 neighbouring communities. The village was then enclosed by a wall (c. 1246) with 3 towers and several gates, but this did not protect it from sieges and pillaging in the 14C. In 1481 Provence was annexed to France, but the village did not receive a governor until 1548. The community enjoyed its greatest period of growth in the 16C, when a monk from Faenza arrived with the secret of faience manufacture. It was on this that Moustiers-Sainte-Marie's fame was based, as the local ware was as good as that of the great French factories. The Viry, Clérissy and Olery were some of the main families of craftsmen. The building of paper mills also increased the town's importance, the population rising to 3,600 in 1780. In 1874, however, faience production came to an end, until Marcel Provence resuscitated it in 1926. At that time the *Musée Historique de la Fayence* was founded (fine pieces from local workshops, 17&18C).

The *parish church* (on the right bank) with its 12C Lombard Romanesque bell tower dominates the whole vicinity. A Gothic choir (started between 1336 and 1361) with three aisles is built on to the single-aisled Romanesque nave; straight-ended, two side apses. The tower (S. side of the nave) is built of light tufa stone on an inclined base wall and has a lower storey and three recessed storeys with round arcades. Inside, the five bays of the nave have a pointed half barrel vault supported by semicircular blind arcades on the side walls. The last two bays were later extended to form a chapel. The blind arcades continue in the choir (simple, untraceried windows), creating a sort of ambulatory around the altar. The interior furnishing includes a processional cross (12C), a carved wooden Christ (14C), the painting by a Provençal master (in the 'Poor Souls' chapel, 1482) depicting the poor souls in purgatory with Moustiers-Sainte-Marie in the background, which makes the painting particularly interesting. The 18C choir stalls have amusing, carved misericords.

The present *Hôtel de Ville* is housed in the former Servite monastery. This was built of stones from the old town wall in 1512, and converted into a house in 1743, when panelling was installed.

Steps hewn out of the rock lead up to a crag above the village, upon which stands the chapel of *Notre-Dame de Beauvoir*. The preceding building probably dates from the time of the arrival of the first monks. The two W. bays are Romanesque, while the choir and the E. bays are of a later date (15C) and both broader and taller, although the five-sided apse is lower and narrower. The N. wall abuts the rock face and the strong walls give the chapel the appearance rather of a fortress. The beautiful, carved door with Renaissance ornaments in the panels is set in an open porch. Above the W. bay is a small square tower with a pavilion roof. The interior is vaulted partly by a barrel vault and partly by a rib vault, over the newer section. A high altar (Italian baroque; 17C) and

Riez, Porte Saint-Sols

two large faience from Moustiers-Sainte-Marie (18C) adorn the interior. Above the chapel stands the *Grotte-Chapelle de la Madeleine*, which offers a beautiful view over the valley. Behind the graveyard is the chapel of *Sainte-Anne*.

Puimoisson (6 km. N.): Old Hospitallers foundation in the middle of lavender fields with a 15C church and the old chapel of *Saint-Apollinaire* (mid-13C).

Saint-André-du-Désert (20 km. NE): 13C *monastery ruins*.

Saint-Laurent-du-Verdon (16 km. S.): 17C *mansion*.

Saint-Martin-de-Brômes (14 km. SW): Small Romanesque *church* with beautiful tower (14C).

Saignon
84 Vaucluse   p.256☐D 5

This beautiful old village, enveloped in the fragrance of the surrounding fields of lavender and perched on its rock secure from all attack, commands a view over the neighbouring countryside as far as Apt and the Calavon valley. Only some ruins, which seem to grow protectively out of the rock, are left of the old *castle*.

Church: The original Romanesque church dating from the end of the 12C was rebuilt and had chapels added to

it in the 17C. At the same time, the original tunnel vaulting was replaced by a groined vault, so that the windows of the nave could be opened. This more or less destroyed the church's Romanesque character, which prior to that had been clearly evident. Its appearance today is a mixture of the baroque and late Gothic, as well as the Romanesque.

Abbaye Saint-Eusèbe: Only the church has survived from the former Benedictine abbey of Saint-Eusèbe a few hundred yards to the E. of Saignon. The latter was founded, or perhaps rebuilt, in 1004, and by the end of the 12C had become one of the richest abbeys in Provence, surpassed only by those of Saint-Victor in Marseille, Montmajour, and Saint-André (Villeneuve). For reasons that we do not know, it was nonetheless abandoned by its monks in 1431 and then made a commendam in 1433. During the Revolution it was seized as national property, after which it was sold off to various private individuals.

Whether the beautiful old *church* is the same one that was consecrated by Pope Urban II in 1096, remains unclear. Today it is used for agricultural purposes and, since it is shared by a number of owners, it has a wall separating the nave from the choir and transept.

Environs: Castellet (7.5 km. SE): Small hamlet containing a beautiful 13C *Romanesque house*.

Plateau des Claparèdes (W.): The site of numerous *bories*, stone huts dating from the Stone Age, and similar structures known as *clapiers*, which have lent their name to the plateau.

Saint-Andiol
13 Bouches-du-Rhône   p.256☐C 6

This is a small, peaceful town whose

Saignon, panorama

populace grows fruit and vegetables and used, in earlier times when danger threatened, to take refuge in the church. The town also contains a Romanesque *graveyard chapel* and a *château* dating from 1642.

Church: This has a single, three-bayed aisle and dates from the 12C. During the 14C, when the Charles V's hordes of marauding mercenaries, known as the 'Grandes Compagnies', were on the loose, it was fortified, on the lines of Les Saintes-Maries-la-Mer; and, indeed, it bears more resemblance to a fort than to a church.

Saint-Blaise
13 Bouches-du-Rhône   p.256☐C 7

On this small, steep-sided, easily defended plateau between the Etang de Berre and the Etang de Lavalduc,

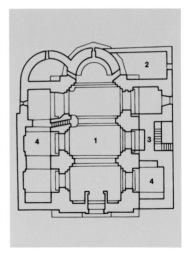

Saint-Andiol, church 1 Romanesque nave with apse directly adjoining (12C) **2** Sacristy (1576) **3** Tower and E. chapel (1752) **4** 19C chapels

archaeologists have excavated 8 separate layers relating to different periods of settlement, from the Neolithic until the Middle Ages. It is extremely interesting that, even before the Phocaeans arrived and colonized the South of France, this town, then known as *Mastramella*, enjoyed a flourishing trade, via Etruria, with Greece and Asia Minor—indeed the Rhône was named after the inhabitants of Rhodes. However, following the foundation of Massalia (Marseille) by the Phocaeans around 600 BC, it became more and more dependent on the new Greek colony, apparently because it functioned as a staging post in Marseille's trade with the Rhône valley. This dependence, however, was not wholly to its disadvantage, for the economic prosperity which Marseille attained in the 4C BC also touched Mastramella. The town recovered from its occupation by the Gauls, of which we are still reminded by the stele and especially by the famous cult columns which contained holes to receive severed heads. It was, however, dealt a heavy blow by Marius' construction in 104 BC of the Fosses Mariennes, which offered a faster route from Marseille to the Rhône valley, and again by the foundation of the town of Fos two years later.

Mastramella's decline was sealed by the Roman conquest of Marseille in 49 BC. Finally, it was itself conquered and destroyed by the Romans. For centuries it lay desolate and it was only when the barbarian invasions began in the early 4C that the people were forced to remember the old strategic sites, and the ruins came back to life. The town was now called *Ugium*, and a new town wall was built; but in 874 the barbarians reduced it to ashes, together with most of the houses. It was again half abandoned and continued to stagnate until 1231, when the Archbishop of Arles built another wall around it. By now it occupied only a quarter of the area of the ancient town and was known henceforth as *Castelveyre*. Even now, however, the new walls could not withstand the onslaught of its enemies, and in 1390 it was once again plundered and once more abandoned, this time for good.

Fos-sur-Mer (Saint-Blaise), ruined castle

There are monuments to visit which represent these various periods of settlement, some of them very well preserved. They include the fine *Hellenistic ramparts* (beginning of the 3C BC), the Christian necropolis, which contains many *rock tombs*, and the *heap of ashes* found in a rectangular tower together with vessels dating from the 7&6C BC, evidently the remnants of some ritual. There is also a small *museum* which displays the earthenware objects discovered in the various strata of the excavations. But what is notably impressive is the *Chapelle Sainte-Blaise*, a small Romanesque building dating from the 12C which is set amongst medieval graves. Its façade was restored on the occasion of the construction of the nearby hermitage in 1608. The chapel was built on the site of an earlier church dating from the 11C.

Environs: Castellan (9.5 km. N.): Old Celto-Ligurian oppidum which acquired the name of *Astromela* when it became a colony of Massalia.
Fos-sur-Mer (16 km. SW): Named after the Fosses Mariennes, the canal dug by Marius in 104 BC so that ships might avoid the spring tide of the Rhône.
Medieval survivals include the still significant remains of the ramparts as well as the ruins of a 14C *castle*, a small, simple Romanesque *church* built in the 11C, and a Romanesque *chapel* near the old graveyard. Today, the construction of the *Europort* means that Fos is in the process of being rapidly developed.
Istres (9 km. N.): Apart from the town centre, which contains a *town gate* dating from 1652, the concentration of industry (foodstuffs, chemicals and, above all, aircraft construction) gives the town a very modern look. The *Musée du Vieil-Istre*, which is housed in the 17C hôtel on the Rue Portail Neuf, is interesting and displays archaeological finds from the district.
Port-Saint-Louis-du-Rhône (39 km. SW): 7 km. from the mouth of the Rhône, this town developed around the tower of Saint-Louis, which the people of Marseille built in 1737 in order to keep watch on the river.

Fos-sur-Mer (Saint-Blaise), church

Saint-Mitre-les-Remparts (3 km. E.): Set in beautiful surroundings, the village retains sections of the old *fortified wall*.

Saint-Chamas
13 Bouches-du-Rhône   p.256□C 7

This little town stands on a site which has been inhabited since remote antiquity. On the hill where it is situated, and which divides it in two, the caves which once housed prehistoric man can still be seen. The town itself retains sections of the old *town wall* and a *fortified gate* dating from the 15C.

Church: This dates from the 17C and has an interesting baroque façade. The altarpiece (1519, the Visitation of the Virgin Mary) is attributed to É.Peson of Marseille.

Chapelle Notre-Dame de Misericorde: The chapel on the hill was built after the plague of 1720.

Fos-sur-Mer (Saint-Blaise), clock-tower

Environs: Berre-l'Étang (13.5 km. SE): This is an old market town, now greatly altered by the advent of oil refineries (the first appeared in 1931) and of the petrochemical industry. It contains a Romanesque *church* and some beautiful *wooden carvings* dating from the end of the 16C in the *Chapelle Notre-Dame-de-Caderot*.

Constantine (7 km. SE): Remains of a Celto-Ligurian *oppidum* which was still inhabited in early Christian times.

Cornillon Confoux (2 km. NE): Pretty village situated on a hill. Its Romanesque *cemetery chapel* contains three Roman stele embedded in the masonry.

Étang de Berre: This lake covers some 38,000 acres and is 26–30 ft. deep at its deepest point. It is surrounded by low limestone hills, which nonetheless descend abruptly. Salt was extracted here from ancient times. Trade with Marseille flourished, and on both shores there were important trade routes to the Rhône valley. Then came farming and fishing, and finally, in modern times, important industries such as oil refineries, the petrochemical industry, and shipyards.

Miramas (5 km. NW): This originated in 1848 as the railway station for the old village of Miramas-le-Vieux, 3 km. away. Thereafter it developed into a town and now has a population of nearly 16,000.

Miramas-le-Vieux (2 km. NW): This village, which is situated on a rocky plateau, has a medieval *fortified wall* and the ruins of a 13C *castle*.

Pont Flavien (1 km. S.): The bridge, named after Flavius who built it, spans the Touloube with a single arch (70 ft. 2 in. long by 20 ft. 4 in. wide), and at each end there is a triumphal arch 23 ft. high.

Vitrolles (24 km. SE): This old village, dominated by a 17C *chapel*, clings to the rocky plateau of the Vitrolles range and looks down on to the large, modern industrial zone. The *church*, which dates from 1744, contains a 17C figure of the Virgin. Remains of an old *fortified wall* can be made out on the steep crag on which the chapel stands.

Saint-Christol d'Albion
84 Vaucluse   p.256☐D 5

In the 12 years that followed the stationing of strategic missiles on the Plateau d'Albion in 1966, the population of Saint-Christol increased from 283 to 1,687, and it has grown from what was originally a modest little village into a small garrison town.

Church: From the outside, this is a rather modest Romanesque church, built in the 2nd half of the 12C, which has suffered from the slightly unfortunate addition of an aisle at the end of the 17C. But the interior achieves a striking effect with the highly unusual *carved decoration* of the apse, which directly adjoins the three bays of the nave and ends with a half-dome.

Also worth seeing: A *fortified house* dating from the 13C (not far from the church).

Environs: Plateaux de Saint-Christol et d'Albion: This plateau is riddled with *caves*, some up to 1,710 ft. deep, including the *Aven de l'Azé* and the *Aven du Cervi*.

Saint-Étienne-de-Tinée
06 Alpes-Maritimes   p.254☐H 4

This popular resort for winter sports is situated in a beautiful Alpine setting on the right bank of the Tinée.

Church: The beautiful square bell tower, which is a fine example of Romanesque architecture in the Alps, survives from the earlier Romanesque church which once occupied the same site. The choir was rebuilt in late Gothic style in the 16C, and during the 17C the nave was rebuilt afresh. An extensive restoration was carried out in the 19C. The church's high altar dates from 1669.

Saint-Sébastien (at the S. entrance to the town): This two-bayed chapel, which was built in the 15C, owes its importance to its *wall paintings* which, according to the inscription on the N. wall, were executed by J.Canavesio and J.Baleison.

Also worth seeing: The *chapel* of the former Trinitarian monastery contains frescos dating from the 16&17C which represent the Battle of Lepanto (1571), the blessing of Don John of Austria, the Immaculate Conception, and other scenes. The *chapel of Saint-Michel* contains a 16C altarpiece.

Environs: Auron (7 km. SE): This is the largest and most important winter resort in the department of Alpes-Maritimes. The 12C chapel of *Saint-Erige* contains frescos painted in 1451 by an unknown artist, which depict scenes from the lives of Sts.Aurigius, Denis and Mary Magdalene.

Isola (14 km. SE): This village is situated at the confluence of the Tinée and Chastillon rivers. As one enters it, one sees the 12C Romanesque *bell-tower* which is all that remains of the former church of Saint-Pierre. The *parish church* has a beautiful portal and contains painted 17C panels.

Sainte-Anne-de-Demandols (7.5 km. SW): There is a very beautiful, though somewhat dangerous, route up to the *chapel*, which is situated at an altitude of 5,112 ft.

Saint-Dalmas-le-Selvage (7.5 km. NW): This is the highest village in the Alpes-Maritimes and is set amidst sheep pastures. The *church*, which was built in the 17C, contains a fine 16C altar of St.Pancratius (16C).

Saint-Maur (2 km. SE): It is the 16C wall paintings that lend interest to the small tunnel-vaulted *church* dating from the early 16C.

Saint-Gabriel (Chapelle)
13 Bouches-du-Rhône   p.256□B 6

Today, this chapel stands on its own between two quarries, but, before the surrounding marshland was drained, it was the place of worship of what seems to have been a very old community of river boatmen, who provided a connection between the trade routes on all sides. However, the area was drained, they became superfluous and left the village, which subsequently disappeared almost without trace. So it is amid a tangle of wild figs and wind-blown bushes, fanned by the fragrance of wild thyme, that we now come across the impressive *faç*ade of the chapel, which stands on a small terrace. This is unornamented, but nonetheless constructed with the greatest care. Its portal is set in a round arch flanked by half-columns, and is preceded by a sort of porch which is just 4 ft. deep. This is crowned by a triangular gable whose apex forms the end of the nave's roof. Above the round arch of the porch there is a cornice and then an upper, smaller arch (a slightly pointed blind arch) encompassing a beautiful *round window*. This is framed by the symbols of the four Evangelists and decorated at its edge with acanthus leaves, rosettes, and masks.
Within the porch, which is decorated with egg-and-dart moulding, is the *portal*. This is clearly modelled on Roman triumphal arches and is a most successful composition; one is only surprised at the relatively unskilled reliefs on the tympanum and pediment, showing Daniel in the lions' den and the Fall (on the tympanum) and, on the pediment, an Annunciation and Visitation, which is incidentally reminiscent of early Christian arch sarcophagi, and may possibly have been taken from a slightly older building. Apart from these features, both the carved decoration (egg-and-dart moulding, Corinthian capitals and acanthus leaves) and the overall construction of the façade itself show great mastery of the architectural language of antiquity.

Saint-Martin-Vésubie
06 Alpes-Maritimes   p.258□I 5

A wholesome climate has made this town a popular resort for bothô summer and winter sports. At one time, the frontier with Italy was only 3 km. from here, but the treaty of 1947 gave France a part of the mountainous border country (which offers the visitor some lovely, long excursions). The town itself is situated in countryside of overwhelming beauty, at the confluence of two mountain streams which join to form the Vésubie, in the middle of the 'Suisse Niçoise'.

Chapelle des Pénitents Blancs (at the end of the Rue du Docteur-Cagnoli): This was built in the 18C. The façade was decorated with a half-relief by Parini in 1847. The interior contains an 18C processional cross and an interesting carved wooden altarpiece.

Church: This was completed and decorated in 1694. Its furnishings include a carved wooden altar of the rosary (1697) and an altarpiece (in the sacristy) which is attributed to L.Bréa and depicts Sts.Peter, Martin, John, and Petronilla. A silver cross decorated with transparent enamel dates from the 15C. There is a side niche on the right which contains a 14C wooden statue clothed in lace. This is taken to Madone de Fenestre at the beginning of the annual pilgrimage.

Also worth seeing: The *Rue du Docteur-Cagnoli* (formerly Rue Droite)

Chapelle Saint-Gabriel

starts from the Place Félix-Faure, where the Hôtel de Ville stands (there is a water channel running along the middle of the road). By the side of this street there is an arcaded *Gothic house* which once belonged to the Ducs de Gubernatis.

Environs: Belvédère (21 km. SE): This is situated at the edge of a plateau and looks down over the Gordolasque and Vésubie valleys. The *church* dates from 1620–1728 and has a square bell tower. It is beautifully stuccoed inside and contains a late-17C altarpiece.

Berthemont-les-Bains (11 km. SE): This remote village is actually a health resort and contains the well-known Christine de France thermal baths.

La Bollène-Vésubie (14 km. SE): This small village is set among chestnut trees beneath Mt. Vallières. The 13C *church* contains some beautiful paintings.

Lantosque (15 km. SE): This old town extends along the top of a ridge. Its *church* was completed in 1668. The font dates from 1605. The front of the altar is of embossed leather (17C).

La Roche (13.5 km. W.): This hamlet contains a *chapel*, built by the Pénitents Noirs, which has beautiful carved choir stalls and a 17C triptych.

Libaret (10.5 km. S.): Starting point for some lovely excursions into the mountains.

Madone de Fenestre (13 km. NE): Here, at the end of a valley surrounded by mountain peaks, there once stood a temple of Jupiter. In 887 a sanctuary was built by Benedictine monks on the temple's foundations, but this was destroyed by the Saracens in the 10C. The sanctuary was restored by the Templars in the 13C,

Chapelle Saint-Gabriel

but was again destroyed during the Revolution. Today's *chapel* has however been once more restored and is the object of a famous annual pilgrimage (15 August and 8 September).

Rimplas (18 km. W.): This small village is situated in a unique mountain setting and its strong *fortifications* look down on it from a crag. The *parish church* contains three altarpieces dating from the 18C. The *Chapelle de la Madeleine* (1834) offers a beautiful view over the surrounding countryside.

Roquebillière-Nouveau-Village (11 km. SE): The Gothic *church* contains a 16C altarpiece.

Roquebillière-Vieux-Village (9 km. SE): The old village was destroyed in 1564 and again in 1926 by landslides. After that, the houses were built in such a way as to support each other and today the place looks as if its tall houses had been piled on top of each other.

Saint-Dalmas-Valdeblore (11 km. W.): The Romanesque *church*, which was built in the 11C, used at one time to belong to the Benedictine monastery of Borgo in Piedmont (in Italy). At the NW corner of this long building there stands a tall, square bell tower with a stone spire, which displays a simplicity typical of Alpine architecture. The interior has something of the look of a basilica, for its round pillars separate the nave into three aisles, each terminating at the E. end in an apse. The whole of the interior was extensively rebuilt in the 17C and a vault replaced the timber roof; only the half-domes above the apses surviving from the first phase of construction. The crypt is considerably older—it dates from the 9C—and is divided into three aisles by eight pillars; it is roofed by a cross vault. The altarpiece behind the high altar was painted by G.Planeta in 1484; that at the end of the left side-aisle depicts St.Francis receiving the Stigmata and was painted around 1520, possibly by A. de Cella. The apse at the end of the right aisle contains a rosary altar dating from the late 16C. The walls of the side apse have paintings which are worth viewing, and whose conception and colouring date them to around 1400. The half-dome shows Christ enthroned in a mandorla, framed by the symbols of the four Evangelists. The scenes beneath show the beheading of John the Baptist and Salome holding his head on a platter. There are two more scenes whose theme is not quite clear, but they may represent Salome in front of Herod and Herodias and the burial of John the Baptist.

Valdeblore-la-Bolline (15 km. W.): The *church* was built in the 17C. Its Romanesque bell tower (1532) was once part of the earlier church which originally stood on this site. The decorations include a simple triptych dating from 1576, a painting by Van Loo which depicts the Virgin appearing to St.James (1704), and an 18C painting of her Ascension. The chapel of the *Pénitents Blancs* contains two paintings of the Madonna dating from the 16&17C, a picture of Christ (18C), and a painting of the Descent from the Cross which dates from 1635 and is attributed to O.Rocca.

Venanson (4.5 km. S.): This small village situated above the Vésubie valley also offers a lovely panoramic view over the Saint-Martin basin. An inscription on the wall of the choir of the chapel of *Saint-Sébastian* tells us that it was built in 1481, after the populace had prayed for an end to the plague which was ravaging them. It is a small building, whose choir directly adjoins the rock face.

Although the chapel is simple and unremarkable enough on the outside, one is struck, on seeing the interior, by its very unusual character, for the entire surface of all the walls, as well as the semicircular tunnel vault, has been painted—painted, actually, with tempera on dry plaster, so that these are not genuine frescos. The wall paintings are the earliest known work of J.Baleison, and are pure examples of 15C French courtly styles. The wall on the N. side is a still life of tools and utensils, which symbolize God's blessing of man's work. The bottom scene on the S. wall shows personifications, now somewhat faded, of the virtues and vices, and also expounds the theme of good and bad prayer. This clearly depicts the contrast between the monk, sunk in prayer in front of the Cross with lines running from his lips straight to the stigmata of Christ, signifying the sincerity of his prayer, and the man of the world, who has lines running from his mouth to a house, field, and vineyard in a rustic setting, showing that, as he prays, his thoughts are turned to the acquisition of material goods. The rest of this wall is devoted to the legend of St.Sebastian. Following the Italian convention, each scene is separated from the next by a bright line. The major part of the choir wall shows the martyrdom of St.Sebastian, to whose left and right we see Bishop Grat with the head of John the Baptist and St.Roch appearing as a pilgrim and showing his sores from the plague. The space inside the round arch depicts the Crucifixion. The vault shows 12 individual scenes from the life of St.Sebastian which have been drawn from the 'Golden Legend' by Jacobus de Voragine. The story begins on the N. side with Sebastian joining the bodyguard of the Emperor Diocletian. As a Christian officer, he preaches, converts pagans to Christianity, and courageously declares his faith to Diocletian. On the S. side, we see the Emperor ordering Sebastian to be beaten with clubs and thrown into the Cloaca Maxima in Rome. The two final scenes depict Sebastian being buried and commanding the plague in Pavia to end. Baleison's emphasis of detail and use of perspective is everywhere remarkable.

Saint-Maximin-La-Sainte-Baume

83 Var   p.256☐E 7

The area around this town was once occupied by a lake which dried up thousands of years ago; later, the site was settled by the Romans. Today, the church is the focal point around which the houses and the little squares with their fountains cluster. The significance of the town derives from a legend that Mary Magdalene, having done thirty years' penance in a cave in the Sainte-Baume, was brought here by angels after her death and buried. The place, thus sanctified, became a place of pilgrimage, and a Cassianite monastery was built here in the 5C. After the Saracen invasions of the 8C, however, it seems to have fallen into oblivion, from which it was later rescued by the Benedictine monks of Vezelay. In the place where she was said to have been buried, they found an empty sarcophagus, apparently hers, as well as that of St.Maximinus, one of her companions, whose name was adopted for the town (12C). In 1279, Charles II commissioned the building of a church here, and the pilgrims began to pour in. The site was taken over by Dominican monks.

Sainte-Madeleine: This is one of the most beautiful Gothic churches in Provence. It was begun by the architect J.Baudici in 1295, but the work was delayed due to lack of money, and was not completed till the 16C. Three separate phases of construction can thus be distinguished.

The exterior is a blend of Provençal Romanesque and cathedral Gothic. On the W. façade there are three portals and a porch. The interior takes the form of a basilica, with a nave and two aisles, ending in a polygonal apse. Although the choir has no windows, the inside of the church is well lit.

The *furnishings* consist of a profusion of altars and sculptures. Mention must be made of the 22 panels of an *altarpiece of the Passion* by F.Ronzen (1520), which includes the oldest painting of the Palace of the Popes at Avignon. The front of a *rosary altar* (1667) by B.Maunier shows scenes from the life of Mary Magdalene (1635) by J.Béguin. A *cope of St.Louis of Anjou* dating from the first half of the 13C is decorated with 30 scenes from the life of Christ and the Virgin. Beyond the choir, the baroque *high altar* (17C) incorporates sculptures by Lieutaud, and the choir itself comprises the last three, central bays of the nave, divided off by the choir screen of 1691. The grilles of the parclose of the choir are topped by a wooden crucifix (1692) and the backs of the choir stalls have been decorated with 22 medallions by V.Funi. The pulpit (1756) depicts scenes from the life of the Magdalene. Finally, the organ and its case, which were built by the Dominican monk, J.-E. Isnard, in 1773, are rare examples of their kind.

A staircase (17C) in the middle of the church leads down to the rectangular, tunnel-valted *crypt*, a burial chamber dating from the late 4C, which contains the sarcophagi of Mary Magdalene and Sts.Maximinus, Marcellus, and Sidonius. The sarcophagi (4/5C) bear reliefs of Biblical scenes. The four marble slabs dating from the 5/6C have been engraved with curious outlines.

Monastery buildings (N. of the church): The construction of the former Dominican monastery began in 1296. During the work of restoration, the monastery guesthouse was converted and became the town hall. The W. section was completely rebuilt at the same time. The E. wing incorporates the sacristy, chapterhouse, and kitchen. The N. wing contains a refectory, a library, and a monk's chapel. The pointed arches of the walks give the 15C cloister a slightly rough appearance.

Also worth seeing: On the Place de Malherbe there is a *fountain* and obelisk (18C). A 16C *house* with a projecting turret survives on the Rue du Général de Gaulle. The S. side of the Rue Colbert is lined by some beautiful *arcaded houses* dating from the 14C.

Environs: Esparron (19 km. N.): The area is dominated by a large medieval *castle*. On the way out of the village stands the Romanesque *Chapelle du Revest*, whose altarpiece is composed of two inscribed Roman tablets.

La Sainte-Baume (21 km. SW): This owes its considerable religious and cultural importance to the legend of the Magdalene, who is said to have lived in a cave during the years of her penance. The existence of a large number of caves in the Sainte-Baume prompted Jean Cassien, the founder of the monastery of Saint-Victor, to settle a small community of monks here in the 5C to foster her cult. The *cave of Mary Magdalene* (or Sainte-

Saint-Maximin-La-Sainte-Baume, Sainte Madeleine, part of the altarpiece of the Passion

Baume) is situated on a steep slope (2,907 ft. high). Behind the main altar there is a passage to a small terrace where the white marble statue of the Magdalene stands (it was carved by Ch. Fossaty in the 18C). There is a *chapel* on the summit of *Mt.Saint-Pilon*, and another one, the 17C *Chapelle des Parisiens*, to its N. The *Grotte aux Oeufs* (25 minutes on foot) takes its name from the strange appearance of the surface of the walls.

Plan d'Aups (24 km. SW): There is an inscribed Roman tablet in the porch of the small 12C Romanesque *church*.

Rougiers (14 km. S.): The old town around the fortress of Castrum Saint-Jean now stands in ruins. In 1250, the town of Vieux-Rougiers grew up nearby. The chapel of *Notre-Dame du Pays-Haut* contains an altarpiece depicting the life of St.Honoratus.

Saint-Zacharie (17 km. SW): The *church*, originally Romanesque, contains a relic of the Virgin—a shoe——which is venerated.

Tourves (7.5 km. SE): On the way out of the town are the ruins of the *Château de Valbelle*, which was built in 1775 in a style modelled on the architecture of ancient Greece and Rome. An old *chapel* was constructed here on the foundations of a Gallo-Roman building.

Saint-Michel-de-Frigolet

13 Bouches-du-Rhône   p.256☐B 5

The abbey was founded in the 10C by Benedictine monks from Montmajour, then passed into the possession of the Bishop of Avignon in the 12C, and was finally declared national property during the Revolution and sold to the Premonstratensians. The church of Saint-Michel and its cloister, and the chapel of Notre-Dame-du-Bon-Remède all date from the 12C, while the new church (which incorporates the 12C chapel as a N. side-choir) and the abbey buildings were built in the 19C.

Saint-Michel: The old roof and the bell tower have been preserved from the old Romanesque abbey church; the façade is modern.

Interior: As soon as one enters the church, one is struck by the absence of bays, which are customary in the Romanesque architecture of Provence, with the result that the nave appears long and unbroken. This impression is emphasized by the straight lines of the choir; but it is mainly due to the fact that the arches of the vault spring from consoles on the cornice, and are not continuous with the pillars. What is typical of Provence architecture, though, is the presence of blind arcades on the walls of the nave and of the narrow N. aisle. The nave and side aisle are divided by low, semicircular arches. The side aisle has a semicircular tunnel vault, the nave a pointed one, and the choir a groin vault. The paintings in the choir and on the wall at the E. end of the aisle date from the 19C.

Adjacent to the S. side is the *cloister*, whose narrow arches supported by broad pillars seem to look like windows. The sculptures may impress at first glance but are not on a level with the works in Montmajour, Saint-Paul, and Arles on which they have been modelled.

Notre-Dame-du-Bon-Remède: Small Romanesque pilgrimage chapel with an octagonal dome supported by squinches. It was sumptuously furnished with wooden panelling inlaid with pictures by Anne of Austria in

Saint-Maximin-La-Ste-B.,
Ste-Madeleine ▷

gratitude for the birth of a son, the future Louis XIV, in 1638.

New church: This was built in the 19C in neo-Romanesque style and isq basilican in plan, with a nave and two aisles; the façade is sumptuously decorated, and there are towers flanking the choir. The abbey buildings and hostels for the pilgrims are in late Gothic style and are crowned by battlements and numerous turrets.

Saint-Michel-de-Frigolet, Saint-Michel

Saint-Michel-de-Frigolet, new church, St.Michael

Saint-Rémy-de-Provence
13 Bouches-du-Rhône   p.256☐B 6

This was the successor to the ancient city of *Glanum*, whose ruins have now been excavated about 1 km. to the S. The new town was founded in the 3 or 4C, after Glanum had been destroyed. St.Remigius, who died in 535, is reputed to have healed a girl of a fatal illness here, and for this reason the place was named *Villa Sancti Remigii*, its present name being adopted in the Middle Ages.

Excavations have revealed Gallo-Greek burial sites and an early Christian church. Not very much has survived of the medieval monuments.

Collegiate church of Saint-Martin: This large church was built in 1825–7 in classical style. One should note the tower, which was part of the earlier church built on the same site at the instigation of Pope John XXII in 1330, and, inside the church, on either side of the choir, the panels which were originally the wings of a triptych dating from 1529 (the Madonna and a Bishop).

Notre-Dame-de-Pitié: Standing some 200 yards S. of the old town wall (some sections still survive from the 14C), this small late Gothic chapel was built in the 15C. Its side chapels were added in the 17C.

Saint-Michel-de-Frigolet, new church ▷

Hôtel de Ville: The town hall is situated in the town centre and occupies an old monastery building; it has a beautiful façade.

Hôtels (Villas): The Renaissance *Hôtel Mistral de Mondragon* dates from 1550 and stands NW of the Hôtel de Ville; it now houses the *Musée des Alpilles* (a museum of local interest). Another museum, the *Dépôt Archéologique*, occupies the 15&16C *Hôtel de Sade*.

Dépôt Archéologique: A collection worth lingering over, it exhibits the antiquities discovered in Glanum dating from the 3C BC to the 3C AD, including sculptures, altars, grave furnishings, and tools. *Glanum* itself, earlier known as Glanon, was destroyed in the 3C AD, after which it fell into ruin. During the 16C, people began to be pay attention to the Roman monuments which had survived and to be interested in the ancient city. Isolated discoveries of statues, urns, and coins soon led to purposeful excavations. During the 18&19C, the name and location of the

Roman city were identified on the basis of inscriptions and coins. Scientifically conducted excavations were begun in 1921 and have been led since 1942 by the archaeologist Henri Rolland. He has proceeded with the greatest care and brought the excavations, which are still far from complete, to their present point. The work is complicated by the fact that three successive periods have been identified, namely the Celto-Greek period during the 3C BC, then the time of Roman influence around 70 BC, and finally the period after the fall of Marseille in 49 BC and the age of Augustus.

The investigations have shown that Glanum arose at the intersection of two important roads, one leading to Spain and the other to Italy, and was laid out around a spring which had been the site of an early cult of the 'mother goddesses' and the god Glanis. The finds go as far back as the 7C BC but the first proper town of which there is any evidence must have been established by the Celto-Ligurian Salluvii in the 3C BC, and seems to have reached a considerable level of

Saint-Michel-de-Frigolet

cultural development by the 1C BC. Its inhabitants were called Glanici and were influenced by Marseille and by Greek culture.

During the 1C BC the Romans came and put up typically Roman buildings. The town was extensively rebuilt and enlarged during the reign of Augustus, and it was at this time that the monuments were erected which still survive today. 300 years later, Glanum was destroyed, probably by invading Germanic tribes.

Glanum The first thing we see, as we head S. from Saint-Rémy-de-Provence to visit the excavation site of ancient Glanum, is the *Plateau des Antiques*, on which stand the Triumphal Arch and the Mausoleum, both very well preserved Roman monuments which were admired as 'antiquities' as early as the Middle Ages.

Triumphal Arch: This was built around 10 BC, slightly before those in Orange and Carpentras. The lower part has been well preserved. The upper part originally resembled a massive platform, and was eventually made into a gable. The level of the soil is lower today than it was then, so that the buildings must have stood deeper in the ground by as much as one-and-a-half layers of stone. The coffered and richly carved vaulting, and the figures of prisoners on both faces, have preserved their beauty to an amazing degree. The corner stones above the opening of the arch show goddesses of victory.

Mausoleum: The mausoleum (60 ft. high), built by the Romans on Greek lines, dates from the same period as similar monuments in Arles, Alleins, and Saint-Julien-les-Martigues, but differs from them in having been outstandingly well preserved. The square pedestal is richly decorated with a bas-relief showing battle scenes beneath garlands of fruit and theatrical masks. The next tier has a semicircular arch, supported by pilasters, on each face, with fluted Corinthian columns at the corners, the whole having the appearance of a temple. The top of this storey is decorated with a relief frieze of tritons and sea monsters. The

Glanum (Saint-Rémy-de-Provence), triumphal arch

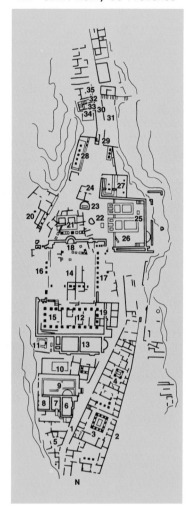

depict Cybele and her companion Atys. Both houses were inhabited from about 200 BC to AD 300 **5** House of Epona. An inscription was found here dedicating the place to the goddess Epona **6-10** Roman baths **6** Caldarium, or hot room **7** Tepidarium, or warm room **8** Frigidarium: the cold room **9** Palaestra (a large courtyard with galleries) **10** Natatio, or swimming pool **11** House in the Greek style with peristyle **12** Basilica dasting from the time of Augustus **13** Probably administrative offices belonging to the basilica **14** Roman forum dating from the same period **15** Pre-Roman temple excavated beneath the basilica **16** Columned hall E. of the forum **17** Columned hall to the W. of the forum **18** The S. wall of the forum incorporates an apse (which probably contained a statue) and two side-doors **19** Pre-Christian House of Sulla, which was excavated beneath the W. parts of the basilica **20** Probably the old theatre **21** Roman square with a paved platform which probably supported a monument **22** Pre-Roman rotunda **23** Roman fountain **24** Pre-Roman building **25** Two temples with altars. These date from about 30 BC and are among the oldest Roman buildings in Gaul **26** Pre-Roman house **27** Pre-Roman assembly building **28** Pre-Roman building **29** Pre-Roman fortified passage to the S. area of the town. It was evidently used as a place of refuge in times of danger **30** Beneath this street there was a covered sewer **31** Roman baths **32** Flight of steps leading down to the spring **33** Deep trapezoid basin (pre-Roman) and spring; probably a cult site **34** Roman temple built by Agrippa in 20 BC at the site of the spring and dedicated to the goddess Valetudo. The inscription 'Valetudini M.Agrippa' still stands on the street **35** Temple of Hercules with six side altars. A statue of the god was excavated here

third and topmost tier is a round tempietto supported by Corinthian columns, above which there is a deep entablature with a floral frieze; the roof is in the form of a scutate cone. The cornice beneath the frieze of tritons bears a funerary inscription which is still clearly legible: SEX. L. M. IVLIEI C. F. PARENTIBVS SVEIS (Sextus, Lucius, and Marcus, sons of Caius, of the family of Julius, in honour of their parents). Inside the tempietto there are two statues of the deceased.

220 yards to the S., behind the Triumphal Arch and the Mausoleum, the extensive excavation site begins (see the plan and key). This area, set amidst hills, pines, and olive trees, is a mass of white ruins and parched grass growing beneath a blazing sun

Glanum (Saint-Rémy-de-Provence), river god ▷

Saint-Rémy-de-Provence, Glanum, excavations: 1 Beneath this street there was a covered sewer **2** Parallel street, also with sewer **3** House in antis built in the Greek style; a fluted pillar with Corinthian capital has survived. Various rooms ran off a central courtyard with cistern which was ringed by columns **4** House of Cybele and Atys. This is a large building with a courtyard surrounded by roofed galleries, rooms to the N., and many rooms to the S. One of the larger rooms, which contained a bench and an altar, was used for worship and was dedicated to the goddess Cybele. Bas-reliefs have been found here which

Glanum (Saint-Rémy-de-Provence)

Glanum, mausoleum

Glanum

and resounding to the evening chorus of cicadas (when it is barely cooler). It is a site that inspires in us dreams of the past, dreams which turn first to the mysterious spring, then the gruesome human skulls which the Celts speared and displayed in specially built niches in the walls as victory trophies, but then to the temples, sculptures, mosaics, and wall paintings, even the furniture, the oil-lamps, vessels and ornaments which have been discovered here. These remains testify, indeed, to a remarkable ancient culture, in which Celtic, Greek and Roman elements alternated and combined to produce a unique blend of styles.

Saint-Paul-de-Mausole: Some 100 yards to the W. of the Triumphal Arch and the Mausoleum is the Monastery of Saint-Paul-de-Mausole (named thus in the Middle Ages after the ancient Mausoleum) which was dissolved during the Revolution and from 1807 to the present day has been used as an asylum. Its most famous patient was the painter Vincent van Gogh, who was treated here from 8 May 1889 to 16 May 1890 and painted 150 pictures during his stay. On the approach to the monastery there is a modern bust of Van Gogh by Zadkine. Virtually nothing is known of the monastery's early history. The first written record of its existence dates from 982. During the early Middle Ages, the monastery church was dedicated to St.Andrew, later to Sts.Andrew and Paul. The monastery itself was originally Benedictine, but was then taken over by the Augustinians in the 11C. During the 12C both monastery and church were renamed simply 'Saint-Paul', and the epithet 'de Mausole' was added. In 1316 Pope John XXII, who was then residing in Avignon, ordered the monastery to be turned into an archdeaconry. It was evidently much respected, but during the 15C it became involved in the turmoil of the Hundred Years' War and lost much its importance, being secularized in 1481. It passed into the hands of the strict Franciscan Order in 1605, and finally became state property during the Revolution. In 1810, when it had been converted into an asylum, nuns

from the Congrégation des Soeurs de Saint-Joseph de Viviers settled here to look after the patients. As one approaches the monastery, one is struck first and foremost by the massive 12C Romanesque *bell tower*, which has a rib vault inside. The church is also 12C and comprises a nave and two aisles (three bays) as well as a transept, a main apse, and two side apses. It was restored in the 19C. The façade dates from the 18C. Chapels were added on to the side aisles at a later stage. On the S. side, the W. chapel dates from around 1500, the one in the middle, beneath the tower, now leads to the cloister, and the E. chapel, which has a domed vault, was built around 1700. The chapels on the N. side are modern.

It is worth visiting the square *cloister*, also built mainly in the 12C, which, though smaller and less sumptuous than those in Arles, Montmajour and Aix, resembles them nonetheless in the way it combines the fragrance of lavender and olives, and the unbelievable brightness of the light—which magically makes the stone seem trans- parent and alive—with a monastic seclusion and tranquillity. The cloisters in Provence are unlike those anywhere else in the world. Saint-Paul's has a heavy tunnel vault, four massive corner pillars, and on each side groups of three arches supported by two pairs of columns. The exception is the E. side, which was the earliest part to be built. Here there are three pillars between which stand two pairs of columns each supporting a two arches and another two pairs of columns supporting a set of four arches. The cloister is entered from the N. side, which was built at the end of the 12C. The columns here have simple capitals decorated with leaves and tendrils. The NE corner pillar is the oldest part of the cloister and may date from the middle of the 12C. Behind the E. walk of the cloister is the still earlier chapterhouse, whose portal has decorated archivolts. The capitals on the E. side are decorated with geometric patterns and leaves, while those on the S. side, which are somewhat older and date from the end of the 12C, are more richly orna-

Saint-Paul-de-Mausole (Saint-Rémy)

Saint-Paul-de-Mausole, cloister

mented and depict water-nymphs, centaurs, and other fabulous creatures. The portal of the refectory behind the W. corner of the S. side of the cloister is also worth viewing. The W. side was built at the end of the 12C, like the S. side, and it has similar capitals; these are decorated with leaves, masks, human figures, and animals, and are reminiscent of the capitals in Arles, Aix, and Montmajour.

Saint-Tropez

83 Var   p.258☐G 8

The ancient Greek settlement of *Athenopolis* was renamed *Heraclea Cacabaria* by the Romans, probably after an oracle and temple to Heracles on this site. The modern name is reputed by legend to derive from a high-ranking officer in Nero's army who was beheaded after making a public conversion to Christianity. His body was buried by a Christian lady called Celerina. He became a saint, and the town was named after him at the beginning of the 4C.

Saint-Tropez was destroyed by the Saracens in 739, and in 888 by the Moors. The conflicts between Louis II and Charles de Duras brought further devastation. The inhabitants then fled, but they were brought back by Jean de Cossa, the Seneschal of Provence, and the town was rebuilt and fortified, with the help of several Genoese families, in such a way as to be able to withstand future attacks. A council of two consuls and twelve councillors was constituted which took charge oft administration. A citadel was built in 1538 and in 1592 it protected the populace from the hostile intentions of the troops of the Duke of Savoy.

Saint-Tropez was still a small fishing village when it was discovered by the painter P.Signac in 1892. From then on, it attracted many artists, and today it has become a fashionable tourist resort with a marina and many shops and cafés.

Tour Daumas (on the harbour):Th-

Saint-Paul-de-Mausole, bust of Van Gogh by O.Zadkine (L.); cloister (R.)

is was built in 880 by William I, Duke of Provence, and was once part of the Château Suffren.

Citadel: This is very well preserved and consists of a 16C fort, which is in the form of a regular hexagon, reinforced by 3 round towers and a wall with bastions (17C).

Church (near the Hôtel de Ville): This was built in 1820 and contains wooden statues dating from the same period, as well as the bust of Saint-Tropez.

Musée de l'Annonciade (Quai de l'Épi): The 17C Chapelle de l'Annonciade was converted in 1955 by the architect L.Suë and now houses the *Musée d'Art Moderne*. This exhibits modern works of art by artists such as Vlaminck, Derain, Rouault, Matisse, Bonnard, Braque, and others.

Also worth seeing: By the side of the abandoned *fishing harbour* (Puncho) there is an old *tower*. In the Rue Gambetta can be seen the *Chapelle de la Miséricorde*, which has a beautiful carved portal (17C). The citadel contains the *maritime museum*, which offers a survey of local maritime history.

Environs: Cavalaire-sur-Mer (18 km. SW): William I built a *watchtower* here. The Dukes of Grimaud fortified the town, which was later destroyed.

Cogolin (9 km. W.): The old town contains a simple Romanesque *church* (11C) which has a square bell tower. Inside there is a triptych by Hurlupin (1540). Only some remains, and an old *gate*, have survived of the fortified wall.

Domaine de Saint-Donat (24 km. NE): The pleasure park contains, amongsth other things, the *Musée de la Musique Mécanique*, which has rare instruments and pieces of apparatus spanning several centuries.

Gassin (10.5 km. SW): This small town is surrounded by a wall. Its Romanesque *church* has a modern cloister (1968).

Grimaud (10 km. W.): The name is derived from the Grimaldi family, which took possession of Grimaud

Saint-Tropez, citadel

Saint-Tropez, citadel

Saint-Tropez, citadel

Saint-Tropez, harbour

after the expulsion of the Saracens. There are the ruins of a medieval *castle* and an 11C Romanesque *church*. The 15C *Chapelle des Pénitents Blancs* contains the relics of St.Theodore.

La Croix-Valmer (12 km. SW): The name derives from a legend that the Emperor Constantine saw a cross of light during his battle here against Maxentius (312), an experience which led to his conversion to Christianity.

La Garde-Freinet (20 km. NW): The *Forteresse de Fraxine* was built by the Saracens on this strategically important site.

Port-Grimaud (6.5 km. W.): This town was built in 1964 in the Gulf of Saint-Tropez by the architect F.Spoerry, who designed it on the model of a medieval town.

Ramatuelle (11.5 km. S.): Originally a Roman settlement, it was occupied by the Saracens for 60 years and in 1056 it passed into the hands of the abbey of Saint-Victor. The backs of the houses form a kind of town wall; within the town there is a square, and narrow, winding alleys. The 17C *church* contains statues of the Madonna and Joseph (16C), and a 17C altar.

Sainte-Maxime (14 km. N.): The old Phoenician settlement of Calidianis was devastated during the Middle Ages by both Saracens and pirates. It was then fortified by the monks of Lérins, who named it after their patron saint, supposedly the daughter of a Duke of Grasse. The *church* was built in 1762; in 1973 it was given a modern ceramic tympanum which had been made in the workshops of Baume. In front of the church stands the square *Tour de Daumes*, which was built by monks.

*Saint-Tropez, church-tower dating
from 1820*

*Saint-Tropez, Chapelle de la
Miséricorde*

Plage de Salins (4.5 km. E.): Near
the beach is the *Château de la Moutte*,
which once belonged to a Government minister, Émile Ollivier.
Verne (20 km. W.): A *Carthusian
monastery* was founded here in 1170
by Pierre Isnard, Bishop of Toulon,
and Frédol d'Anduze, Bishop of Fréjus. During the Revolution, the
monks fled to Italy and the buildings
fell into decay. The site was bought
by the state in 1961 and has been
undergoing restoration since 1969. A
large monumental gate (17C) leads
into the inner courtyard, which is surrounded by 18C buildings, guest
rooms, a lovely kitchen (12C) with a
herring-bone vault, a bakery (16C), a
refectory, a chapel, and a small
cloister. The Romanesque chapel
(which has been damaged) dates from
the period of the monastery's foundation. The large cloister leads to the

monks' cells and the garden. The
Carthusians' old observatory ('pavillon') stands 600 yards to the SE.

Salin-de-Giraud
13 Bouches-du-Rhône   p.256□B 7

This village was founded at the end of
the 19C and although it has now been
incorporated into Arles. It was the
first example in Provence of the kind
of planned, modern workers' town
which had been introduced farther
North. As its name suggests, it owed
its existence to the sea salt which
began to be extracted here on a large
scale during the last century, and
when the Belgian company Solvay
established itself here it brought with
it the idea of workers' settlements laid
out in rectangular grids of identical

houses and with the town hall, post office, school, police station, and church all concentrated in the centre. 1.5 km. to the S. there is an *observation tower* which provides a good view of the salt-works.

Salon-de-Provence
13 Bouches-du-Rhône   p.256☐C 6

This grew up near a Celto-Ligurian oppidum at Salonet and was first mentioned in the 9C as being the property of the Bishops of Arles. It was fortified during the period of the Saracen and Norman incursions. In 1032 it passed, together with the Kingdom of Provence, to the Holy Roman Emperors, as we are still reminded by the name of its castle, the 'Château de l'Emperi'. Being directly subordinate to the Emperor, it enjoyed tax favours and soon prospered greatly; it had four markets in the 14C, and was able to make its voice heard. Today, as capital of the Crau, it is still a centre for the shipment of local agricultural produce (wine, fruit, early vegetables), though its modern prosperity is primarily due to the oil trade.

Collegiate church of Saint-Laurent (Rue Maréchal-Joffre): This was built in 1344 by the Dominicans, an order comprising preachers and mendicants who had set themselves the task of winning back the Albigensians, and who were especially strong in the South of France. The church is a typical example of Dominican Gothic. Its undecorated, compact walls contrast with the beautiful and richly ornamented tower, which has two Romanesque and two early Gothic storeys. Despite these almost non-Gothic features, its solid lines do give it an unmistakable Gothic character.

The *interior* is also typical of Dominican Gothic in its resemblance to a hall: it consists of a single aisle of six broad bays with pointed vaults which ends in a five-sided apse (there being no choir or transept). This impression is further emphasized by the unusual difference in height between the nave and the chapels between the buttresses.

Saint-Cannat (Salon-de-Provence), pre-Christian sarcophagus inside the church

Salon-de-Provence, Saint-Michel

Salon-de-Provence, Saint-Laurent

Saint-Michel (Rue de l'Horloge): Despite its simplicity, this is an unusually striking church, which was built in 1220/30, during the period of transition from Romanesque to Gothic. One is especially impressed by the W. façade, with its beautiful portal and its windowless square tower ending in a sharply pointed bellcote. This is balanced at the E. end by the freestanding wall between the nave and the slightly higher apse; this wall culminates in two tiers of semicircular arches and a steeply angled gable. The *interior* consisted originally of a single aisle, to which the S. aisle was added in the 15C.

Castle: The Château de l'Emperi, which stands on a crag above the town, was built in its present form by Archbishop Jean des Baux (1233–58). After the Papal Palace in Avignon and the castle in Tarascon, it is one of the largest and most important castles in Provence. Even though it has been stripped of its battlements and three of its towers during the course of the centuries, its huge bare walls still give it the appearance of an unassailable stronghold. The castle is 558 ft. long, and has several towers on the E. side, where the ground falls away steeply. It has three courtyards, namely an *outer bailey*, which until 1860, when the castle was converted into a barracks, was separated from the main part of the castle by a moat, and two inner courtyards. A ramp leads into the *outer works* (the portal was rebuilt in 1585 and the watch-house added in 1656) and thence through a barrel-vaulted room in the *gate-house* along a passage and into the first inner courtyard. This *passage* is covered with stone slabs and closely spaced rectangular ribs and deserves special notice inasmuch as the idea for it is thought to have been brought from Syria by the Crusaders. Here, in the *first inner courtyard*, we can clearly see the various phases of the castle: it was originally built in the 1st half of the 10C, then rebuilt, as a fortress, by the Bishops of Arles in the 12&13C, but was converted by its later owners into a stately residence. The N. and W. wings are fronted with elegant pillared arcades with broad, flat arches surmounted by galleries; indeed, even

Salon-de-Provence, Tour de l'Horloge

Saint-Cannat (Salon-de-P.), church

the enlarged windows testify to the embellishments made by Archbishop J.Ferrier (1499–1521). One passes from this beautiful courtyard, known as the Cour d'Honneur, in which the *Festival de Salon* is held annually, through the N. section into the *second inner courtyard*, the Cour de l'Emperi, which is the oldest part of the entire building, and was severely affected by the earthquake of 1909. It contains the *chapel*, which was rib-vaulted in the 13C and converted into a double chapel typical of medieval castles and palaces.

Today, the castle houses a *museum* (entered via the chapel) which has a small collection of paintings and incorporates a very well stocked military museum.

Also worth seeing: The *Hôtel de Ville* (1655–8) is built in the French Classical style and has a stately appearance befitting its role as the Town Hall. In front of it there stands a statue of Adam de Craponnes (1525–76), who dug the irrigation canal which has been named after him. The *Porte du Bourg Neuf* (Cours Victor Hugo) constitutes one of the last remnants of the town wall, which was demolished in the 17C. It is a square tower with a gallery and machicolations. The 17C *Tour de l'Horloge* (17C) has a beautiful and typically Provençal wrought-iron belfry.

Environs: Alleins (16 km. NE): This old village contains a Romanesque *cemetery chapel* and also the ruins of a 16C *château*.

Aurons (7 km. NE): Small village with a tiny Romanesque *church*. In front of the village stands the former priory of *Saint-Pierre-des-Canons*, a huge complex of buildings which also has a beautiful 17C garden.

Eyguières (9 km. NW): Pretty market town at the foot of the Alpilles which has a Romanesque *graveyard chapel*.

Fare-les-Oliviers (14 km. SE): Remains of an old *castle*.

Grans (5.5 km. SW): The olive harvest is pressed in November and December (Rue Émile Zola). There are some beautiful 18C *façades*.

Lamanon (6.5 km. N.): During the

Sault, Saint Sauveur

Tertiary era, the Durance burst through the defile known as the *Pertuis de Lamanon* on its way to the sea; eventually, over thousands of years, the pebbles and scree which it deposited brought formed the Crau plain.

Lançon-Provence (7.5 km. SSE): This old village contains the ruins of a *castle* built in the 12C by the lords of Baux. There are also ruins of some beautiful old *houses* and of the old *fortifications*. On the N119 can be seen the notably beautiful and charming *Chapelle Saint-Cyr*, an 11C Romanesque chapel.

Roquemartine (11 km. NW): 17C *castle*. On the N569 there are the ruins of the old castle known as *Castellas de Roquemartine*.

Sénas (12 km. N.): This contains a beautiful 14C Gothic *church*. It has a Romanesque S. aisle, which was probably the nave of the older church which once occupied the same site.

Vernègues (10 km. NE): Small village destroyed by the earthquake of 1909 and then rebuilt farther down. 1 km. N. of the old village are the ruins of a Romanesque *church* and of a *castle*.

Saint-Cannat (16 km. E.): For a village with a population of barely 2,000, the *church* is astonishingly large. It has a richly decorated 15C tower.

Sault
84 Vaucluse   p.256□D 5

This began life as the ancient *Saltus* and became the seat of a barony in the Middle Ages and of a county in 1561. Today it is a small market town, whose lavender mills and factories pervade the whole town with a sweet aroma.

Parish church of Saint-Sauveur: This Romanesque church was built in the 12C and originally possessed a single aisle, to which a side aisle was added in the 16C. The neoclassical stone pavilion roof of the tower is a later addition. The carved moulding of the round window in the otherwise plain W. end is a specific feature of Provençal Romanesque architecture. The slender columns of the portal's

Sénanque

round arches are an early pointer to the Gothic style. The *interior* achieves a harmonious unity even though the three bays of the nave have a pointed barrel vault, while the choir and side aisle have a slender rib vault.

Castle: Only some towers have survived from the original 16C castle.

Museum: This displays Celtic and Gallo-Roman finds from the area, including weapons, coins, etc.

Environs: Château-Reybaud (6 km. NNE): There is a 13C *keep* in the pass between Luire and Ventoux.
Gour des Oules (9 km. NNE): This is a wild, rocky ravine looking down to the valley of the Toulourenc.
Monieux (6.5 km. SW): Tiny village situated at the entrance to the Nesque gorge. It has an old signal-tower and a Romanesque church.
Nesque gorge (Gorges de la Nesque): The road winds dramatically between the huge, precipitous crags, which are honeycombed with caves, and passes the *Rocher du Cire*, a cliff-face nearly 1,300 ft. high which was made famous by Frédéric Mistral's poem 'Calendal'.
Saint-Trinit (7 km. NE): 12C Romanesque *church*.
Ventoux (26 km. NW): From the mountain, which is nearly 6,550 ft. high and ranges from a zone of lush vegetation at the bottom to barren scree slopes at the top, there is a stunning panoramic view extending from Marseille to Mont Blanc and from the Cevennes to the Italian border.

Sénanque

84 Vaucluse   p.256□C 5

Cistercian abbey: On the bleak and barren Plateau de Vaucluse between Venasque and Gordes one may still find bories; the stone huts with corbelled roofs and holes for door and window, which were built here since time immemorial right up to the 18C by local farmers and shepherds, and are still used from time to time as overnight shelters. The Cistercian abbey is in a valley basin in this thinly populated region, which has more

Sénanque, cloister

stones, bushes, and heather than cultivated fields, amidst hills overgrown with trees and surrounded by lavender and gorse—as well as carefully sown grain. Built from the local limetone, its normal grey colour changes in the midday sun to a reddish yellow.

The Cistercian Order was founded in Cîteaux in 1098 and in 1112 its severe rules were laid down by St.Bernard of Clairvaux (1090–1153), who reacted against the excesses of the Cluniac Order, which itself had originally been given an ascetic rule when it was founded in 910. He insisted upon seclusion from the world and complete renunciation, including that of worldly goods. The order rapidly expanded until, by the time of his death, there were more than 350 Cistercian abbeys.

The abbey at Sénanque was built by twelve monks who came here in 1148 from the abbey at Mazan (now in the department of Ardèche). They faithfully copied the design of the new abbey from their old one, Mazan, which had been founded from the order's first abbey in Cîteaux (Mazan was totally destroyed in the 19C). The poverty and isolation of the place suited the Cistercians' needs; moreover, it contained the only river in the whole region, the Sénancole, although today this is very low and is often completely dry.

The construction of the church began around 1160. Except that its choir is on the N. side (because of the direction of the river and the valley) and that it has a semicircular apse, like the church at Le Thoronet, it is a traditional Cistercian basilica with a nave and two aisles. The altars were consecrated some time before 1178. Alterations were made at the end of the 12C—possibly in order to bring somef light into the nave, which is very dark—the wall of the nave being built upwards and windows being opened in the new upper wall. Despite its complete lack of ornament, the church is actually very expressive. The nave and aisles are five bays long and have a barrel vault. From the nave, three steps lead up to the square crossing which has an octa-

*Sénanque, E. arm of transept containing the tomb of the lord of Vénasque (L.);
dormitory (R.)*

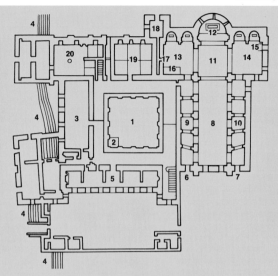

Sénanque, Cistercian monastery 1 Cloister **2** Vaulting pillar from the old well **3** Refectory **4** Channels for the Sénancole which the monks dug here towards the end of the 12C **5** The old kitchen and workrooms, now used as exhibition rooms and offices **6, 7** Gates leading into the abbey church **8** Nave **9, 10** Side aisles **11** Crossing and dome with squinches **12** Apse (at N. end) **13** W. arm of transept with two choir chapels **14** E. arm of transept with two choir chapels **15** Tomb of the lord of Vénasque dating from the 13C **16** Staircase to the dormitory **17** Door to the sacristy **18** Sacristy **19** Chapterhouse **20** The monks' room, also called the warm room or calefactory. The dormitory is above the chapterhouse and the monks' room

gonal dome; the arms of the transept contain four altars, one of which is Romanesque, the others being copies. Two more steps take us up to the raised apse, whose three windows symbolize the Holy Trinity.

The *cloister*, which has been as well preserved as the church, has capitals decoratively carved with leaves, flowers, and tendrils, with necking beneath the capitals; there are no figurative motifs, apart from one animal mask on the N. side. The capitals date from various periods, ranging from roughly 1180 to 1220.

The *dormitory* is above the chapterhouse and the monks' room, and appears as a continuation of the W. arm of the transept. Like the church, it has a pointed barrel vault. All the monks slept in the single room and it was approached by two staircases, one leading directly into the church and the other into the cloister.

The rectangular *chapterhouse* was the Order's assembly-room. Every day, a chapter from the Rule of the Order or from the Holy Scriptures would be read out and commented upon. The rib vaulting was probably not added

until the 13C but the rows of stone seats along the walls, where the monks sat, are original.

The *monks' room* was the only room to be heated; there is still a fireplace here which dates from the original period of construction. This is why it is usually referred to as the 'calefactory'; in fact, the monks used it as a place to work and write.

The *refectory* was destroyed in 1544 and rebuilt in the 17C in the original style; it has recently been faithfully restored.

All Cistercian churches answer the requirement of poverty by a lack of ornament but the perfect simplicity of this church, which has a symbolic value over and above its technical precision, is an overwhelming success. Through their expression of the renunciation of everything that is superfluous, both the church itself (which has survived in outstanding condition) and indeed the whole abbey (parts of which have been restored in the original style) radiate harmony and clarity of thought. The abbey flourished up to the middle of the 13C, but grew farther and farther

Sénanque, cloister

Sénanque, monks' room

apart from the Cistercian rule of poverty, and was eventually reorganized in 1470. Meanwhile, the villages of Mt.Lubéron were being settled by the Vaudois, who wanted to reform the Church but were horribly persecuted by both nobility and clergy. They took revenge by attacking Sénanque in 1544 and setting fire to part of the abbey. Then, in 1580, the plague wrought its havoc. Everywhere, the Cistercian order was losing its recruiting appeal, until a new reform was introduced by Abbot de Rancé in the abbey of La Trappe. From now on, Cistercian monks were called Trappists. Sénanque, however, became more and more dilapidated, until the Abbot de Béthune had it rebuilt at the end of the 17C. The abbey was sold during the Revolution, but in 1854 was acquired by the Abbé de Barnoin, who built a novitiate, workshops, a large guesthouse, and a farm building. In 1880 and again in 1902, the monks were driven out of Sénanque by the law against monastic communities, but some resettled there between 1926 and 1969. A Society of the Friends of Sénanque was founded which finally rescued the abbey.

Today it houses an institute for medieval research and an institute for research into the Sahara. Gregorian chants are studied and performed, and there are also other musical events.

Seyne-les-Alpes
04 Alpes-de-Haute-Provence   p.254□G 4

One's main impression is of the stone houses, the high bell tower of the church, and the citadel; all of which are in the old part of this mountain town on a terrace above the left bank of the river Blanche. An old 15C *gate* (Rue Basse) has survived from the town walls.

Citadel (17C): This fortress was built by Louis XIV and restored by Vauban. Since then it has fallen into ruin.

Chapelle des Pénitents (17C): The old Dominican chapel stands on the Place de la Chapelle. It was later enlarged, and now contains several paintings and reliquaries.

Parish church (Beginning of the 13C): A Romanesque church, 130 ft. long, 30 ft. wide, and 45 ft. high, it closely resembles the church of Notre-Dame de Bourg in Digne. Its walls are built of small, regularly laid blocks of stone and a square tower on the S. side looks down on the steeply gabled roof. There are three beautiful *portals*; that to the S. has three orders and is similar to those in Digne and Sisteron. Two semicircular arches spring from the buttresses on either side, and there are narrow eaves above. Parts of the ornamentation have been much restored. The pointed tympanum is empty and is framed by archivolts. The N. portal has been walled up; its tympanum is decorated with a leaf motif in the form

Selonnet (Seyne-les-Alpes), church

of a cross. The W. end contains a huge *rose-window*, 16 ft. in diameter, with sumptuous moulding. Parts of the delicate tracery have been renewed.

The interior consists of a single three-bayed aisle which has a pointed barrel vault with powerful ribs. The side walls are decorated with pointed blind arcades. There is no transept, and the nave goes straight into the half-barrel-vaulted choir, with which the church ends. There is a triumphal arch at the beginning of the choir, which is borne by columns with interesting figurative capitals. The square chapels on either side of the choir have rib vaults and were added in the 13C. Only a small amount of light is able to penetrate the church through the narrow windows in the S. wall and the two round windows in the wall of the choir. The furnishings include a large font (13 ft. in circumference), choir stalls, and a striking 17C high altar.

Environs: Barles (23 km. SW): a *ruined castle* stands above the church on the right bank of the river Bès.

Saint-Vincent-les-Forts (17 km. N.): The massive *fortress* once dominated two valleys.

Selonnet (8 km. NW): The *church* has an unusual bell tower.

Silvacane (Abbey)
13 Bouches-du-Rhône   p.256□D 6

The name originated from the Latin *Silva cannorum*, which means literally 'forest of reeds'. The marshland was drained in the 11C, and in 1150 this was chosen as the site for the youngest of the three Cistercian abbeys which comprise the 'Sisters of Provence' (following those in Sénanque and Le Thoronet). The church was built in 1175–1230 and the cloister and other abbey buildings in 1250–1300; the abbey being complete by 1300. However, shortly after the construction of a new refectory in 1420 it was abandoned by most of its occupants. The abbey was owned by the cathedral chapter of Aix from 1413, and not long afterwards its church was made the parish church of Roque d'An-

Silvacane, Cistercian Abbey

Silvacane, Cistercian Abbey

théron. During the Revolution it was sold off, but it was acquired once more by the State in 1846 and restored.

Church: This plain, undecorated, purely functional building, with its clear arrangement of space, appears, at first glance, typically Cistercian on the outside. It is a basilica with a nave and two aisles, a marked transept, a low choir and four chapels on the E. side of the transept. The only exception to the strict rule of having no decoration is the W. end, which incorporates a recessed portal and prominentö moulding around the window. The small, square tower with round arches for the bells today looks somewhat unconventional; originally, it probably had a flat stone helm roof. The compact *interior* also displays the features characteristic of Cistercian architecture, namely its fine masonry, clear lines, its renunciation of ornamental detail which would merely distract the attention, the harmony of its proportions and its use of mass, and its very intuitive use of light (for example, the typical group of three round-arched windows at the E. end, and the inevitable round window above them which is repeated at the W. end).

Cloister (Entrance in the E. bay of the N. aisle): This is also entirely Romanesque in character, although the decorations on the consoles etc. are a harbinger of Gothic. Nonetheless, the date of construction is put between 1250 and 1300.

The *abbey buildings* date from the same period. Their E. wing was connected to the church by means of a staircase leading up from the N. arm of the transept to the *dormitory* on the first floor, which made it easier for the monks to perform their nightly worship. Under the staircase is the *library*, and beneath the dormitory, a few steps lower than the level of the cloister, is the *chapterhouse*, which occupies six bays and has a rib vault.

We come next, on the N. side, to the stairwell, beneath which there was a small prison, and the *parlatory*, a barrel-vaulted passage between the cloister and the garden which was the only place where the monks were allowed to talk. Next to it is the *monks' room* or calefactory, which was heated by a fireplace and was also used for writing. The *refectory*, a rib-vaulted room of four bays, was in the N. wing, and this too has survived. By contrast, there is not much left to see of the S. wing, which housed the lay brothers.

1.5 km. SW, in the parish of **La Roque d'Anthéron**, there is a *château*, flanked by towers, which was built in 1605 and now accommodates a health centre.

Environs: Cadenet (3.5 km. NNE): This is situated at the foot of a hill riddled with caves which used to be inhabited, and was the birthplace of the troubadour Elian de Cadenet (1160–1239). It has a pretty Romanesque *church* with a Provençal bell tower dating from 1538. The outstanding feature is the *font*; which has been made from one half of an ancient

Cadenet (Silvacane)

marble bath, on which is depicted the horned Gallic god Cernunnos sitting on his throne surrounded by Roman deities—evidence that the two cults must have been temporarily intermingled.

Meyrargues: (18.5 km. SE): This village has a medieval *castle* which was rebuilt in 1638 and is now a hotel. To the E. can be seen the remains of the old *Roman aqueduct* from Traconnade to Aix.

Peyrolles-en-Provence (24.5 km. SE): Old town with three fortified towers, one of which was converted in the 17C into a belfry. Large *château* (now the town hall). *Church* with beautiful Romanesque vault. The 12C *Chapelle du Saint-Sépulcre*, bears a marked resemblance to the Chapel of Sainte-Croix in Montmajour.

Simiane-la-Rotonde
84 Vaucluse   p.256□D/E 5

Picturesque little village. The fort, whose walls are not very strong, is 11–16C. On the highest point stands the *rotunda*, which is the most controversial Romanesque building in Provence and has long puzzled the experts.

Rotunda: The function for which this was built has been the subject of intense dispute. Some see it as a keep, others as a mausoleum, and still others interpret it variously as a castle chapel, a double chapel, a chapel and mausoleum, or a combination of weapon-room, store-room, reception room and state apartment. It is a heavy, relatively low building, which is encompassed by three separate layers of wall, and is semicircular on the outside and polygonal towards the courtyard. It has two storeys (although there is no dividing ceiling inside), of which the lower is wholly void of ornament, with a completely plain wall, and the upper is richly decorated in comparison, with a wall containing 12 niches formed by semicircular barrel vaults. The high dome, which rests on the continuous cornice, also has 12 sides, and is supported by 12 slightly spiralling ribs. The ribs run down from the lantern at

Simiane-la-Rotonde, panorama

the top of the dome to the columns which separate the niches, at which point they meet the grotesque or grimacing human masks which are the only sculptural decoration in this room (apart from the capitals, which are decorated with leaves, and the rosette around the round window at the top).

Environs: Cañon d'Oppedette (9 km. SE): *Ravine* 15 miles long and up to 400 ft. deep.
Ferme de Boulinette (5 km. SE): This contains some beautiful large houses and farm buildings which were built in the 17C by the monks of Valsaintes after they had abandoned their monastery.
Valsaintes (6 km. SE): This was originally a Cistercian abbey which was founded in the 12C and abandoned in the 17C. It is now a farm.

Sisteron
04 Alpes-de-Haute-Provence   p.256☐E/F 4

This site in the valley where the Buech joins the Durance was settled at an early date. The Romans called it *Segustero* and the Via Domitia ran past it. Nothing has survived from Roman times except a *mausoleum* (near the station) which contains sculptures and a cemetery on which the present cathedral now stands. The suburb of Faubourg de la Baume developed during the Middle Ages at the foot of the Rocher de la Baume, extending as far as the river and encompassing the small suburb of Faubourg Saint-Jaume. The 'Grandes Compagnies' did not spare this region from their depredations, and in the face of this menace the fortified wall was restored in the 14C. At the same time, the suburbs outside the wall had to be partly or entirely abandoned. Today, all that remains of this wall are a few towers.

During the early Middle Ages, a citadel was built on the fortified rock overlooking the picturesque old quarter of the town. Its position on the defile of the valley led to its having considerable military importance from the 16C onwards.

Sainte-Marie-et-Saint-Thyrse:

Sisteron, citadel

Sisteron, clock-tower

The well-preserved *former Cathedral* is a typical example of Provençal Romanesque (12C), with Lombard elements (and shows the unmistakable influence of the cathedral at Embrun). The choir cannot be identified from outside because of the high walls but the apses are low and plain and have conical roofs. The octagonal tower over the dome in the last bay of the nave is a Lombard feature and it has a row of columns resembling a dwarf gallery. Behind the N. aisle there is a two-storeyed bell tower with pointed arches in the belfry storey and a pavilion roof. The round windows in the side aisles and the round-arched windows in the wall of the choir have been either renewed or enlarged at a later date. The round window at the W. end, which has a prominent moulding (though its tracery has been lost), was put in later. Beneath it is a delicate, round-arched *recessed portal* which once led into a porch. The outer order of the portal has a beautiful Romanesque frieze decorated with animals but the tympanum is now bare. The side chapels were added to the church in the 16C.

There is no carved decoration in the interior, whose effect is achieved by the stone walls. Those of the side aisles are high and have the usual Provençal blind arcades. There is an octagonal dome, which has no windows and is supported by squinches, above the last bay of the barrel-vaulted nave. After that come the short choir and the semicircular apse. The choir is very low, and the blind arch on its end wall was originally the triumphal arch.

Towers: (S. of the cathedral): The town wall incorporates several massive semicircular towers built of irregular stone blocks. These contain embrasures, a few slits, and the remains of galleries with machicolations supported by consoles.

Citadel: The large, terraced citadel was built in the 16C on the site of the

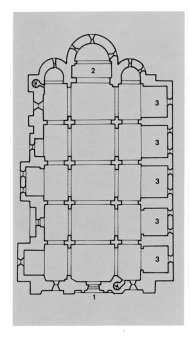

Sisteron, Sainte-Marie-et-Saint-Thyrse **1** Recessed portal **2** Choir **3** Side chapels

medieval fortress (on the S. slope of the hill) by Henry IV's military architect, J. Erard. The supporting walls are high, with semicircular arcades, and are defended by bastions. There are two towers, of which the higher has a platform and performed the function of a *keep*. On the E. side of the keep can be seen the remains of a Gothic chapel, built in the 14C but largely destroyed by bombing in 1944. An underground staircase leads from the NE corner of the fortress to the Porte Dauphiné.

Also worth seeing: The closely clustered houses, winding alleys, and little squares of the *old town* are a picturesque sight. The chapel of *Saint-Jacques*, a much restored

erre Ecrite

Saint-Geniez de Dromon (Sisteron), Défilé de Pierre-Écrite

Romanesque church built in the style typical of Provence, stands on the road running N. from the Faubourg de la Baume along the embankment.

Environs: Montfort (*c.* 18 km. S.): On the D101 stands the former monastery church of *Saint-Donat* —now abandoned and in a poor state —it is one of the outstanding early Romanesque buildings of Provence. Donatus, to whom the present church was later to be dedicated, is supposed to have lived here as a hermit in the 6C. In 1018, the church came into the possession of the monastery of Saint-André in Villeneuve-lès-Avignon, and after that was mentioned several times in documents as the 'ecclesia Sancti Donati'. Later (up to 1778), it belonged to a priory attached to the monastery of Gânagobie. During the Revolution, it was declared national property and sold off, after which the church fell into ruin and the monastery buildings disappeared.

The church is a columned basilica, with a nave and two aisles, a transept, and three semicircular apses. The outside is simple and unpretentious, and its surface has been worn down by the weather. There is a saddle roof over the nave and aisles. The transept is considerably lower, and its S. arm was rebuilt at a later date. An extension of the nave, which has since become dilapidated, and a bellcote above the E. wall of the crossing, were also added later. Inside the church, the nave is 14 ft. wide and the side aisles 5 ft.; the arcades which separate them are borne by simple round pillars. The side aisles, which are 7 ft. lower, have half-barrel vaults. The nave supports a barrel: vault, and the crossing a transverse barrel vault. The semicircular apses have half-domes and narrow windows.

Saint-Geniez de Dromon (16 km. NE): At the foot of Mt.Dromon is a half-ruined 17C *chapel*. It has an important trefoil crypt, which is Merovingian or Carolingian period and was built in honour of the Prefect Dardanus. Dardanus and his wife lived as hermits, trying in their lives to bring about the City of God envisaged by St.Augustine. The crypt has a barrel and half-dome vault resting on capitals which incorporate interesting depictions of peacocks and rams' heads. On Mt.Dromon itself can be seen the remains of a Celtic *oppidum* and of a *shrine*.

Solliès-Ville

83 Var   p.258☐F 8

This old town stands on a hill amid lovely scenery, and is separated from Solliès-Pont in the plain below by the winding course of the river Gapeau.

Church: This simple Romanesque church, dating from around 1200, possesses the unusual feature of having two rectangular aisles of equal height ending in a straight-sided choir. The aisles are divided into three bays by 2 pillars and support a ribbed vault with striking cross ribs, although the construction of the vaults is somewhat clumsy. The walls of the choir contain narrow, round-arched windows.

Also worth seeing: Ruins of the *Château de Forbin*. A *museum* is housed in the holiday home of the writer J.Aicard.

Environs: Belgentier (8 km. NW): The 16C *château* was decorated by P.Puget.
Cuers (10.5 km. NE): The *church* (1524) on the site of the Roman Castrum de Corio contains a gold-mounted relic of St.Peter.
La Garde (11 km. S.): There are a Romanesque *church* and a *ruined*

castle in the old town. The *J.Aicard Museum* contains, among other things, a collection of Clément Massié's ceramics.
La Pauline (13 km. S.): The neo-Gothic *chapel* (19C) contains sculptures by Pradier.
Solliès-Pont (2.5 km. E.): 17C *Château*.
Solliès-Toucas (2 km. N.): *Church* dating from the 17C.

Sospel

06 Alpes-Maritimes   p.258☐K 5

This charming little town lies amid fertile river-meadows surrounded by bleak mountains. The new part of the town extends along the left bank of the Bévéra; it contains beautiful arcaded houses and, in the centre, the Place Saint-Nicolas, in the middle of which stands a fountain dating from the 15C. An old bridge links it to the medieval town on the right bank. Here, the old cathedral is surrounded by narrow streets, in which some of the houses are Gothic.

Bridge: This was built across the Bévéra in the 11C and severely damaged in World War 2. It was extensively restored in 1945. It comprises two arches, and has a tower in the middle.

Saint-Michel: Only the Lombard Romanesque bell tower has survived from the original 11C church, but the design of the present one built in 1641 was influenced by its predecessor; extensive restoration work was carried out in 1888. The outside is classical, although the façade displays Italian baroque features. There are two fine altarpieces: the Pietà in the chapel of the Pénitents Blancs is by an unknown Provençal artist (the wings depict Sts.Catherine and Nicholas); more important is the altar in the left choir chapel, which dates from 1555 and is attributed to F.Bréa.

Also worth seeing: Only a few remains and a 14C *tower* have survived from the medieval *fortified walls*. Above the square on which the church stands are the ruins of a *Carmelite monastery* which was destroyed in 1728.

Environs: Breil-sur-Roya (23 km. NE): A village typical of the Alpes-Maritime. Only certain sections, as well as a gate (*Saint-Antoine*, to the W.), have survived from the medieval *town wall*. The large 18C church of *Sancta Maria in Albis*, is impressive and it contains an altar dedicated to St.Peter (1500).

L'Escarène (23 km. SW): This old village stands on the banks of the Paillon and is dominated by its large 17C church.

Lucéram (*c.* 33 km. W.): The Romans built a salt road past here, and it was this which brought Lucéram its wealth and its importance. On this road was discovered the *tomb of Julius Valens*, the Roman governor of Alpes Maritimae. The *remains of the fortifications* and a *watch-tower* (the Grosse Tour) date from the 14C and individual *Gothic houses* still survive. The Romanesque-Gothic *church* (1487) was rebuilt in the 18C in Italian rococo style. Even so, it still appears simple when compared with the extraordinarily rich furnishings inside. The most important of the altars are those produced by the School of Nice, in other words by the Bréa brothers and their workshop. St.Margaret's altar is attributed to L.Bréa and dates from 1500. Its predella and wings are now in the Museum in Nice. St.Bernards's altar (1510), which depicts the Crucifixion, St.Bernard, and four other saints, is probably by A.Bréa. The altar of St.Lawrence dates from 1560 and is thought to be by F.Bréa. Another altar, which represents St.Anthony of Padua, seems to be the work of Canavesio. On the other hand, we do not know who created the altar of Sts.Peter and Paul (around 1500), nor the altar of St.Claudius (1566), which depicts the Annunciation, the Crucifixion, and Sts.Lawrence and Pancratius. The treasury contains, among other items, a silver statue of St.Margaret (16C), a gilded wooden statue of the same saint (17C), two silver reliquaries (16&17C) containing relics of Sts.Margaret and Rosalie, a beautiful 16C monstrance, and a processional cross dating from the 17C. All in all, the furnishings are copious enough to fill a small museum. 1.5 km. S. of Lucéram is the simple *Chapel of Notre-Dame de Bon Coeur*. It is worth noting the frescos inside the chapel, which date from the late 15C. Those in the nave depict scenes from the life of the Virgin and from Jesus's youth. Those in the choir have been somewhat damaged, but one can still recognize Sts.Michael and Anthony beneath a figure of Christ, here shown as the Man of Sorrows. The best preserved of all the frescos are those in the porch. On the right wall we see the Crucifixion, and on the left wall Sts.Sebastian, Crispin, and Pons with various tools. Since the same motif appears in the frescos in Venanson, we may assume that these are also by J.Baleison. The same artist was probably also responsible for the wall paintings (around 1480) in the *Chapel of Saint-Grat* (880 yards outside Lucéram). The chapel itself is not significant except for its wall paintings, which were painted in tempera on dry plaster. Those which have been preserved are on the straight wall of the choir and on four segments of the ribbed vault. Here, the arrangement resembles that of an altarpiece. In the centre is the Madonna, seated on her throne, with Sts.Sebastian and Grat at either side. Beyond that are Sts.Catherine and Denys. The whole is reminiscent of the refined art of the 15C courts.

Piene-Basse (28 km. NE): This small old town, which is situated near the frontier, is dominated by its medieval *ruined castle*.

Tarascon
13 Bouches-du-Rhône   p.256☐B 6

This little Rhône town was made famous beyond the borders of France by Daudet's celebrated show-off Tartarin, whose colourful adventures brought a smile to the lips of many a reader ('Tartarin de Tarascon', 1872). The Celto-Ligurian foundation on the Rhône island of Jovarnica (the present suburb of Jarnègues), barely more than a trading post of Phocaean

Marseille in pre-Roman times, achieved sudden importance through the building of the Rome-Nîmes-Narbonne road. Secured by a Roman castrum, the river crossing soon developed into an important port, linked by pontoon bridge to Beaucaire opposite. The town was thus able to take control of its own administration around the middle of the 12C and govern itself, in spite of all attempts at interference from outside, up until the Revolution; consuls being elected by lottery from the nobles and citizens.

Collegiate church of Sainte-Martha: St.Martha, together with Lazarus and the Marys, an important figure to Christians in Provence, is supposed to have arrived in the S. of France around AD 48, bringing with her the true religion. Her deeds include the subduing of the Tarasque, a notorious man-eating monster, half-crocodile, half-lion, which she miraculously tamed by sprinkling with holy water and holding up the Cross so that she was able to put her girdle around its neck and lead it away from the people of Tarascon. The latter, of

Tarascon, castle

course, did not hesitate from butchering the monster with their lances. In 1469 King René established a festival in memory of this legendary event, which was to be held in two stages: A parade of the dragon on the second Sunday after Whitsun, in which the monster furiously thrashed around with its tail, and a festive procession on the Feast of St.Martha (29 July) in which the monster let himself be lead through the streets in a calm and docile fashion by a young girl. Today these festivals are combined and held on the last Sunday of July as the highlight of a series of variety performances, bull runs, fireworks, dance displays and so on.

Given this adoration of St.Martha, it is not surprising that the 'discovery' of her relics in the predecessor of the present collegiate church in 1184 attracted so many believers that the building of a larger church was necessary. This was consecrated as early as 1197, as can be seen from an inscription on the right-hand side of the S. portal. In its present form, however, the church dates mainly from the 14C (nave) and the 15C (bell

tower, sacristy, buttresses). In the 17C the crypt was rebuilt and two chapels added. Finally there was the restoration following the bombing raids of 1944, which resulted in the church's isolated position.

Exterior: The various phases of the building have resulted in a not entirely convincing mixture of styles and very unbalanced proportions. Only the *S. portal* is of interest, which, apart from the W. and S. walls, is the sole survival from the Romanesque building. The S. portal is also the main portal, since the church faces the town. This elegant Romanesque structure is reminiscent of Saint-Gilles and Saint-Trophime in Arles, with acanthus leaf and eagle capitals on slender columns in the recessed portal, and consoles supporting the sharply projecting entablature, which are embellished with animal heads, fabulous creatures and human figures.

Inside the basilica, which has a five-bayed nave and two aisles, the various phases melt into a uniform impression. The most striking feature is the ascending height of the ceiling

Tarascon, Porte de Condamine

from the side chapels to the aisles and to the nave, which drops again perceptibly in the apse. The following are the most interesting features: St.Francis of Assisi by C.Van Loo (third chapel of the right aisle) and the beautiful grille from the 15 or 16C, which encloses the reliquary behind the pulpit (second chapel of the left aisle); also scenes from the Life of St.Martha by Vien (1716–1809) and paintings by Mignard (1612–95), Parrocel (1670–1739) and Sauvan (1698–1792). The *crypt* in the lower church below the W. part of the N. aisle is a long, narrow room with a flat-ceilinged, semicircular apse and small chapels like transept arms. The beautiful tomb of Jean de Cossas (d. 1476) on the landing on the right is an interesting product of the Italian Renaissance in France, which is attributed to F.Laurana or his school. Also note the tomb of St.Martha (16C) in the first bay on the right, which is flanked by two large 14C Gothic figures of Christ and St.Front. The bas-reliefs depict the saint with the Tarasque and again being carried by angels and also Lazarus as a bishop. Two holes in the base of the tomb allowed the sarcophagus to be seen and touched with pieces of cloth. It has since been moved to the apse, where, in 1653, a marble tomb with an altar and recumbent figure of St.Martha was installed, having been commissioned by the Archbishop of Arles and made in Genoa. The famous Tarasque can be seen during the summer months at the Syndicat d'Initiative (Rue de Roi René/Rue de la République).

Castle: Rising beside the Rhône as if growing from the very rock and separated from the town by a wide moat is one of the most beautiful and best preserved castles in France. It was one of the border fortresses built to protect Provence from the French sphere of influence beginning in Beaucaire on the other side of the Rhône. Unfriendly and threatening, the high, battlemented walls, with their few, barred windows and projecting machicolations gaze down on the town and river, giving no hint of the elegance and comfort, which so forbidding a building offers within. It was begun around 1400 by Louis II of Anjou, Count of Provence and King of Sicily, in place of the Roman castrum and all the subsequent structures, which had, in the course of time, been destroyed by the Saracens and rebuilt and extended by the Kings of Arles. Completed in 1447–9, the castle then became the setting for wild festivals.

After the death of this monarch the castle and the town fell to France together with the rest of Provence. From then on the castle served as the seat of the royal governor until it was converted into a prison in the 18C. In 1926 it was acquired by the state and restored.

Exterior: Some 328 ft. long and, in parts, up to 164 ft. wide, the complex is divided by a moat into a 'basse-cour' (outer ward) and main castle. The latter, like a massive keep, consists of 4 dissimilar wings, nearly 160

Tarascon, Sainte-Martha

ft. high, strengthened on the landward side by round—and on the river side square—towers, which enclose an irregular, rectangular court. Adjoining to the N. are the walls of the basse-cour, only half as high, which are overtopped by higher rectangular towers on the landward side.

Inside the *basse-cour*, on the river side, are the outbuildings and accommodation for the castle garrison, as well as a large court, which was used for training and probably for the festivities as well. The only *entrance* to the castle lay between the N. round tower of the main castle and the first rectangular tower of the basse-cour, except that in the Middle Ages, instead of the present stone bridge there was probably a drawbridge over the moat, the water in which is taken from the Rhône. From this gate steps led to a platform and from there either through a narrow gate into the basse-cour or via a bridge through a square tower block into the *main castle*. The court of the main castle, although small and enclosed by sheer walls, displays all the charm of the Flamboyant style, as exemplified by the portal (pointed arch), the large traceried window of the chapel in the S. section, and the reliefs of King René and his second wife, Anne de Laval, which look down on the court from an escutcheoned double arch. Next to the old well in the SE corner there is a slender staircase tower which is adjoined on the E. side by a rib-vaulted porch. Above this open ground-floor hall are the residential apartments, two on the middle floor with timber ceilings and two on the upper floor with rib vaults. The W. wing had three enormous state rooms running its full length, the lower storeys again having wooden ceilings, while the upper room, with windows framed by figures, has a beautiful rib vault resting on carved consoles. The S. wing is mainly given over to the obligatory chapels, which no medieval castle could be without.

Also worth seeing: *Porte de la Condamine* (on the Avignon road). The only notable remnant of the 14C fortifications. *Hôtel de Ville*, an elegant building from 1648. Church of *Saint-Jacques* (17C) with a painting by J.-B

Tarascon, Sainte-Martha, portal

Tarascon, Sainte-Martha

Van Loo (St.Martha Taming the Tarasque).

Environs: Notre-Dame-du-Château (8.5 km. SE): 11C Romanesque *chapel*, which was the object of a pilgrimage, famous throughout the Camargue, on the first Sunday in May.

Tende

06 Alpes-Maritimes   p.258☐K 5

Tende lies above the Roya valley and its position on steeply sloping ground necessitated the terraced, amphitheatre-like arrangement of its houses. The community was always part of the county of Nice; but lying as they do on the borders between France and Italy, which were long disputed, the mountain valleys of the Roya, Vésubie and Tinée found themselves under Italian rule for 87 years. The people of the region had chosen French status in 1861 but Napoleon III left the decision to the King of Italy Victor-Emmanuel II, so that it was not until 1947 that a plebiscite finally assured the region's affiliation to France.

Château des Lascaris: A 66 ft. high wall is all that remains of this castle, which was built in the 14&15C and destroyed in 1692. The wall is connected through a legend to Beatrice of Tende (15C), who had her own husband murdered in order to possess it.

Notre-Dame de l'Assomption: This church was built between 1474 and 1518 under the direction of the architect Lazzarino. In the lintel of the green slate Renaissance portal there are small figures of Christ and the Apostles. To the left of the choir is the funerary chapel of the Lascaris, Counts of Tende and Vintimille. Here too is the tomb of the Duke of Savoy, René le Bâtard.

Also worth seeing: On terraces next to the ruined castle extends the *old cemetery*, which commands a beautiful view of the neighbourhood. In the Rue de France there is an old *town gate* and next to it, on the left, a small *chapel*.

Environs: La Brigue (6.5 km. SE): Apart from the ruins of the *Château des Lascaris* and a few green slate door lintels (13&14C) the most interesting feature of this village in the Levence valley is the Romanesque *church*. There is uncertainty about the exact date of its construction but it was some time in the late 12C or early 13C. The beautiful Lombard Romanesque bell tower is somewhat later and has the semicircular blind arcades typical of the style. A sexpartite rib vault appears to have been installed some time after 1300 and the interior contains a number of Italianate items. The high altar is gilded wood; there is an altar depicting a Crucifixion and an altar of the Virgin (only the central panel remains) by artists of the Bréa school. By L.Bréa himself is the altar of the Nativity of Christ. The altar of St.Martha was influenced by the Italian Renaissance and the predella depicts the arrival of the saint and her brother and sister, Margaret and Lazarus.

Fontan (12 km. S.): The Fouze springs here are the most fluoride-rich waters in the whole of Europe.

Les Mesches (14 km. SW): From here one can walk to the *Vallée des Merveilles* below Mont Bégo in which steep slabs of slate have been covered with *prehistoric engravings*. There are more than 100,000 individual images, some indecipherable, probably dating from the Bronze and early Iron Ages and presumably the work of Ligurian tribes (2000–1500 BC). They comprise stylized depictions of animals, people, tools and geometric figures.

Maurioun (16 km. SW): Following a devastating outbreak of plague the surviving inhabitants of this little village erected a *chapel* (1631) in fulfilment of a vow.

Morignole (11.5 km. E.): Outside the village is a 15C Genoese *bridge*, which is remarkable for its unusual approach ramp.

Notre-Dame des Fontaines (5 km. N.): In a lonely spot at the source of the Lavenza there has been a shrine since early times, although it was not officially documented until 1357. There is a legend which tells that the seven springs here dried up in an earthquake, but that at the intercession of the Virgin they began to produce water again. The villagers thereupon vowed to build a *chapel*, which became the object of a famous pilgrimage. A pilgrim hospice was also built in 1475. The present chapel consists of a narrow, rib-vaulted choir (14C) and a nave (18C). The hall-like interior (52 ft. 6 in. × 59 ft.) has no windows and no wall articulation—the ideal requirements for *wall paintings*. The extraordinarily well-preserved tempera paintings were executed on dry plaster by four different artists. Less important are the exterior frescos (God the Father and Saints) by C.Alberti and the Sibyls (inner wall) by G.Ruffi (1745). The scenes inside are much earlier and were possibly the combined work of J.Baleison and J.Canavesio. An inscription on the N. wall only mentions Canavesio as artist, but the paintings on the choir walls display Sienese influence and thereby the hand of Baleison. The works in the choir were only recently discovered under several layers of overpainting. In the entrance arch are the busts of the four Church Fathers, Ambrose, Jerome, Augustine and Gregory as counterparts to the four Evangelists in the cells of the vault. The arch of the altar wall is occupied by the Assumption of the Virgin with her flower-filled tomb below and St.Thomas, who reported the miracle. Thomas offered hope to pilgrims with eye afflictions since Christ made the doubting Thomas able to 'see'. On the N. and S. walls of the choir there are scenes from the Life of the Virgin (Dormition, Entombment and Assumption). The cycle of the Virgin is continued on the E. end wall in the nave and linked to scenes from the Childhood of Christ (11 scenes). The Passion cycle is depicted in two parallel rows (26 scenes) and on the W. wall is the Last Judgement with the Raising of the Dead and the Heavenly Jerusalem, where Christ passes judgement over the dead souls.

Saorge (14 km. S.): The present small town grew up in the 15C on a good strategic site NW of the former settlement. The houses, high above the Roya valley, literally cling to the steep slope. Steps link the narrow, twisting streets. A 17C *Franciscan monastery* stands on the way out of Saorge. Its *church* was built in a rustic baroque style and there is an onion-domed tower. Only parts of the monastery are open. The *parish church*, built around 1500, contains 17C altars and a 15C font. The former parish church, *Madone del Poggio*, was built in early Romanesque style (11C). The square tower (belfry), with semicircular blind arcades, is a beautiful example of Lombard art.

Toulon, Place d'Armes, gate

Toulon

83 Var p.258☐E 8

The Romans were the first to recognize the favourable coastal position, of this town and stationed a fleet here. They also set up productive purple dye houses. The Roman name for Toulon was supposedly Telo Martius. From 718 to 1197 it was repeatedly plundered by the Saracens. In the Middle Ages the town belonged to the Vicomtes de Marseilles, who then ceded it to Charles of Anjou. In 1481 Toulon went over to the French crown, together with the whole of Provence. The medieval town wall reputedly ran right into the sea but these ramparts were later turned into streets. Louis XII was the first to begin building a proper harbour, the harbour entrance then being guarded by the *Grosse Tour de la Mitre* (1514). These defences, however, proved inadequate during the struggles with Charles V. Under Henry IV (*c.* 1600) the governor of Provence, the Duke of Epernon, had fortified piers constructed. The 100 ft. wide entrance to the Darse Vieille (inner harbour) could be blocked by a chain and an arsenal and a dockyard were built in the shelter of the ring of walls. Under Louis XIV, who had his own navy, the harbour was further extended and, under the supervision of Cardinal Richelieu, dockyards were built for the building and repairing of warships. The growing importance of Toulon as a port resulted in a further extension based on plans by Vauban. Toulon was now able to withstand even a double siege, on land and at sea, during the War of the Spanish Succession (1707). In the course of the 18&19C the town walls were further fortified and extended as far as Cap le Mourillon, where the strong Fort La Malgue was built. Further forts, dry docks and harbours were built. Toulon is now the most important naval port in France. In spite of heavy war damage the New Town clearly stands out from the medieval quarters.

Arsenal Maritime (along the Darse

Toulon, cathedral, detail of façade

de Castigneau and Darse Neuve): The monumental entrance portal was built by Maucord in ancient Greek style in 1738. A clock-tower with wrought-iron campanile rises above the complex.

Grosse Tour de la Mitre (Cap le Mourillon): This *tower*, surrounded by a wide moat, was built in 1514 by Italian architect J.-A. de la Porta. Housed within is a small *Naval Museum*.

Hôpital Civil (behind the Jardin Alexandre Ier): The two statues of the founders are on the façade of the small *hospital chapel* (1678).

Saint-François-de-Paule (Place L.Blanc): This small *baroque church* was built in 17C style in 1744–9. Following the destruction of 1944 the building was restored. Inside is a 17C altar and an 18C wooden bust of St.Cyprian.

Sainte-Marie-Majeure (Place de la Cathédrale): The Romanesque cath-

edral, built in the 12&13C, has an awkward appearance as a result of a 17C enlargement. The rib-vaulted, three-bayed nave has barrel-vaulted aisles and a choir built in the medieval tradition. The lavish interior furnishing includes a baroque sunburst (1682), a relief (Entombment of the Virgin) by Verdiguier, the Glorification of the Eucharist by J.B.Van Loo and an Annunciation (1650) by P.Puget.

Place d'Armes (N. of the Porte Principal): Colbert had this rectangular square (590 ft. × 295 ft.) laid out in 1683. The *gate* itself was built in 1689.

Place Puget (E. of the Place d'Armes): The site of the large *Fontaine de Trois Dauphins* (1782), on which the architect Toscat and the sculptor Chastel collaborated.

Musée-Bibliothèque (Boulevard du Général Leclerc): Installed in a Renaissance house is the *Museum d'Histoire naturelle* and the *Musée*

Toulon, tower of the savings bank (1897)

Toulon, Grand Théâtre

d'Art et d'Archéologie. Exhibits include Egyptian and late Roman sculptures, coins and Celto-Ligurian works. The picture gallery contains works by Italian, Dutch (16&17C), French (17&18C) and modern artists.

Musée Naval (Quai de Stalingrad): A series of models of famous ships and works by French seascape painters provides a general view of naval history.

Musée de Vieux Toulon (Cours Lafayette): The former bishop's palace contains items relating to the city's history, a library and a folklore collection.

Also worth seeing: The façade of the *Grand Théâtre* (1862, Place V.Hugo) was adorned with interesting figures by local artists. The beautiful grounds of the *Jardin Alexandre Ier* (Place G.Péri) contain diverse sculptures and busts of local personalities. At the *Porte d'Italie* (end of the Rue Garibaldi) there are still remains of the town wall of Henry IV to be seen.

Environs: Balaguier (12.5 km. S.): The *fortress*, built on the orders of Richelieu in 1636, has housed a *maritime museum* since 1971. The key position of the fort in the defence of Toulon earned it, together with the *Fort Napoléon*, the title of 'little Gibraltar'.

Le Brusc (15 km. SW): This may well have been the site of the ancient Greek port of *Tauroentium*, a remnant of which survives in the form of an underground water channel (6 ft. high).'

L'île des Embiez (W. of Le Brusc): On the small island are the *ruins* of the medieval *Château de Sabran* and the *Observatoire de la Mer.*

Notre-Dame du Mai (19 km. S.): A *chapel* was built in 1625, next to the ruins of a *watch-tower*, and it now contains an interesting collection of local votive offerings.

Le Revest-les-Eaux (8 km. N.): At the foot of Mont Caume the Carthusian monks of Montrieux built the *church of Saint-Christophol* (1674–9). 17C *château* flanked by elegant corner towers. The square *watch and bell tower* is medieval. The *Château de*

Toulon, Place d'Armes, gate, detail

Dardennes, which was built on the foundations of an old Celto-Ligurian tower, is not open to the public.

Seyne-sur-Mer (7 km. S.): The former fishing village of La Sagno is now a modern shipbuilding centre. From 1580 onwards the town was administrated by the abbots of Saint-Victor in Marseille. In 1614 it became a parish and in 1657 self-administering, whereupon its own church, *Notre-Dame du Bon Voyage*, was built (1674). The *Musée Municipal de la Mer* displays examples of Mediterranean marine flora and fauna.

Six-Fours-les-Plages (11 km. SW): On the road from Toulon stands the old collegiate church of *Saint-Pierre* (9C). The *local church* was built in Provençal Romanesque style and Gothic additions and alterations were made at the start of the 17C. In the Romanesque choir there is a 16C Madonna, attributed to Jean de Troyes. The high altar (17C) by Guillaume Grève depicts Christ's investiture of St.Peter. Further altarpieces from the 15&16C are also contained in the church. N. of the Old Town is the chapel of *Notre-Dame de Pépiole*, a rustic building from the 10 or 11C with a nave and two aisles.

Valette-du-Var (2 km. N.): The former Vallis Laeta is today an important suburb of Toulon. The 16C Gothic nave of the *church* contains beautiful windows (16C) and a painting by Guillaume Grève. The choir dates from the 12C and was pierced by embrasures in the 14/15C. The half relief, St.John writing the Apocalypse, above the portal, is attributed to P.Puget.

Tour d'Aigues
84 Vaucluse   p.256☐D 6

This old village on the right bank of the Lèze is famous for its *château*, which is one of the most beautiful Renaissance examples in southern France. Built in 1545–75 by the Italian architect Ercole Nigra, incorporating the medieval castle (E. side, wing, keep), the building was destroyed by fire in 1782 and, after being rebuilt, was burned down once again

Toulon, portal of the old town hall by P.Puget (L.); Musée Naval, ship's figurehead (R.)

just 11 years later in the Revolution (1793). Fortunately, among the parts that survived, was the W. front, which the architect had completely rebuilt as the main front facing the village. The pedimented *portal*, almost classical in its elegance, is flanked by two old corner towers converted into three-storeyed residential pavilions. Strengthened at the corners by two colossal, fluted pilasters, the portal is composed of two splendid storeys. The lower one, with a semicircular archway framed by victories in the spandrels, has four columns with Corinthian capitals, round-arched niches and rectangular panels —as does the upper storey, where this pattern is basically repeated, except that it is considerably smaller and the columns are replaced by pilasters. Particularly splendid, however, and reminiscent of the triumphal arch in Orange, is the frieze of trophies carved in high relief which divides the two storeys.

Church: Well worth seeing too is the little Romanesque church with its two facing apses, one of which dates from the early 13C, the other from the 17C. The side chapels of the nave, which is single-aisled and spanned by a pointed barrel vault, are also of a later date. Note the 17C *carved pulpit* and the 15C *painting of Christ* (Italian school).

Environs: Barrage de Cadarache (19 km. NE): Dam at the confluence of the Durance and Verdon. On a terrace above the dam, fortified in the 14C, is the *Château de Cadarache*, built by Louis de Villeneuve in 1475. To the E. of this is the *Centre d'Etudes Nucléaires de Cadarache*.

Grambois (6 km. NE): Charming little village with an interesting church, which combines various styles and houses in the choir a very beautiful triptych (1519) of the Life of John the Baptist. Also note the 13C fresco of St.Christopher.

Mirabeau (10 km. SE): Little village made famous by the 17C château of the Counts of Mirabeau.

Pertuis (6 km. SW): Old town on the left bank of the Lèze with remains of a medieval castle, the present *clock-tower*, and a tower from the old town

Tour d'Aigues, château

wall of the 14C. The Gothic church of
Saint-Nicolas, where Mirabeau was
baptized, is of interest particularly for
its contents: beautiful 16C triptych,
18C marble altar, numerous reliquaries etc.

Notre-Dame-de-Consolation (17
km. SE): Romanesque chapel.

Sainte-Madeleine (11.5 km. SE):
Charming 12C chapel with a record of
the 1239 solar eclipse in Latin and
Provençal on the façade.

Saint-Eucher (16 km. SE): Chapel,
rebuilt in 1704. A hermit of this name
is supposed to have lived in the neighbouring cave around the middle of the
5C.

Saint-Paul-lès-Durance (16 km.
SE): Small village between the
Durance and its canal, the church of
which contains beautiful 17C wood
carvings.

Trets

13 Bouches-du-Rhône   p.256☐E 7

Mentioned in Roman times as *Trittia*,
this picturesque little town is now
entirely medieval in character:
remains of the old town wall and
gates, protected by square 14C
towers, Romanesque houses and
narrow alleys. And of course there is
the *castle*, a tall, forbidding 15C
building. The *church*, dominated by a
massive, unfinished 15C bell tower, is
partly Romanesque. The transepts
were added in the 15C, while the S.
aisle and the apse were extensively
rebuilt in the 17C.

Environs: Peynier (3.5 km. W.):
Romanesque church; early pointed
vault in the chapel of Saint-Pierre by
the cemetery.

Pourrières (8 km. NNE): The name
of the village is not, as is claimed, derived from those who fell during Marius's famous victory over the Teutons
(102 BC) and 'pourirent' (decom-
posed) here, but, much more prosai-
cally, from 'porree', leek.

Puyloubier (9 km. N.): Small village
dominated by the ruins of a medieval
castle.

Tour d'Aigues, detail of portal of No. 9, rue de l'Église

Vaison-la-Romaine

84 Vaucluse   p.256☐C 4

Standing on the banks of the river Ouvèze, a tributary of the Rhône, the site of this town, surrounded by wooded hills W. of Mont Ventoux, protected from the Mistral and set in fertile land fed by numerous springs, was settled in early times, possibly even in the Neolithic. Ligurians lived here later, and from the end of the 4C BC the Vocontii, a Celtic tribe, who developed the place as their capital ('Vasio Vocontiorum'). The Romans invaded in 124/3 BC, captured Vasio and annexed it in 118 to the province of Gallia Narbonensis. In 58 BC Caesar made Vasio a Civitas Foederata (a city linked with the Roman people), whereupon, thanks to its setting and pleasant climate, not only public buildings, but also lavish private villas, baths, theatres and everything which made life pleasant for the cultivated Roman of that time was built. Viticulture and agricultural produce from the nearby hillsides helped further prosperity. Local stone was used as building material for houses and temples.

For 400 years until the fall of the Roman Empire and the onslaught of the Visigoths, Ostrogoths and Burgundians during the Barbarian Invasions, Vasio was a flourishing town. It then decayed and was covered by the alluvial sands of the Ouvèze, until the excavation works were begun in 1907. All that remained intact was the 56 ft. long, single-arched Roman bridge over the Ouvèze, which is still in use today.

In the meantime, however, Christianity had arrived early in the town and increasingly established itself alongside the Mithras and Cybele cults. By the end of the 3C there was already a Christian community and a bishop. In the course of the centuries the town was ruled by various peoples, but thenceforward the real power came from the church until finally, in 1160, the Counts of Toulouse captured the town and built a secure castle on a rocky slope on the left bank of the Ouvèze. They returned the bishop's rights and left him the old, already mostly ruined town. The inhabitants, however, now settled on the other side of the river under the protection of the counts' castle. A new church was built here in 1464, which served as the bishop's church until the disso-

Notre-Dame de Nazareth

Notre-Dame de Nazareth ▷

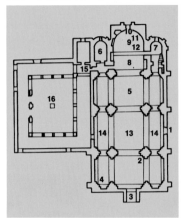

columns with Corinthian capitals and Romanes-que coping stones **10** Early Romanesque altar table with early Christian marble slab **11** Bishop's throne elevated on Roman base **12** Sarcophagus of St.Quenin, who was Bishop of Vaison in the 6C **13** 12C nave with pointed barrel vault **14** Narrow side aisles dating from the 12C with barrel vault **15** Way into cloister **16** 12C cloister

Vaison-la-Romaine, Cathedral of Notre-Dame de Nazareth 1 Entrance through the S. portal **2** One of the fluted pillars with sculpted figures **3** Small porch dating from the late Middle Ages **4** The foundations of what was probably an ancient temple were excavated here. A double column with Corinthian capital has been preserved **5** Square E. bay beneath an octagonal dome without windows **6** N. side apse with early Christian marble altar table decorated with reliefs **7** S. side apse **8** 12C choir **9** The apse (shown by recent research to date from the 10 or 11C) has a straight end wall dating from the 11C. There are stone seats for the priests, and above these are Romanesque blind arcades supported by Roman

lution of the bishopric in the Revolution.

This town, then new, but now almost totally abandoned, survives in its impressive medieval uniformity, but with many ruined buildings, above the Ouvèze. There, between the fortified ramparts, life in Vaison went on, while the Roman town gradually disappeared and faded into oblivion, until in the 18&19C a slow resettlement began with the building of a new town above the Gallo-Roman one, which by now had been reduced to rubble. In 1897 the church on the left bank was abandoned and in 1907 the town's administration was also transferred back to the other side of the river. In the 20C the varied history of the town took another turn as interest in the history of art, archaeology, excavations, museums and cultural

Notre-Dame de Nazareth

events on the ancient site led to Vaison becoming a tourist attraction and cultural centre.

Notre-Dame de Nazareth: To the left as one enters Vaison from Orange to the W., behind a park, stands the well-preserved medieval cathedral. For a long time it was believed that the E. end, the semicircular apse, encased on the outside by an 11C rectangular block, and the two side apses, dated back as far as the 5 or 6C. Now, however, it is thought to date from the 10C at the earliest, while the W. part is reckoned to be 12C. What is certain, however, is that the whole church is based on an older Roman structure, maybe even a former cult building. The Romanesque walls were built on Roman column stumps, capitals and rubble. Even the buttresses of the Romanesque masonry rest on Roman foundations (particularly evident in the main apse). In the W. part of the left aisle there is still a Roman double column with a Corinthian capital. From the outside the basilica, built of ashlars, with a nave, two aisles and four-cornered bell tower, appears to date fairly uniformly from the 11&12C. Moulded eaves, fluted pilasters and sculpted cornices are typical of the architectural style of that time in Provence. Inside the transeptless basilica, which nevertheless has an octagonal dome over the E. bay, the apses are surprising for their early Christian and early Romanesque features. In 1951, when the choir was restored to its original level, i.e. lowered by nearly 3 ft., the bishop's seat next to the altar and the three Spartan stone rows of seats for the priests, upon which Roman columns were placed, again came to light. On both sides of the choir and in the N. of the apse there are three wall tombs for bishops from the 14&15C with notable reliefs depicting figures. Particularly impressive is the N. apse with a beautiful marble altar, probably early Christian or Carolingian, decorated in relief with chi-rho monograms, doves, chalice and vines. Small windows in the S. aisle and the nave provide, apart from the later Gothic choir window, the meagre lighting of the church. The fluted pillars have Corinthian

Notre-Dame de Nazareth, cloister, figures in relief on marble sarcophagus

Notre-Dame de Nazareth, crucifix

capitals. Relief slabs under the imposts of the vault ribs bear carved animal and plant motifs.

Cloister: Adjoining the N. side of the basilica is the 12C cloister, which may be on the site of a 10 or 11C one, and was rebuilt in the 19C. Barrel and groin vaults rest on chevroned or fluted piers. Between each of these there are 3 arches supported by two sets of small double columns standing on a single plinth and with a single entablature, although each has its own foliate capital. Some of the columns are originally from Roman buildings, others were added in the 19C in place of damaged on ... However, these replacements ble... in well in this most romantic of cl... ters. It is now a small *museum*, with a. splays along its walks of *sculptures, inscriptions* and *architectural fragments* from early Christian and medieval times.

Saint-Quénin: About 660 yards NW of the town centre on the road to Valréas stands the chapel of Saint-Quénin, surrounded by a low wall. Not so long ago it stood alone on open ground but today a new development has grown up around it. It is thought —as a result of a few tomb finds—that there was an early Christian cemetery on this site and that it was perhaps the burial place of St.Quentin, Bishop of Vaison 556–78, who was revered as a saint soon after his death; hence the building of a memorial chapel. The present building with its triangular apse, which looks so unusual from the outside, dates from the 2nd half of the 12C. The W. part was rebuilt entirely in Romanesque style in 1630–6; indeed only the upper part of the bell tower above the W. front displays baroque features. The E. end was carefully built of ashlars, using in part Roman building material. It is interesting that the decorative forms on the outer half-columns (fluted, chevrons, Corinthian capitals) are based around Roman models. The capital above the half-column in the NE corner has a frieze of Abraham sacrificing Isaac and one with Hercules and the Lions. Above the capitals of the pillars of the choir bay, which serve only as supports for the upper outer wall, there are reliefs of figures over the entrance. In the W. there is an early Christian or at least early Romanesque bas-relief of vines with grapes, chalice and a Cross. The chapel inside was rebuilt, again in Romanesque style, in the 17C.

Former bishop's church in the Upper Town (Rue Principale): This church, which served as cathedral from the 15C to the Revolution of 1789, was built in 1464 under Bishop Pons de Sade and extended by two chapels in 1601. The façade dates from 1776. The interior, the furnishing of which is mainly 18C, has a Gothic nave with 8 side chapels.

Museum ▷

Castle: At the top of the hill there still lie the remains of the castle, which the Counts of Toulouse built at the end of the 12C and which was then altered in the 14, 15 and 16C. It comprises an inner court surrounded by three main wings and a massive keep.

Upper Town: The whole of the Upper Town, which is in a state of decay, is surrounded by ramparts. Very recently, renovation work has got under way on some of the pretty 16–18C houses and mansions, the small squares and the fountains.

Lower Town: In the Lower Town, which began to be resettled in the 17C, there are still new buildings being built. In parallel with this, from 1907 onwards, excavations of the old Roman town have been carried out and today the two Roman quarters of Le Puymin, above the Place du 11 Novembre, and La Villasse, below this square, can be visited.

Puymin: The excavations in this area are fenced-in along the Rue Burrus up the slope of the Puymin next to the Rue B.Noël. The entrance is in the Place de l'Abbé-Sautel, behind the Office de Tourisme.

Immediately on entering the excavation area one crosses an old pavement to the **Maison des Messii**, of which there remain some ruined sections and re-erected columns, and which was originally a distinguished house with an atrium and peristyle court. The trapezoid hall of the house leads on the left to the baths, and on the right to a reception room formerly adorned with a mosaic pavement. A passage leads to the atrium with what was a water basin in the middle. To the N. is a temple with a beautiful mosaic pavement, which was dedicated to the lares (household gods). SE of the atrium lies the tablinum (work room). Adjoining the tablinum to the E. is a large peristyle with a pond and garden (to the S.), then the large dining room, in which columns and remnants of frescos survive. To the N. are a series of living-rooms and a large oecus (living-room) decorated with various marbles, and W. of this (under a modern roof) is a narrow

Excavations

Excavations

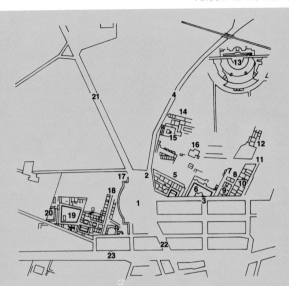

Vaison-la-Romaine, excavations of the Roman town 1 Place du 11-Novembre **2** Place de l'Abbé de Sautel **3** Rue Burrus **4** Rue Bernard-Noël **5** House of the Messii **6** Portico of Pompey **7** Large theatre street **8** Small Nymphaeum street **9** Rented houses **10** Rented houses **11** Large Nyphaeum street **12** Nymphaeum **13** Ancient theatre **14** Residential rooms with frescos **15** Praetorium **16** Museum **17** Entrance to the Villasse excavations **18** Street with shops **19** House with the silver bust **20** House with the dolphin **21** Avenue du Général-de-Gaulle **22** Grande Rue **23** Avenue Jules-Ferry

room with wall frescos. Here there are also two inscriptions indicating that the villa belonged to members of the Messius family.

E. of the House of the Messii stands **Pompey's Portico**, a large public building, which—as indicated by an inscription—was donated by the Pompeia family. Only the N. part of the 170 ft. long portico has so far been excavated. The covered part served as a lobby, which apparently surrounded a garden with a central square building. In the excavated N. gallery there are copies of statues in niches (Empress Sabina, Hadrian)—the originals are in the museum.

Steps lead from Pompey's Portico to the broad road which runs to the theatre. On the E. side of the road are the **apartment houses**, which rich Romans rented out to individuals or families. A large provisions urn (dolium) has been set up again here.

Nymphaeum: Continuing down the Theatre Road, to the NE on the upper slope above a retaining wall, is the old nymphaeum with its rectangular basin, which was covered by a roof supported by four columns. The spring, which supplied the fountain with water, still flows today.

Theatre: The road to the ancient theatre leads W. from the nymphaeum through a tunnel and then down again on the other side of the Puymin hill. Coming out of the tunnel, which forms an upper ambulatory around the auditorium, into what was a covered colonnade and surveying the whole theatre, one is overwhelmed by the size of the complex, which—although smaller than the one at Orange—is cut into the natural slope of the N. side of the Puymin hill, like an ancient Greek theatre. From the stage and orchestra 34 semicircular rows of stone seats rise up to the surviving columns of the portico. On the bottom three rows, which are also wider, the armchairs of the guests of honour were placed. The very spaciousness of this imposing complex in front of its splendid natural backdrop is still an experience in itself. In 1911–13 excavations were begun on the theatre, which was probably built around AD 20 during

Museum, satyr (L.); Bacchus (R.)

the reign of Tiberius, rebuilt in the 3C and apparently destroyed in the 5C. The back wall of the stage appears, according to the finds, to have been laid out as in Orange. Like the central statue of Augustus there, one of Tiberius is supposed to have stood here—it is now in the museum. During excavations the sculptures which decorated the front of the stage were discovered in 12 large rooms which originally lay under the stage and were used for storing props and machinery, whence also figures could rise from the Underworld. These statues are now also in the museum. The semicircle of the theatre has a diameter of 312 ft. and rises to a height of 82 ft. Of the former high stage back wall there remain only the foundations, of the pulpitum (forestage) the W. part is still visible, including the 12 channels from which the curtain rose, the hyposcenium (the stage itself) and the remains of the stone barrier which separated the auditorium from the orchestra.

Archaeological Museum: Nearby lies the museum, which just a few years ago replaced a smaller one built in 1927, and which displays finds from the excavation areas: coins, ceramics, utensils of various kinds, weapons and jewellery, various sculptures and fragments as well as the statues, most of which were discovered in the theatre, above all the statue of Tiberius and the two more than life-size marbles of the Emperor Hadrian and the Empress Sabina.

Villasse: 110 yards SW of the excavation site of Puymin lies the second excavation area, Villasse. This has been systematically cleared of trees since 1924 and takes its name from an 18C château, which stands at the end of the ancient avenue of plane trees. This château now houses students and archaeologists, as well as finds. Immediately ahead, upon entering the the excavation site, lies the broad, paved N.–S. street, which also had pavements. Parallel to this and running further W. is a smaller, originally covered street for pedestrians. This also has steps and was the former shopping street, on both sides of which there are still some recogniz-

Museum, Venus (L., 2C BC); Empress (R., 2C BC)

able foundations of closely packed little rooms and even the odd shop counter. A statue of Mercury stands here.

The house of the silver bust: To the W. lie the ruins of a villa, in which the silver bust of a Roman patrician was found (now in the museum). The entrance is flanked by two pillars. There follows a paved hall with the statue of a toga-clad man and then an atrium bordered by 12 columns, around which are grouped the private chambers. Here stands a copy of the statue of the Emperor, which was found in the theatre. Of note is a room with a mosaic pavement and marble slabs in the four corners. To the S. there is a peristyle with basin and colonnades, and at the foot of the last hill on the excavation area there are two rooms lying next to each other, which also have interesting mosaics depicting geometric patterns and figures.

House of the dolphin: Adjoining to the NW is a 2C villa, excavated in 1949–54, with a large peristyle surrounded by 18 columns and 3 semicircular exedrae on the N. side, where the marble sculpture of Cupid riding on a dolphin was found (now in museum). This house, which was also luxuriously furnished, was built on the site of an older one.

The remaining excavations, such as the **trade basilica** E. of the large paved street, with a spacious, 41 ft. wide room and the N. wall with a decorative arched gateway, are only partly finished. Drains and baths are discernible.

There are other Roman ruins apart from the Puymin and Villasse sites in the town. Baths, for example, with a caldarium, tepidarium and frigidarium, have been discovered to the N. of Vaison.

Theatre: Vaison is now known as a tourist and cultural centre, above all for its festival, which has been held each summer for the last 25 years in the **ancient theatre** (4,500 seats). The popular international 'Gala folklorique', in which 30 nations have so far taken part with traditional music and dance, takes place here, as well as highly entertaining productions of drama, opera and ballet. Modern theatre pieces, as well as stylishly pro-

Venasque, baptistery

duced baroque operas are also held in the **Théâtre des Fouilles**, in the nymphaeum in the Puymin site.

Vauvenargues
13 Bouches-du-Rhône   p.256☐D/E 7

The Château de Vauvenargues, a 16&17C Renaissance building flanked by two round towers and surrounded by a 14C wall, stands on an isolated hill in the valley. It largely owes its fame to two of its owners: the French moralist Luc de Clapiers de Vauvenargues (1715–47), known to the French as a friend of Voltaire and Marmontel, but who may also be viewed as a forerunner of Nietzsche, and Picasso (1881–1973), who acquired the château in 1958 and had himself buried on the terrace here.

Environs: Pain-de-Munition (12.5 km. SE): Important Celto-Ligurian oppidum with three surrounding ramparts.
Saint-Marc-Jaumegarde (7 km. W.): 16C château flanked by three round towers and an older square one called the 'Templar Tower'.
Sainte-Victoire (c. 5 km. S.): The mountain made world-famous by Cézanne, the name of which does not, however, have anything to do with Marius' victory over the Teutons, as one repeatedly hears around here, but is derived from the much older word ventour (see Ventoux).
Prieuré de Sainte-Victoire: Small priory situated at 2,913 ft. with a chapel, built between 1656–61 on late medieval remains. At the end of April each year it becomes the goal of a pilgrimage by the 'Venturiers', the friends of the mountain.

Venasque
8 Vaucluse   p.256☐C 5

Whether or not this village, which has one of the most colourful histories in Provence, dates back to prehistoric times, as some suggest, or is a 5/6C foundation, as others believe, is uncertain. Still impressive today, the little rocky eyrie above the Nesque shelters behind a massive rampart, fortified by three towers, on the one easily accessible spot. One certainty is the early medieval link with Carpentras, and it may well be that the bishops of the larger town moved their seat to Venasque at the time of the Barbarian Invasions in the 6–10C.

Church of Notre-Dame: This small Romanesque church looking down into the valley was built in a number of stages. Portal and façade date from the start of the 13C (the porch, however, is 17C), the three-bayed nave with a pointed barrel vault and typical octagonal dome on squinches from a somewhat earlier period, and the rectangular apse from the 11C. The side chapels between the buttresses and the bell tower (17C), on the other hand, were not added until the 17&18C. There is a beautiful *Crucifixion* of the school of Avignon, 1498.

Venasque, baptistery

Baptistery: The so-called baptistery on the N. side of the church, to which it was once connected by a vaulted passage, was, according to present opinion, never a baptistery at all, as had previously been supposed, but a funerary chapel. Furthermore, it was not built in the 6C at the instigation of St.Siffrein, but in all probability in the second quarter of the 11C. Unfortunately greatly disfigured by later additions, the 'baptistery' has the ground plan of a centrally-planned building drawn into a trapezium with four apses of unequal size, originally forming a Greek cross. *Inside*, the apses, vaulted by half-domes, are separated from the groin-vaulted central area by arches. Their walls have semicircular blind arcades, the pink and grey marble columns of which are antique works, as are the tall columns of the apse arches and a part of the Corinthian-style capitals.

Notre-Dame-de-Vie: This chapel by the bridge at the foot of the mountain houses a rare treasure, the Merovingian *tombstone* of Bishop Boethius (d. 604), a slab decorated with wheels

Vence, Place Peyra, fountain

and rosettes and divided into squares by cross ribs. Above it is an inscribed plaque crowned by a gable, which is also filled with wheels and rosettes.

Vence
06 Alpes-Maritimes   p.258 □ I 6

The strategic position of the plateau, already settled by the Ligurian Nerusii, induced the Romans in the 2C BC to set up a sort of military outpost, under the name of Vintium, for the conquest of Gaul. Under Roman protection the town flourished, with the result that Bishop Eusebius founded a diocese here as early as 374. At the entreaty of St.Veranus the Goths and Vandals (5C) spared the population, but in 578 the Lombards so devastated the country that it did not recover until the expulsion of the Saracens (9C). Raymond Bérenger V, Duke of Provence, handed the town over to his capable minister (13C) Romée de Villefranche. Throughout the Middle Ages there was an endless dispute between the town's administrators and the bishop—the latter wielded remarkable power. The quarrelling did not end until Provence was united with France. That Vence was not of particular importance in the Middle Ages is proved by the fact that for centuries it did not grow beyond its boundary walls. During the Wars of Religion (1592) Vence was one of the Catholic strongholds. In 1704 Imperial troops occupied the town, but in the War of the Spanish Succession (1746) Bishop Surian successfully interceded on behalf of the population. The diocese, which had for centuries had famous and capable bishops, was dissolved during the Revolution.

Town wall: The medieval walls form an oval around the Old Town and are still completely intact. To the E. and SE are the *Porte d'Orient* (1592) and the *Porte Signadour* from the 13C.

The *W. town gate* with embrasures and machicolations was additionally fortified by the *Porte du Peyra* (12/13C). The *Portail Lévis* (Place Thiers) was built at the same time.

Chapelle du Rosaire (Avenue Henri-Matisse): This simple shrine was built in 1950 at the Dominican convent in the NE of the town at the instigation of Henri Matisse, who also provided the interior decoration: St.Dominic, the Madonna and Child and the Stations of the Cross, painted on white glazed tiles. The interior is further enlivened by colourful stained-glass windows.

Former cathedral (Place Clemenceau): Dedicated to *St.Veranus*, it is dated back to the 11C on stylistic grounds. The lower floor of the battlemented tower (N. side), with an arcaded belfry, also dates from this time. In the 17C the choir was widened and two further aisles added. The sacristy (SE corner of choir) was added in the 13C and the façade dates from 1879. Set into the outer walls there are reliefs from Merovingian or Carolingian times. The unimpressive interior appears squat because of the galleries and aisles installed in the 17C. On the walls there are relief slabs similar to those outside. In the second S. chapel is the sarcophagus of the canonized Bishop Lambert (12C) and in the next chapel a 5C sarcophagus, which is reputedly that of St.Veranus. In the barrel-vaulted nave there is a large crucifix dating from the 16C.

Of particular note are the choir stalls, carved between 1455–9 (in the W. gallery from 1499), with humorous misericords by Jacotin Bellot of Grasse. The beautiful singer's desk is from the same century.

Also worth seeing: Within the town walls lies the *Old Town*, unchanged since the Middle Ages, with narrow alleys, squares and fountains. The 15C *Place Peyra* (fountain of 1822) was possibly once the forum of the Roman settlement. The *New Town*, with the central *Place du Grand-Jardin*, is in obvious contrast to the

Cagnes-sur-Mer, Renoir's house, bronze statue

Cagnes-sur-Mer, Chapelle N.-D.-de-Protection

medieval town centre. The former *Château Seigneurial* (N. of Tour du Peyra) was superseded by a large château in the 17C. Only the tall square tower remained from the 14C. The *Chapelle des Pénitents Blancs* (Place F.Mistral), built in 1614, has a large Renaissance bell tower, which serves inside as an exhibition room.

A small *open-air museum* shows Gallo-Roman finds.

E. of Vence is the chapel of *Sainte-Elisabeth*, which was painted throughout by Jacques Canavesi in 1491.

Environs: Bonson (*c.* 35 km. NE): This little village stands on a hill above the confluence of the Var and Vésubie. The *church* contains a triptych (1517) by Antoine Bréa depicting John the Baptist flanked by St.Clare and St.Catherine.

Bouyon (*c.* 22 km. N.): The *church* of this beautifully situated village has an interesting Virgin, which was painted by the Nice school in the 15C.

Le Broc (*c.* 16 km. NE): There is a beautiful view from this village, the *church* of which was built in the 16C.

At the village exit stands the chapel of *Saint-Antoine*, which has a 14C sculpture of St.Anthony.

Cagnes-sur-Mer (*c.* 10 km. S.): This rocky coastal height was settled first by Ligurians, then Romans. In the 5C the monks of Lérins built a monastery here, but this was abandoned in 1050. In the 12C the town was enclosed by a *wall*, secured with gates: *Porte de Saint-Paul, Porte d'Antibes* and *Porte de Nice*. Rainier I, ruler of Monaco, began building the *castle* in the 14C. This was extended by one of his successors into a stately seat in the 16C. The château, badly damaged in the course of the centuries, was acquired by the town in 1939 and restored to its former state. The buildings are towered over by a hexagonal keep and enclose a triangular inner court. In the large staircase there is a Renaissance relief depicting Francis I at the Battle of Marignano. The state rooms of the piano nobile still retain part of their original decoration. The ceiling painting (1625) of the banqueting hall is by a member of the Carlone family. On the ground

Saint-Paul-de-Vence, Fondation Maeght

floor, next to a small ethnographic collection, there is the little *Musée de l'Olivier*, devoted to the region's main product—the olive. Two rooms on the first floor contain a few works by Auguste Renoir. The *Musée d'Art méditerranéen moderne*, with works by such artists as Matisse, Chagall, Kissling etc. is housed on the second floor. The chapel of *Notre-Dame de Protection* was a small prayer-house in the 14C, which was extended by the Grimaldis in 1642 (Place Planastel). The Gothic choir had a bay, a porch and a tower added, while apse and vault were painted with scenes from the Life of the Virgin and Biblical figures. The modest church of *Saint-Pierre* (next to the château) has a Gothic nave and another from the 17C.

Carros (*c.* 12 km. NE): The *château* with its four little towers was built in the 13C and extended in the 16C. The *church* contains a beautiful carved wooden tabernacle and a bell tower with a square ground plan.

La Gaude (*c.* 10 km. E.): The Knights Templars built a *castle* here,

but this is now a ruin. The *church* dates from the 18C.

Gilette (*c.* 30 km. NE): In the 12&13C the Dukes of Provence built a *castle* below the village to protect the valley; only *ruins* remain.

Saint-Jeannet (*c.* 5 km. NE): At the entrance to this little town at the foot of the Baou stands the chapel of *Sainte Pétronille*, which contains a 15C sculpture and a 17C altarpiece. The *church* was completed in 1666. At the W. exit from the town stands the chapel of *Saint-Jean-Baptiste* (1753), with a beautiful 18C sculpture and a Beheading of John the Baptist (1834) by Féraud.

Saint-Paul-de-Vence (5 km. S.): Pillaging Teutons, Saracens and Normans eradicated all traces of the site's first settlers. Castrum Sancto Paulo, first officially documented in the 10C, became self-administering in the 13C and a *town wall* was built in 1401, of which the only part still standing is a high tower with battlements and machicolations. The present walls, which enclose the medieval Old Town on the hill, were built at the insti-

Saint-Paul-de-Vence, Fondation Maeght (L.); Place de la Grande Fontaine (R.)

gation of Francis I (1537–47) by the two military architects François Mandon and Vauban. Entrance to the strong fortress, which withstood enemy attacks, is via the *Porte Royal* and the *Porte de Vence*. The former *collegiate church* was built in sober Romanesque style in the 12&13C. The vault was rebuilt in the 17C and a square bell tower added on to the S. side in 1740. The interior, with a nave and two aisles (straight-ended choir) contains numerous works of art, including an alabaster Madonna (15C) on the font, a St.Catherine (16C) by Tintoretto, St.Clare by Guido Reni, 17C wooden busts, walnut choir stalls (16C) etc. The chapel of *St.Clement* (1681) in the left aisle has lavish stucco decoration. The church treasure is kept in the sacristy and includes beautiful silver items, reliquaries and a painted, hexagonal pyx of 1595.

The modern *Fondation Maeght* provides a marked contrast to the medieval town and is itself an unusual example of its kind. It is a large cultural centre, built by José Luis Sert, an American architect of Spanish origin, with the financial support of the artists exhibiting here. It is named after its founders, Aimé and Marguerite Maeght, and was built in 1964 as a single storey building and in a style which achieves harmony with the surrounding countryside. The centre comprises rooms for permanent and rotating exhibitions, a house for artists, a photograph archive, and a library. The exhibits, some of them displayed in the open air, include paintings, sculptures, faience tiles, prints, and other forms of art by such artists as Braque, Miro, Chagall, Arp, and Kandinsky. The small *Chapelle Saint-Bernard* is dedicated to the founders' son and contains stained-glass windows by Ubac and Braque. Concerts, ballets, and poetry readings are also held the whole year round in this place, which is virtually unique as a tourist attraction and artistic centre. The **Auberge de la Colombe d'or**

has a small museum with paintings by Utrillo, Vlaminck, Bonnard, Braque, Matisse, etc. The *Musée des curiosités mécaniques* (Place de Mêriers) contains an extensive collection of mechanical musical instruments, musical boxes, accordions, and so on, ranging from 1750 to 1930. The *Musée provençal*, which is accommodated in a 16C house on the Place de la Grande-Fontaine, displays reconstructions of the living conditions of past centuries. On the road leading southwards out of town is the 12C *Prieuré de Canadel*, built by the monks of Lérins, which has a beautiful Romanesque chapel and a fortified gate. 1.5 km. out of town on the D7 can be seen the *hermits' chapel of Saint-Donat* (17C), and 2 km. further along the same road is the small settlement of *Colle-sur-Loup*. According to tradition, some 700 houses in Vence were destroyed during the construction of its town walls in the 16C, and the families thus left homeless resettled themselves here, building a *church* in the 17C whose windows are by Gesta. On the road leading SE out of town is a 16C country house called the *Château de Montfort*.

Tourrette-sur-Loup (6.5 km. W.): The houses here are so arranged as to constitute a kind of town wall in themselves, with a 14C church in the middle which has a single aisle. It contains a Roman altar of Mercury which dates from the 3C. The former *castle* of the Marquesses of Villeneuve-Tourette has wall paintings above the staircase dating from the period of the Revolution. The *Chapelle Saint-Jean* was built in 1959 and contains frescos in the naive style by Ralph Soupault.

Villeneuve-Loubet (*c*. 12 km. S.): On a hill above the left bank of the Loup stands a 12C *castle* whose ownership changed several times over the course of the centuries. It is crowned by a square keep and defended by corner towers. A second wall, added in the 16C, encircles the castle at a lower level than the first.

List of places mentioned in the text. Those which have a separate entry are marked △, while those which are mentioned in the environs sections are indicated by the → symbol.

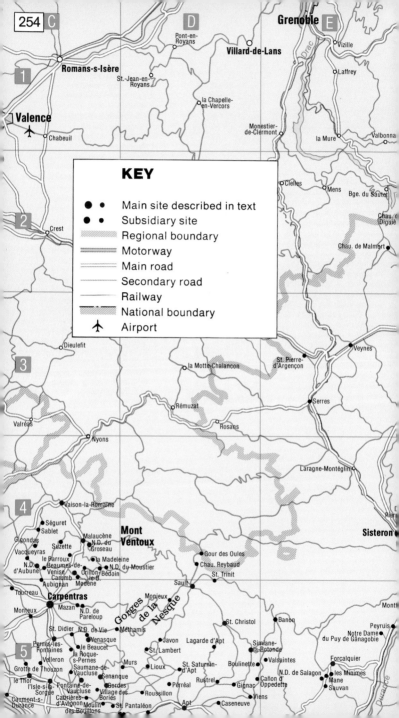

KEY

● ●	Main site described in text
● ●	Subsidiary site
▨▨▨	Regional boundary
▬▬▬	Motorway
═══	Main road
───	Secondary road
───	Railway
▨▨▨	National boundary
✈	Airport

Romans-s-Isère
St.-Jean-en-Royans
Pont-en-Royans
Villard-de-Lans
la Chapelle-en-Vercors
Vizille
Laffrey
Valence
Chabeuil
Monestier-de-Clermont
la Mure
Valbonna
Clelles
Mens
Bge. du Sautet
Chau. d Diguiè
Crest
Chau. de Malmort
Dieulefit
Veynes
la Motte-Chalancon
St. Pierre-d'Argençon
Valréas
Rémuzat
Serres
Rosans
Nyons
Laragne-Montéglin
Vaison-la-Romaine
Sisteron
Séguret
Sablet
Gigondas
Malaucène
N.D. du Groseau
Mont Ventoux
Suzette
Vacqueyras
le Barroux
la Madeleine
N.D. d'Aubune
Beaumes-de-Venise
Caromb
Crillon-le-B
N.D. du Moustier
Gour des Oules
Chau. Reybaud
Aubignan
Bédoin
Medene
St. Trinit
Tourreau
Sault
Carpentras
Mazan
Monjeux
Gorges de la Nesque
Monteux
N.D. de Pareloup
St. Christol
Banon
Peyruis
Notre Dame du Puy de Ganagobie
St. Didier
N.D. de Vie
Méthamis
Venasque
Javon
Lagarde d'Apt
Pernes-les-Fontaines
le Beaucet
St. Lambert
Simiane-la-Rotonde
Forcalquier
Velleron
la Roque-s-Pernes
Murs
Lioux
St. Saturnin-d'Apt
Boulinette
Valsaintes
N.D. de Salagon
les Minimes
Grotte de Thouzon
Saumane-de-Vaucluse
Mane
le Thor
Fontaine-de-Vaucluse
Sénanque
St. Christol
Rustrel
Cañon d'Oppedette
Sauvan
l'Isle-s-la-Sorgue
Cabrières-d'Avignon
Bordes
Village des Bories
Pérréal
Roussillon
Viens
Gignac
Caumont-s-Durance
Moulin des Bouillons
St. Pantaléon
Apt
Caseneuve

Valence ✈
Chabeuil
Crest

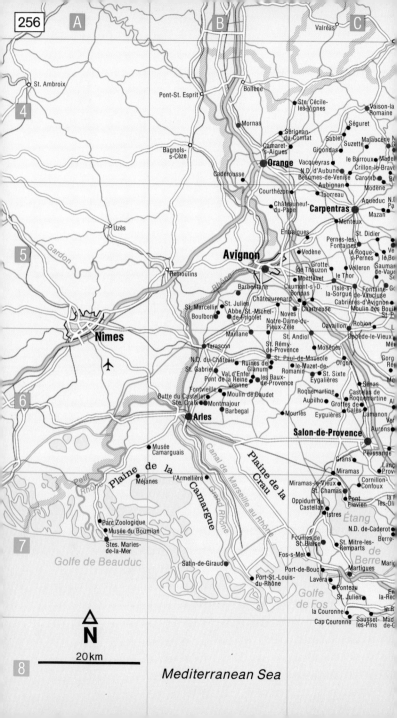

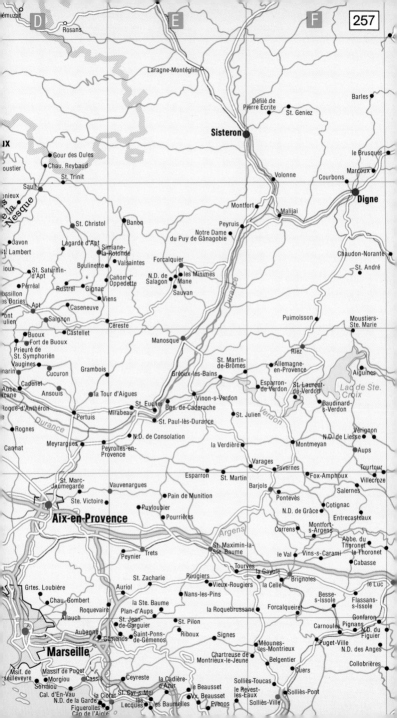

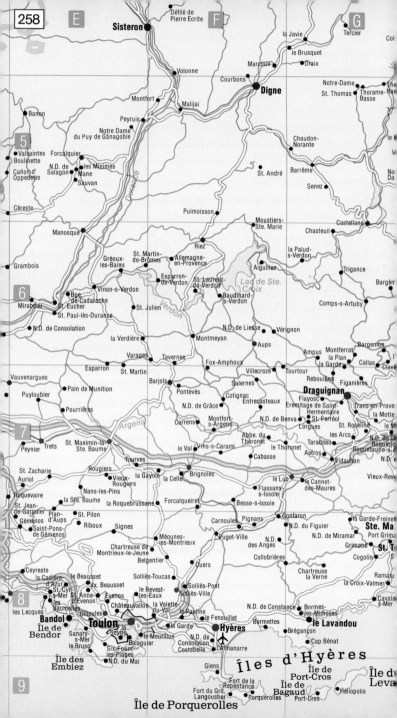